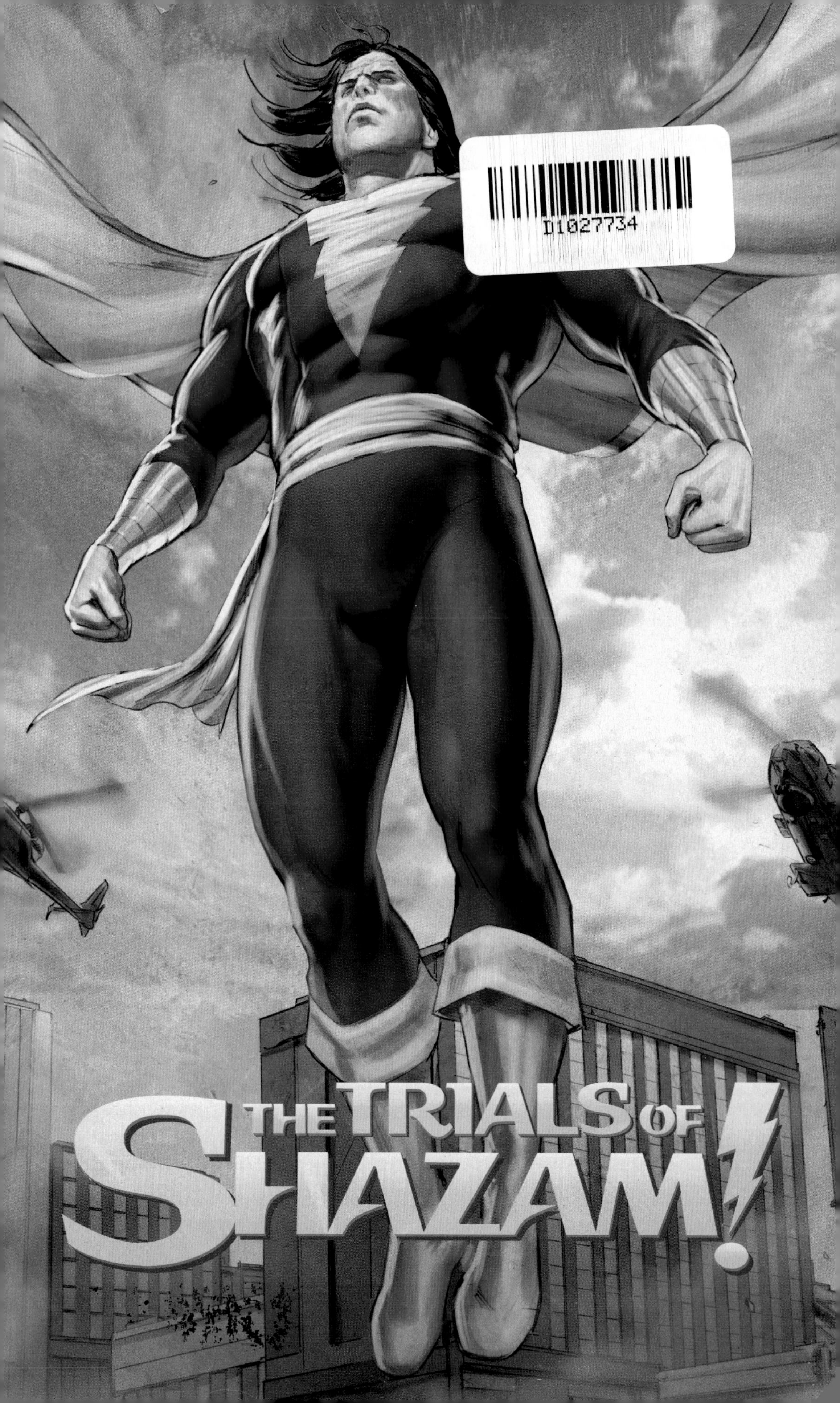
THE TRIALS OF
SHAZAM!

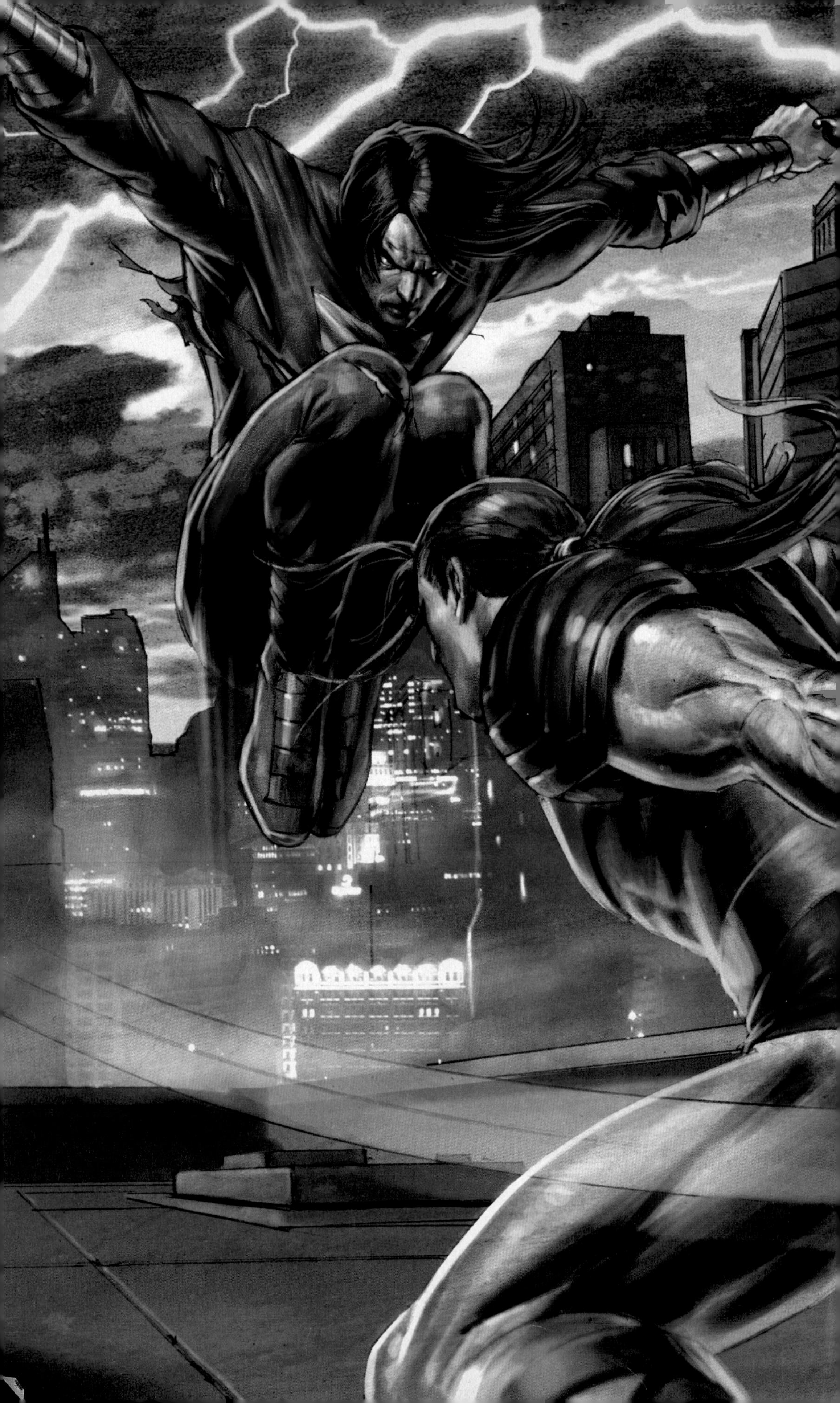

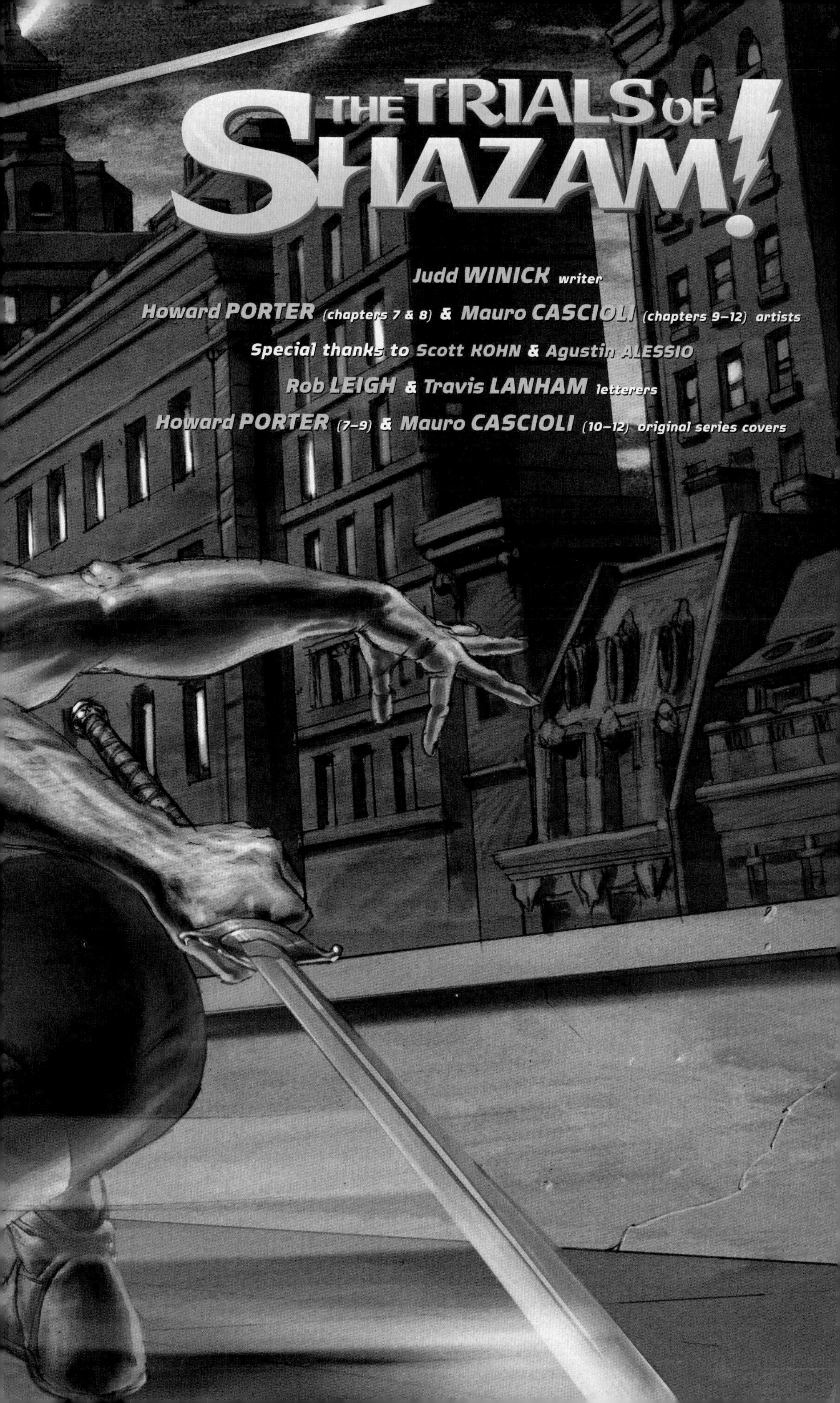

THE TRIALS OF SHAZAM!

Judd WINICK writer

Howard PORTER (chapters 7 & 8) & Mauro CASCIOLI (chapters 9–12) artists

Special thanks to Scott KOHN & Agustin ALESSIO

Rob LEIGH & Travis LANHAM letterers

Howard PORTER (7–9) & Mauro CASCIOLI (10–12) original series covers

Dan DiDio
Senior VP-Executive Editor

Mike Carlin
Editor-original series

Tom Palmer Jr.
Associate Editor-original series

Bob Joy
Editor-collected edition

Robbin Brosterman
Senior Art Director

Paul Levitz
President & Publisher

Georg Brewer
VP-Design & DC Direct Creative

Richard Bruning
Senior VP-Creative Director

Patrick Caldon
Executive VP-Finance & Operations

Chris Caramalis
VP-Finance

John Cunningham
VP-Marketing

Terri Cunningham
VP-Managing Editor

Alison Gill
VP-Manufacturing

David Hyde
VP-Publicity

Hank Kanalz
VP-General Manager, WildStorm

Jim Lee
Editorial Director-WildStorm

Paula Lowitt
Senior VP-Business & Legal Affairs

MaryEllen McLaughlin
VP-Advertising & Custom Publishing

John Nee
Senior VP-Business Development

Gregory Noveck
Senior VP-Creative Affairs

Sue Pohja
VP-Book Trade Sales

Steve Rotterdam
Senior VP-Sales & Marketing

Cheryl Rubin
Senior VP-Brand Management

Jeff Trojan
VP-Business Development, DC Direct

Bob Wayne
VP-Sales

Cover art by Mauro Cascioli
Publication design by Amelia Grohman

THE TRIALS OF SHAZAM! VOLUME TWO
Published by DC Comics.
Cover and compilation Copyright
© 2008 DC Comics. All Rights Reserved.

DC Comics, 1700 Broadway, New York, NY 10019
A Warner Bros. Entertainment Company
Printed in Canada. First Printing.
ISBN 13: 978-1-4012-1829-4

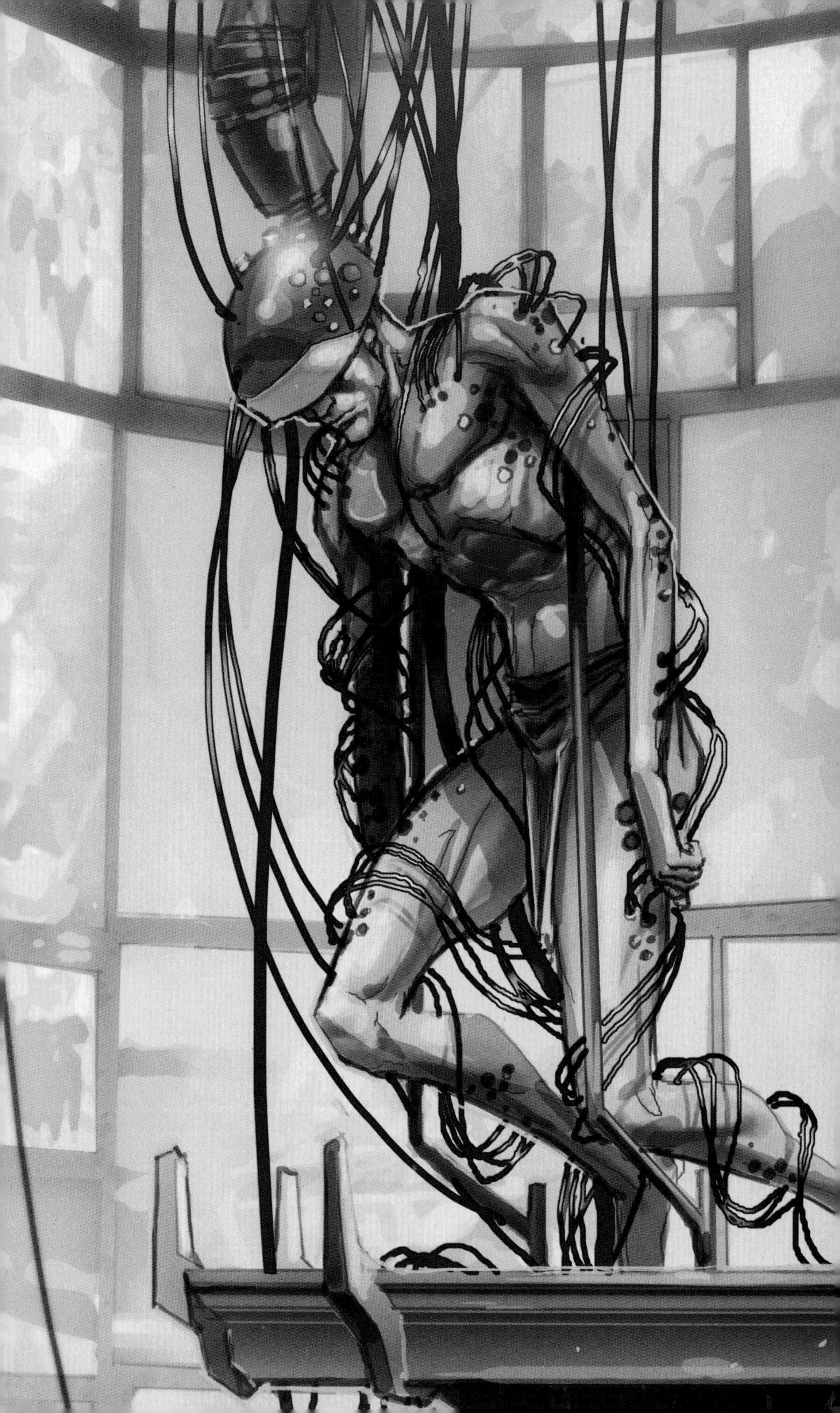

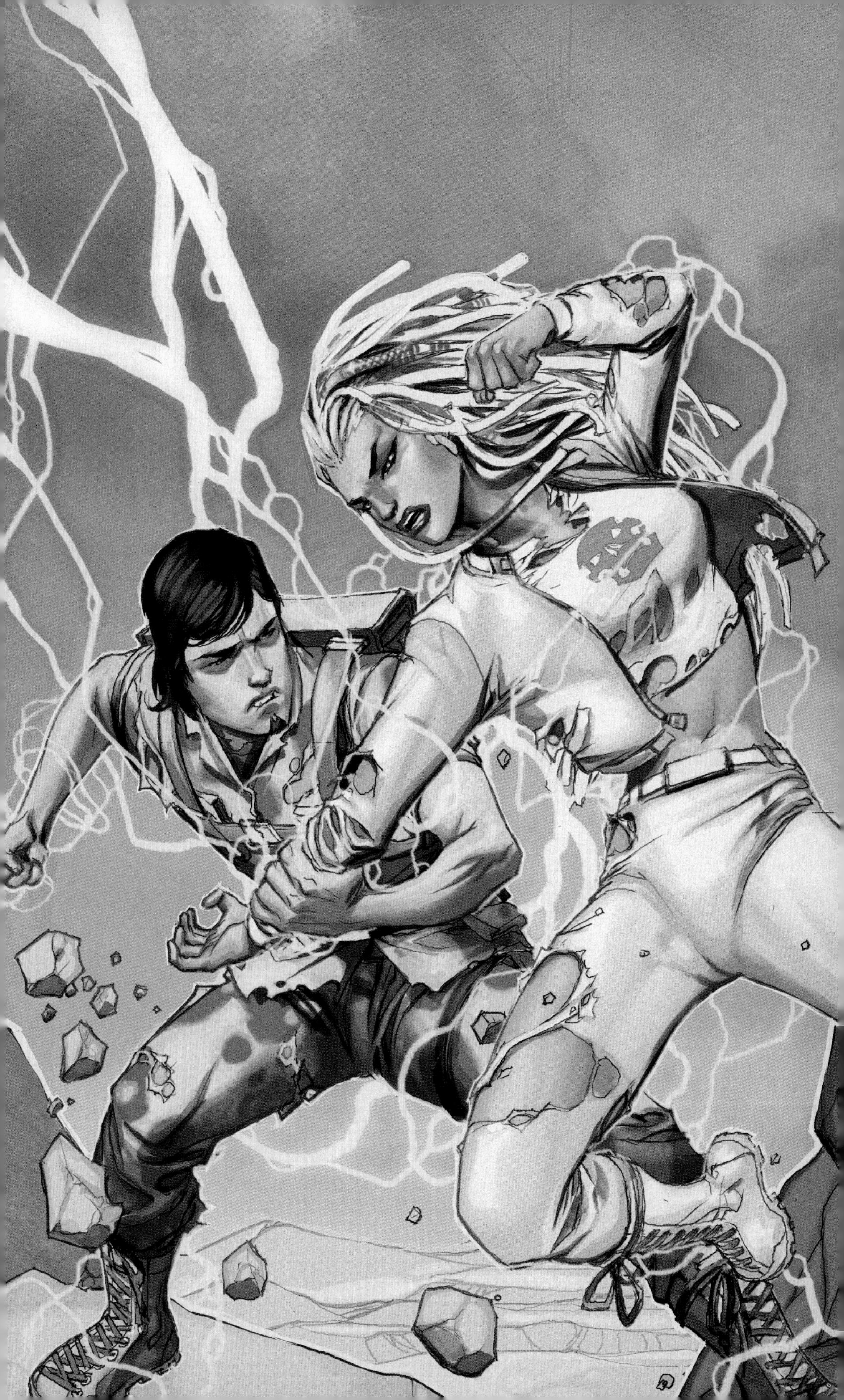

CHAPTER SEVEN:

NURTURE
Vs.
NATURE

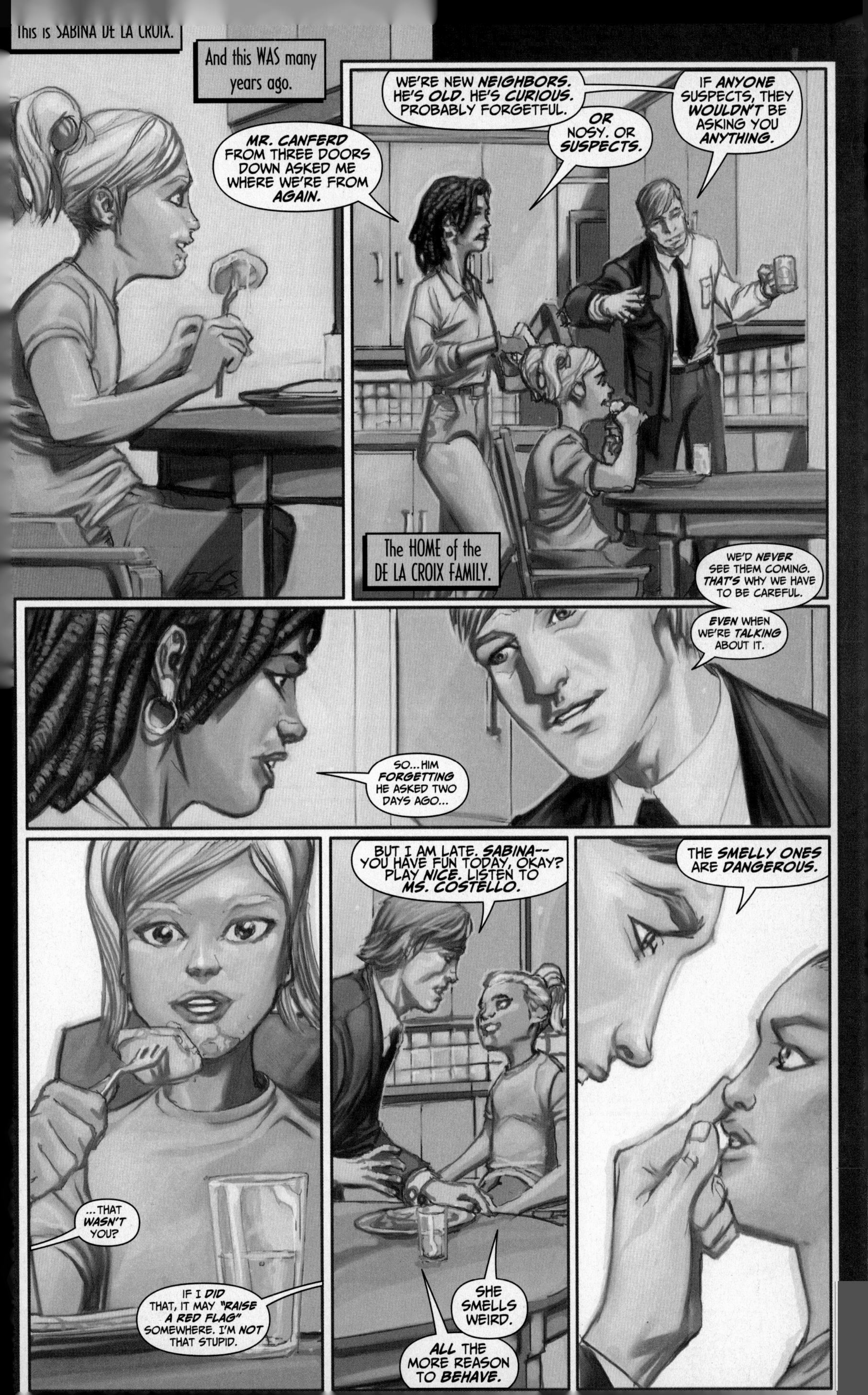
This is SABINA DE LA CROIX.
And this WAS many years ago.
MR. CANFERD FROM THREE DOORS DOWN ASKED ME WHERE WE'RE FROM AGAIN.
WE'RE NEW NEIGHBORS. HE'S OLD. HE'S CURIOUS. PROBABLY FORGETFUL.
OR NOSY. OR SUSPECTS.
IF ANYONE SUSPECTS, THEY WOULDN'T BE ASKING YOU ANYTHING.
The HOME of the DE LA CROIX FAMILY.
WE'D NEVER SEE THEM COMING. THAT'S WHY WE HAVE TO BE CAREFUL.
EVEN WHEN WE'RE TALKING ABOUT IT.
SO...HIM FORGETTING HE ASKED TWO DAYS AGO...
...THAT WASN'T YOU?
IF I DID THAT, IT MAY "RAISE A RED FLAG" SOMEWHERE. I'M NOT THAT STUPID.
BUT I AM LATE. SABINA-- YOU HAVE FUN TODAY, OKAY? PLAY NICE. LISTEN TO MS. COSTELLO.
SHE SMELLS WEIRD.
ALL THE MORE REASON TO BEHAVE.
THE SMELLY ONES ARE DANGEROUS.

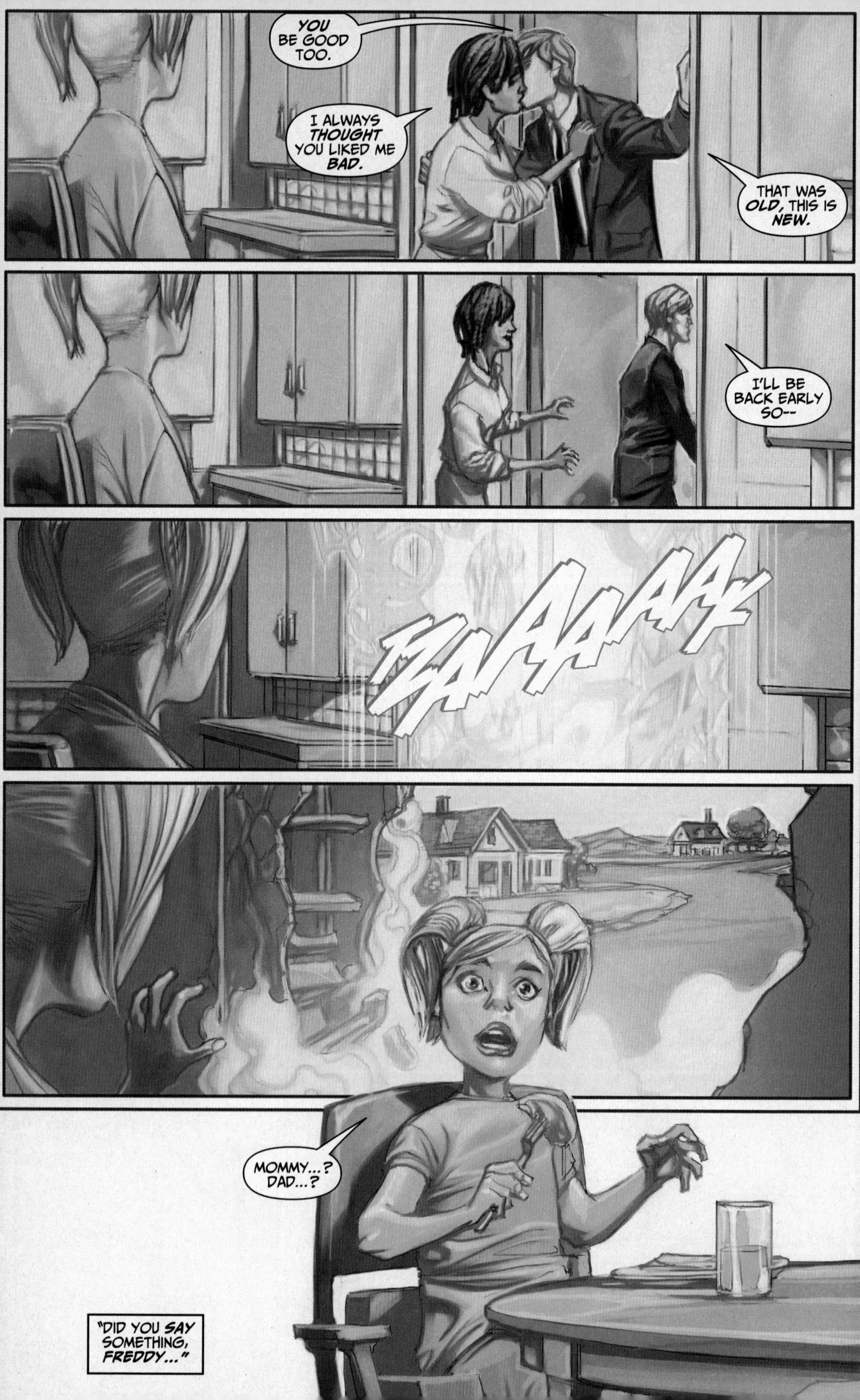
YOU BE GOOD TOO.
I ALWAYS THOUGHT YOU LIKED ME BAD.
THAT WAS OLD, THIS IS NEW.
I'LL BE BACK EARLY SO--
ZZAAAAAK
MOMMY...? DAD...?
"DID YOU SAY SOMETHING, FREDDY..."

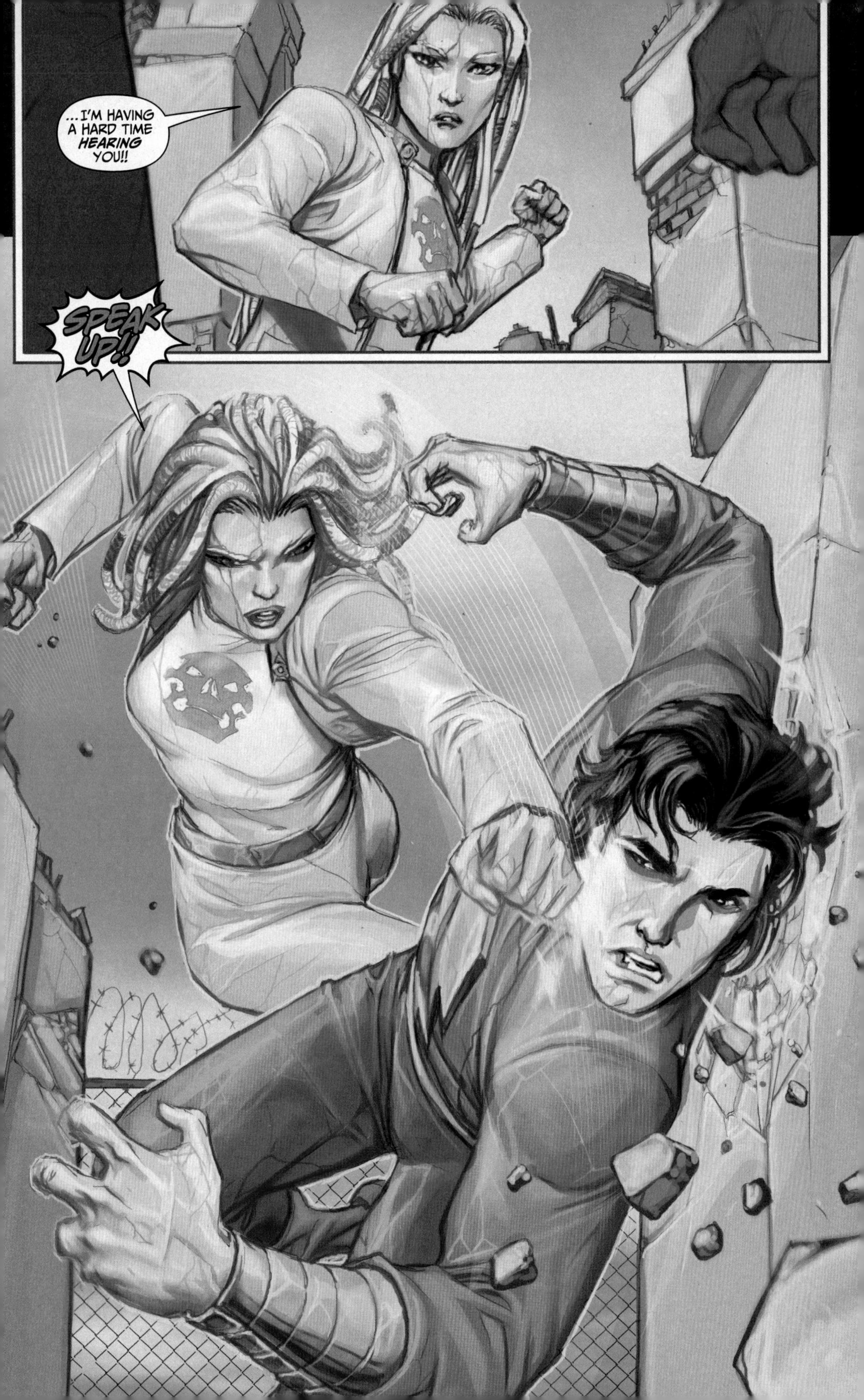
...I'M HAVING A HARD TIME HEARING YOU!!
SPEAK UP!!

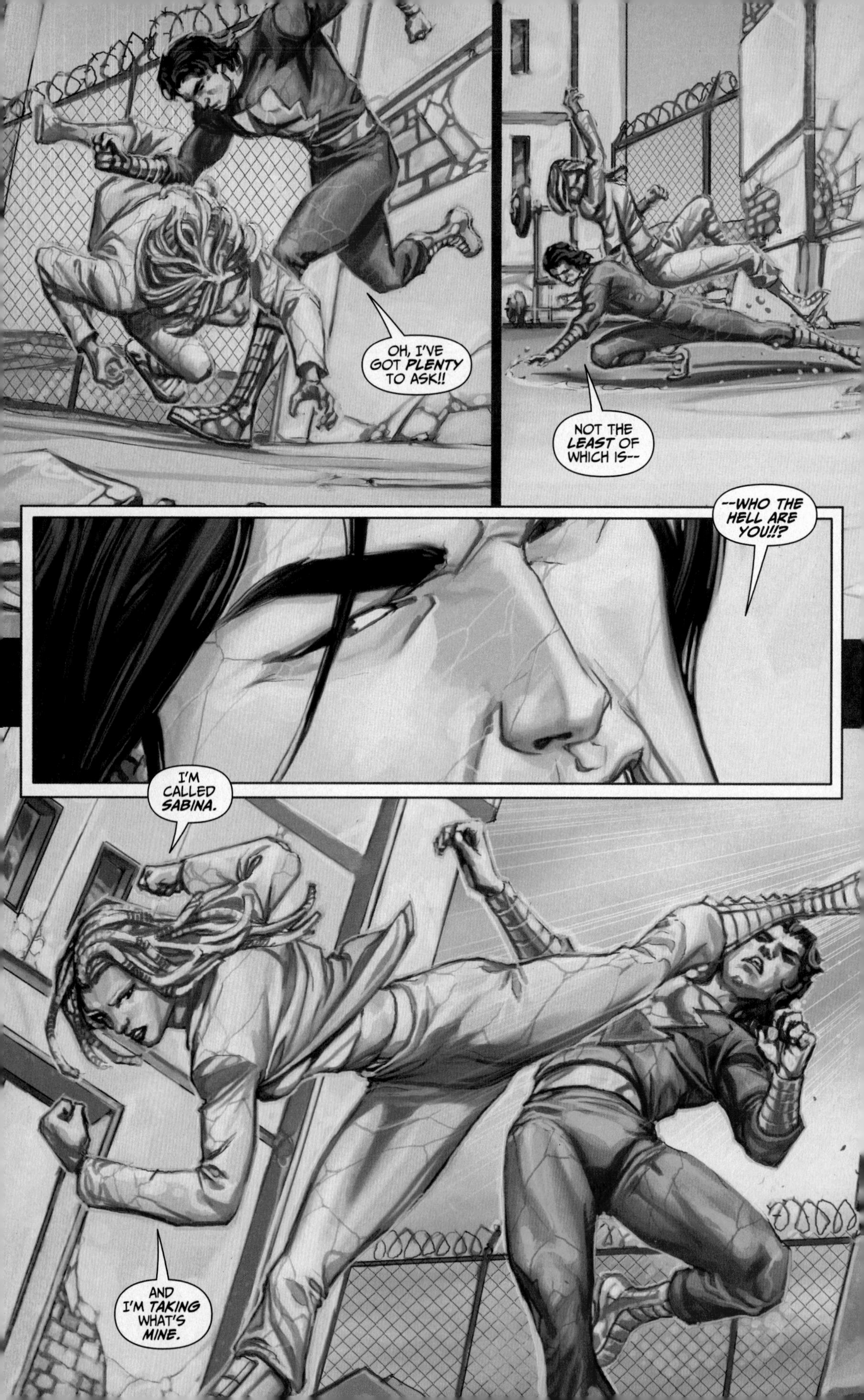

OH, I'VE GOT PLENTY TO ASK!!
NOT THE LEAST OF WHICH IS--
--WHO THE HELL ARE YOU!!?
I'M CALLED SABINA.
AND I'M TAKING WHAT'S MINE.

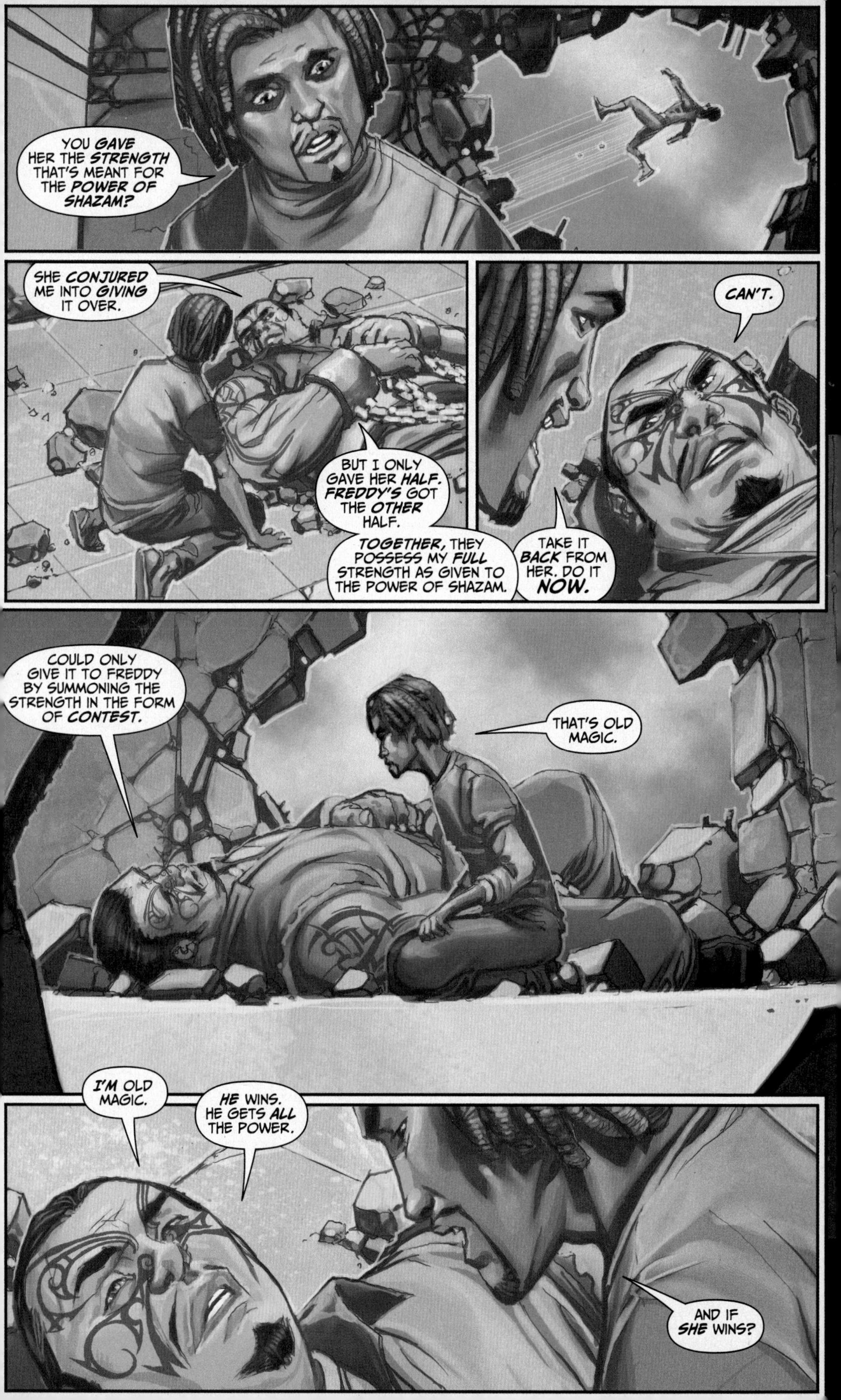
YOU GAVE HER THE STRENGTH THAT'S MEANT FOR THE POWER OF SHAZAM?
SHE CONJURED ME INTO GIVING IT OVER.
BUT I ONLY GAVE HER HALF. FREDDY'S GOT THE OTHER HALF.
TOGETHER, THEY POSSESS MY FULL STRENGTH AS GIVEN TO THE POWER OF SHAZAM.
TAKE IT BACK FROM HER. DO IT NOW.
CAN'T.
COULD ONLY GIVE IT TO FREDDY BY SUMMONING THE STRENGTH IN THE FORM OF CONTEST.
THAT'S OLD MAGIC.
I'M OLD MAGIC.
HE WINS. HE GETS ALL THE POWER.
AND IF SHE WINS?

"THEN SHE *KEEPS* WHAT SHE'S FAIRLY *STOLEN.*"

Years ago.

I *SAID* TO *STAY* AWAY FROM HIM!

HE *DOES* NOT AND HE *IS* MY BOYFR--

I *HEARD* YOU, BUT HE'S *NOT* YOUR *BOYFRIEND,* AND I CAN'T HELP IT IF HE *LIKES* TO HANG WITH ME.

LISTEN, JUST BECAUSE YOU *LET* HIM *MESS AROUND* WITH YOU AS MUCH AS HE DOES DOESN'T *MAKE* HIM YOUR *BOYFRIEND.*

AND *YOU'RE NOT THE ONLY ON* WHO CAN *MES* AROUND.

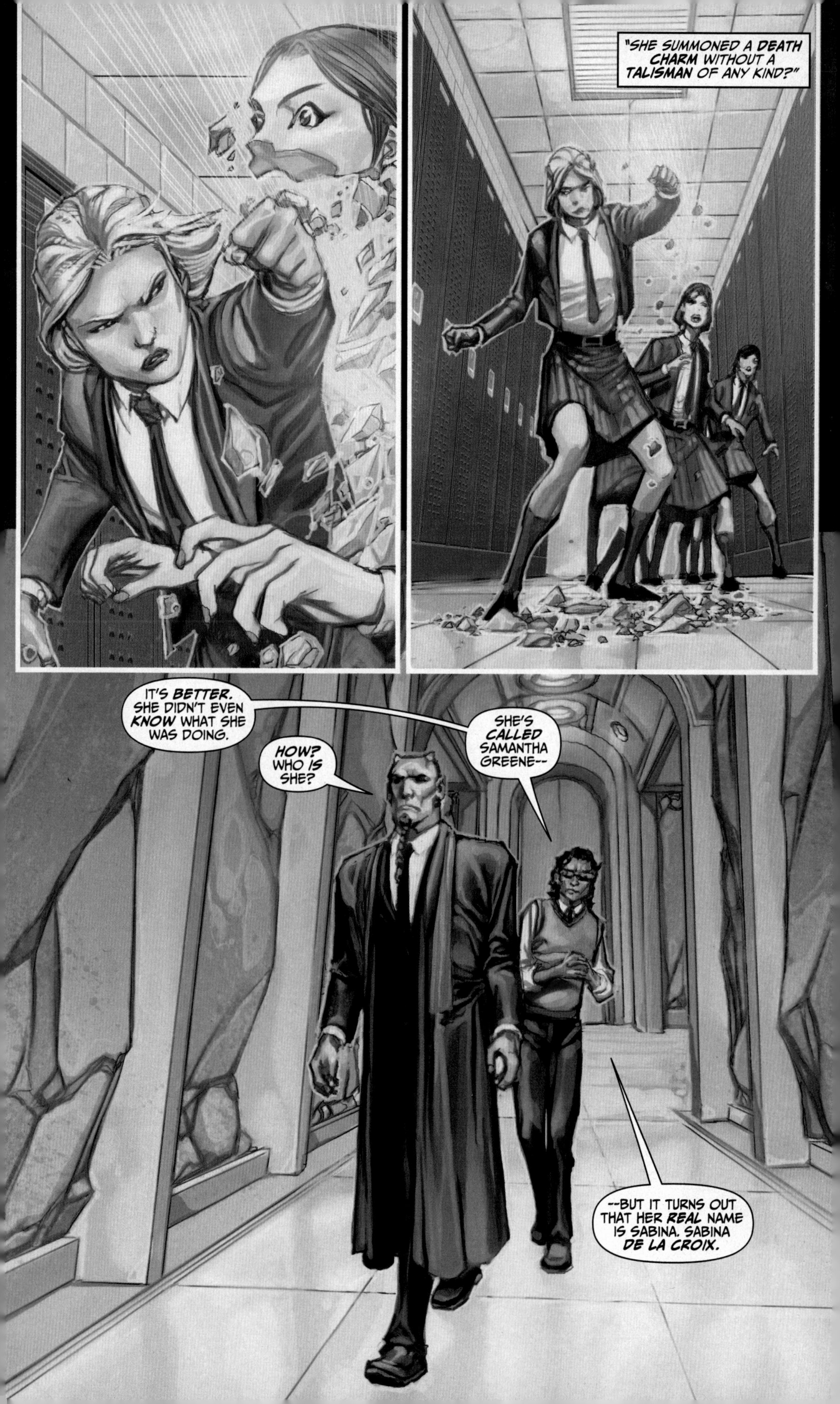
"SHE SUMMONED A DEATH CHARM WITHOUT A TALISMAN OF ANY KIND?"
IT'S BETTER. SHE DIDN'T EVEN KNOW WHAT SHE WAS DOING.
HOW? WHO IS SHE?
SHE'S CALLED SAMANTHA GREENE--
--BUT IT TURNS OUT THAT HER REAL NAME IS SABINA. SABINA DE LA CROIX.

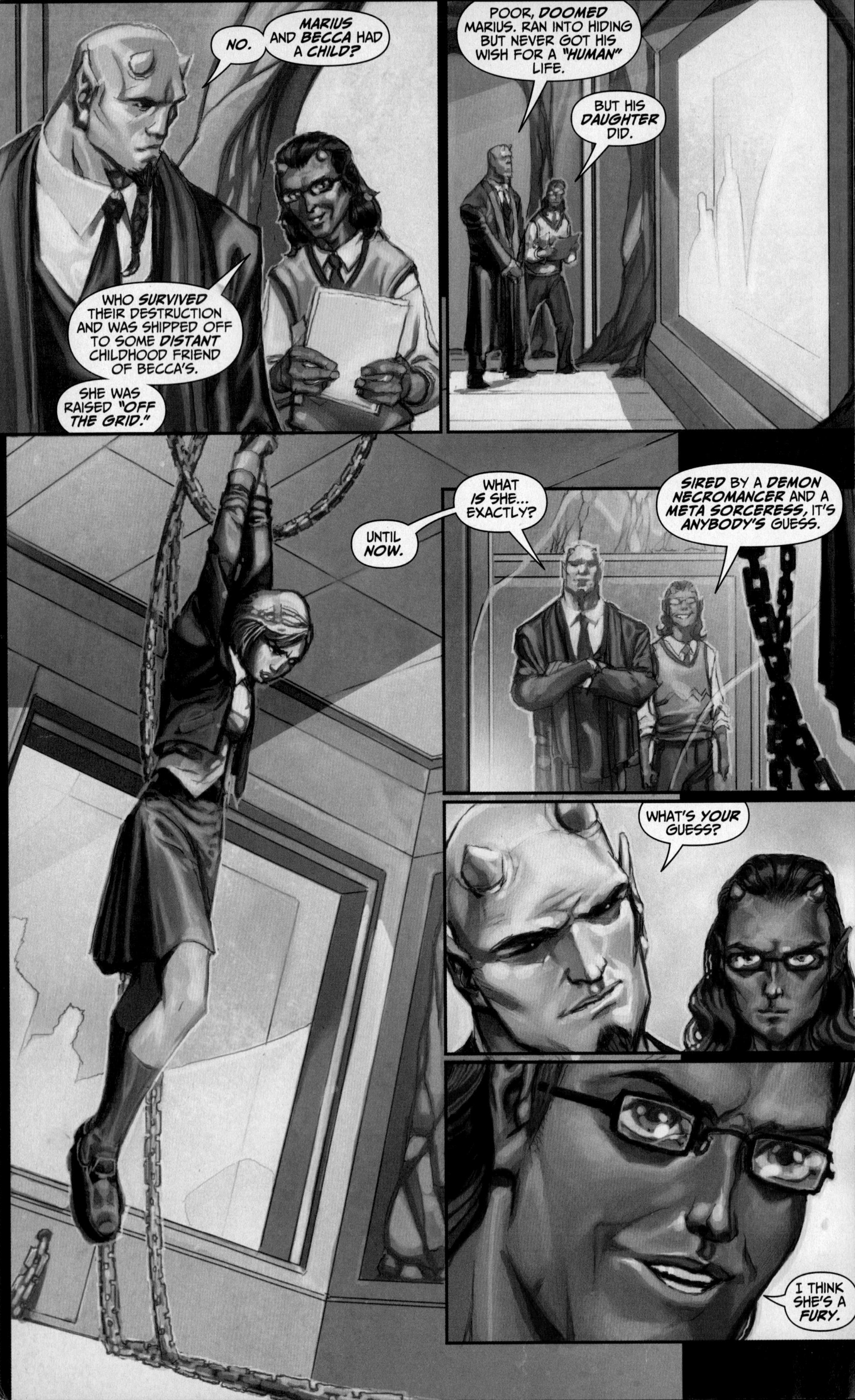

NO.
MARIUS AND BECCA HAD A CHILD?
WHO SURVIVED THEIR DESTRUCTION AND WAS SHIPPED OFF TO SOME DISTANT CHILDHOOD FRIEND OF BECCA'S.
SHE WAS RAISED "OFF THE GRID."
POOR, DOOMED MARIUS. RAN INTO HIDING BUT NEVER GOT HIS WISH FOR A "HUMAN" LIFE.
BUT HIS DAUGHTER DID.
UNTIL NOW.
WHAT IS SHE... EXACTLY?
SIRED BY A DEMON NECROMANCER AND A META SORCERESS, IT'S ANYBODY'S GUESS.
WHAT'S YOUR GUESS?
I THINK SHE'S A FURY.

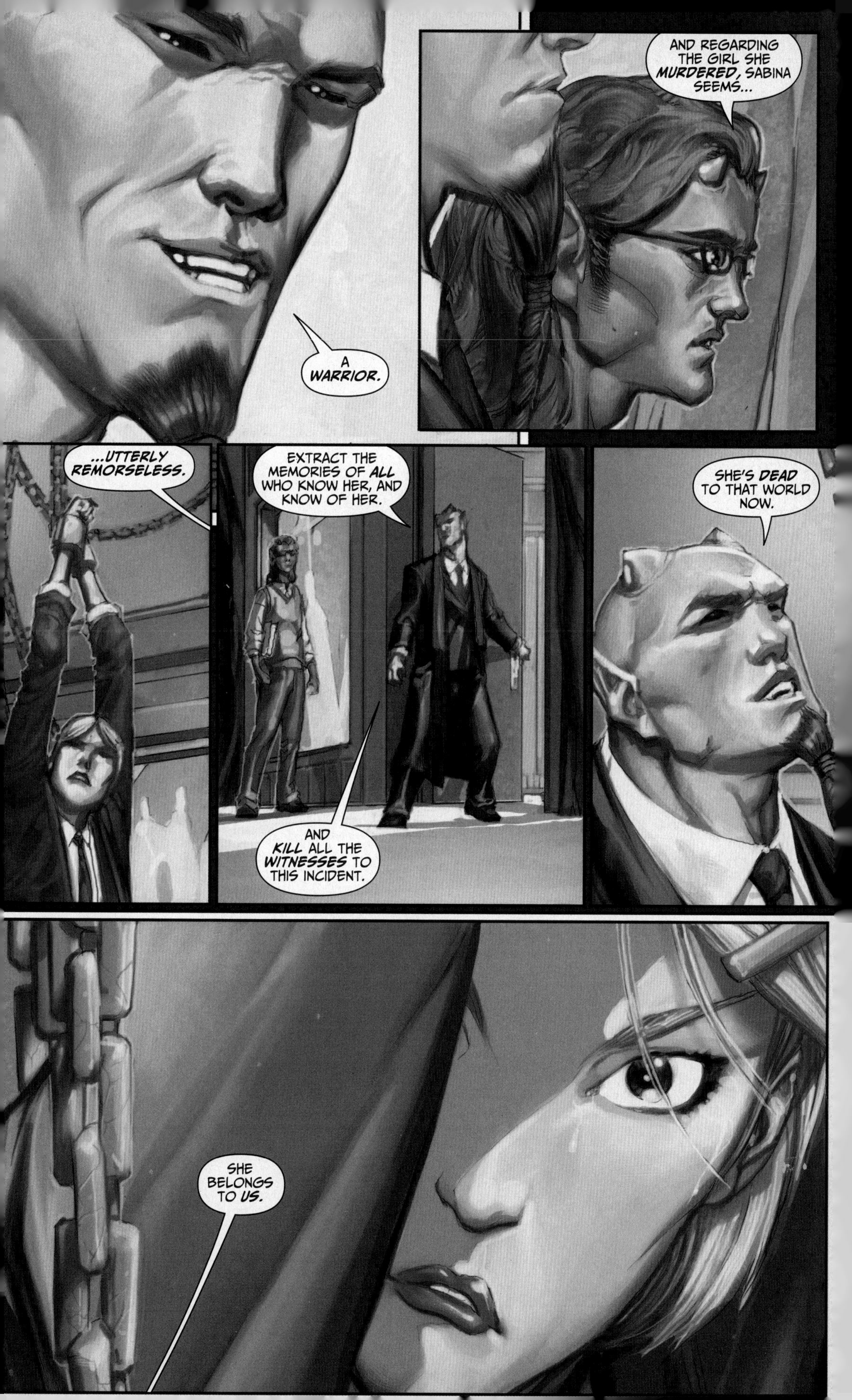
A *WARRIOR.*
AND REGARDING THE GIRL SHE *MURDERED,* SABINA SEEMS...
...UTTERLY REMORSELESS.
EXTRACT THE MEMORIES OF *ALL* WHO KNOW HER, AND KNOW OF HER.
AND *KILL* ALL THE *WITNESSES* TO THIS INCIDENT.
SHE'S *DEAD* TO THAT WORLD NOW.
SHE BELONGS TO *US.*

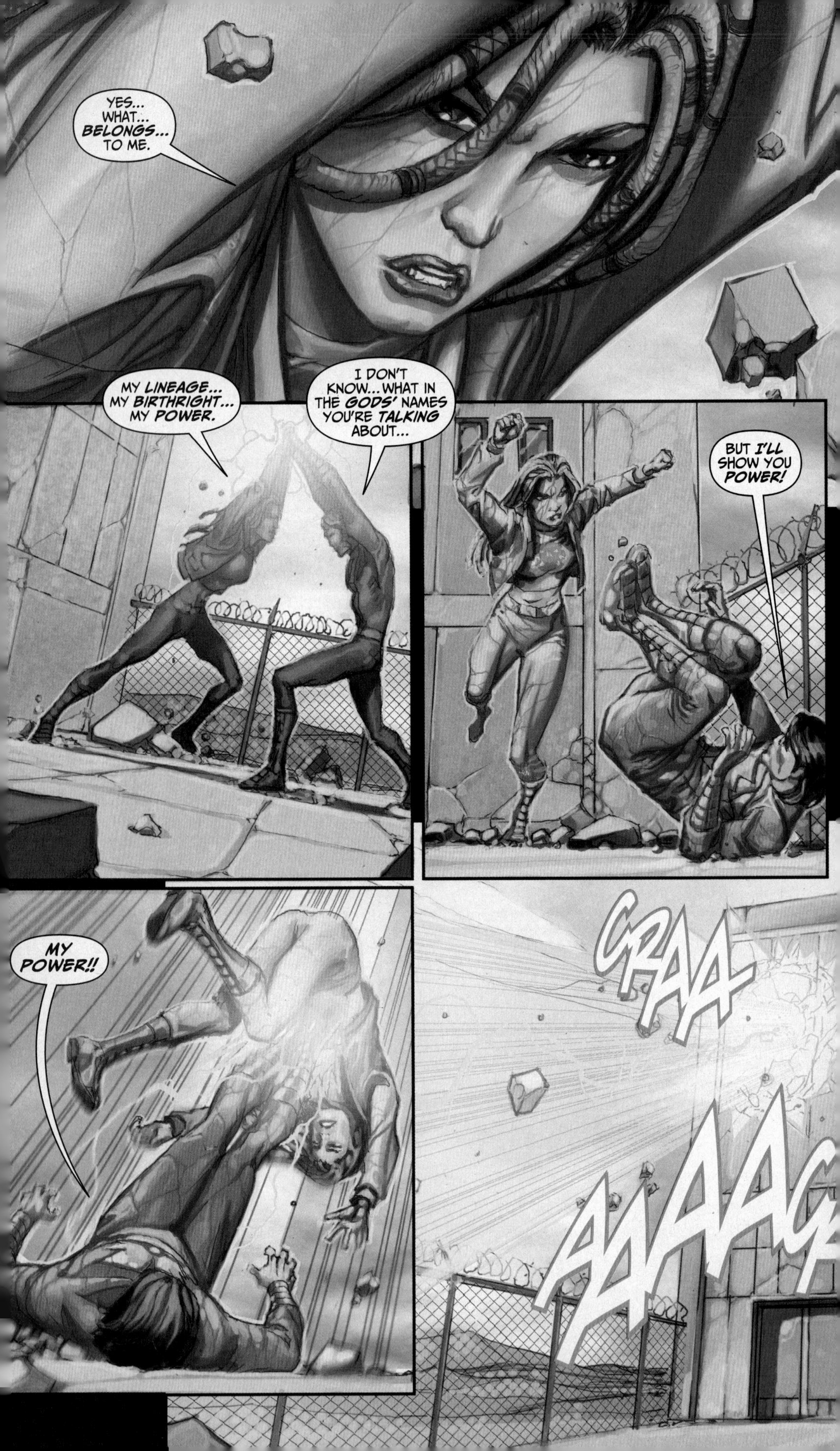
YES... WHAT... BELONGS... TO ME.
MY LINEAGE... MY BIRTHRIGHT... MY POWER.
I DON'T KNOW... WHAT IN THE GODS' NAMES YOU'RE TALKING ABOUT...
BUT I'LL SHOW YOU POWER!
MY POWER!!
CRAAAAAAAG

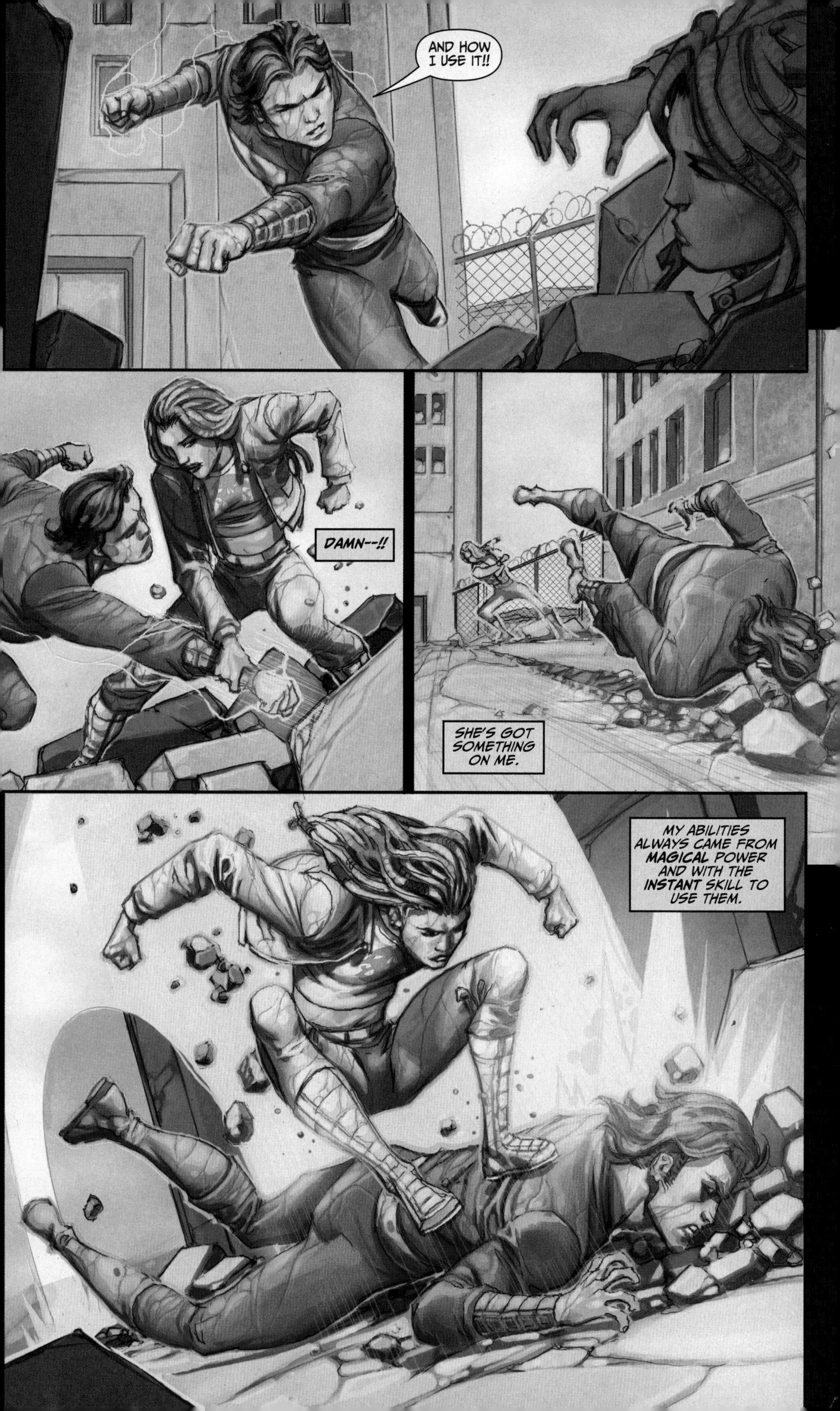

AND HOW I USE IT!!
DAMN--!!
SHE'S GOT SOMETHING ON ME.
MY ABILITIES ALWAYS CAME FROM MAGICAL POWER AND WITH THE INSTANT SKILL TO USE THEM.

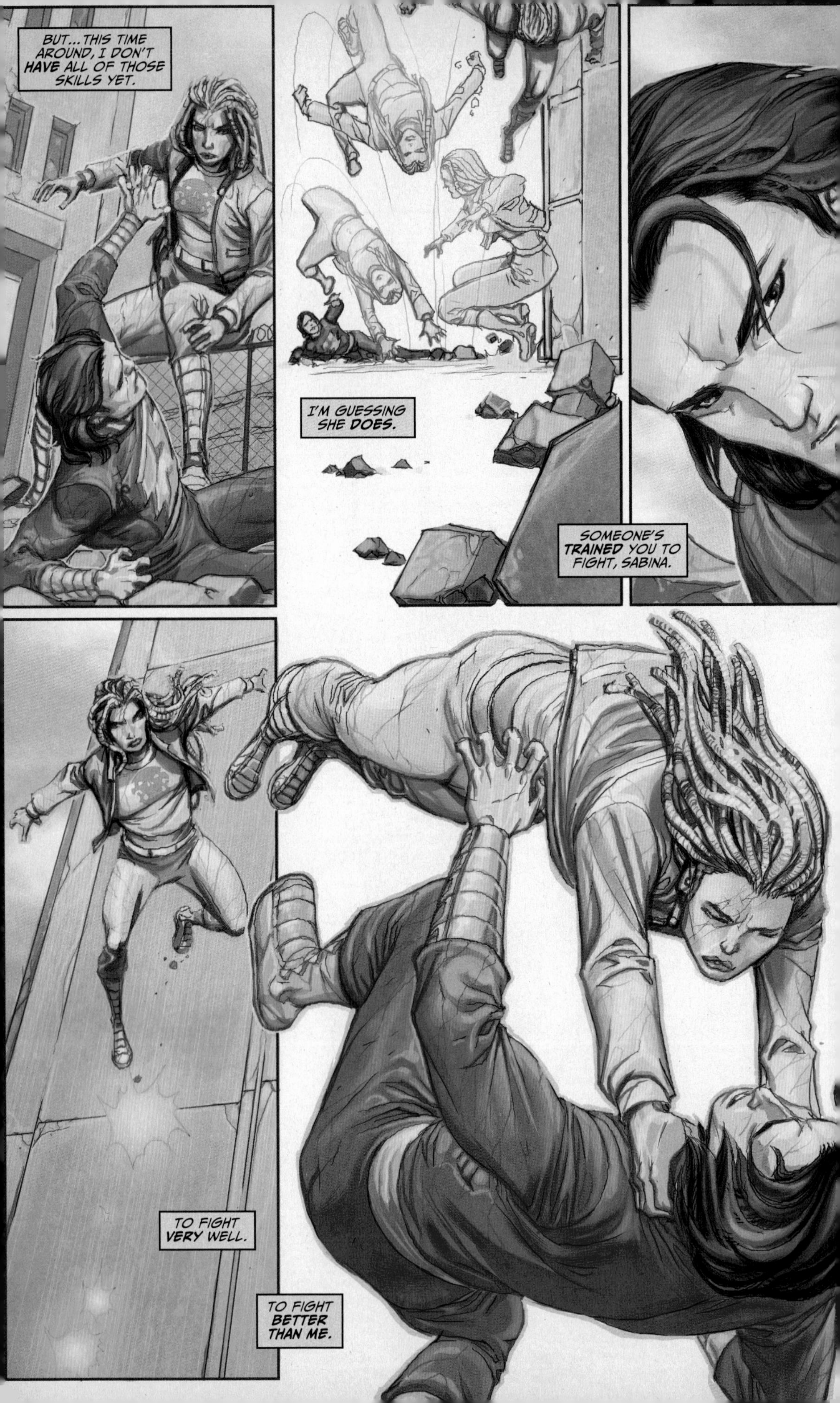

BUT...THIS TIME AROUND, I DON'T HAVE ALL OF THOSE SKILLS YET.
I'M GUESSING SHE DOES.
SOMEONE'S TRAINED YOU TO FIGHT, SABINA.
TO FIGHT VERY WELL.
TO FIGHT BETTER THAN ME.

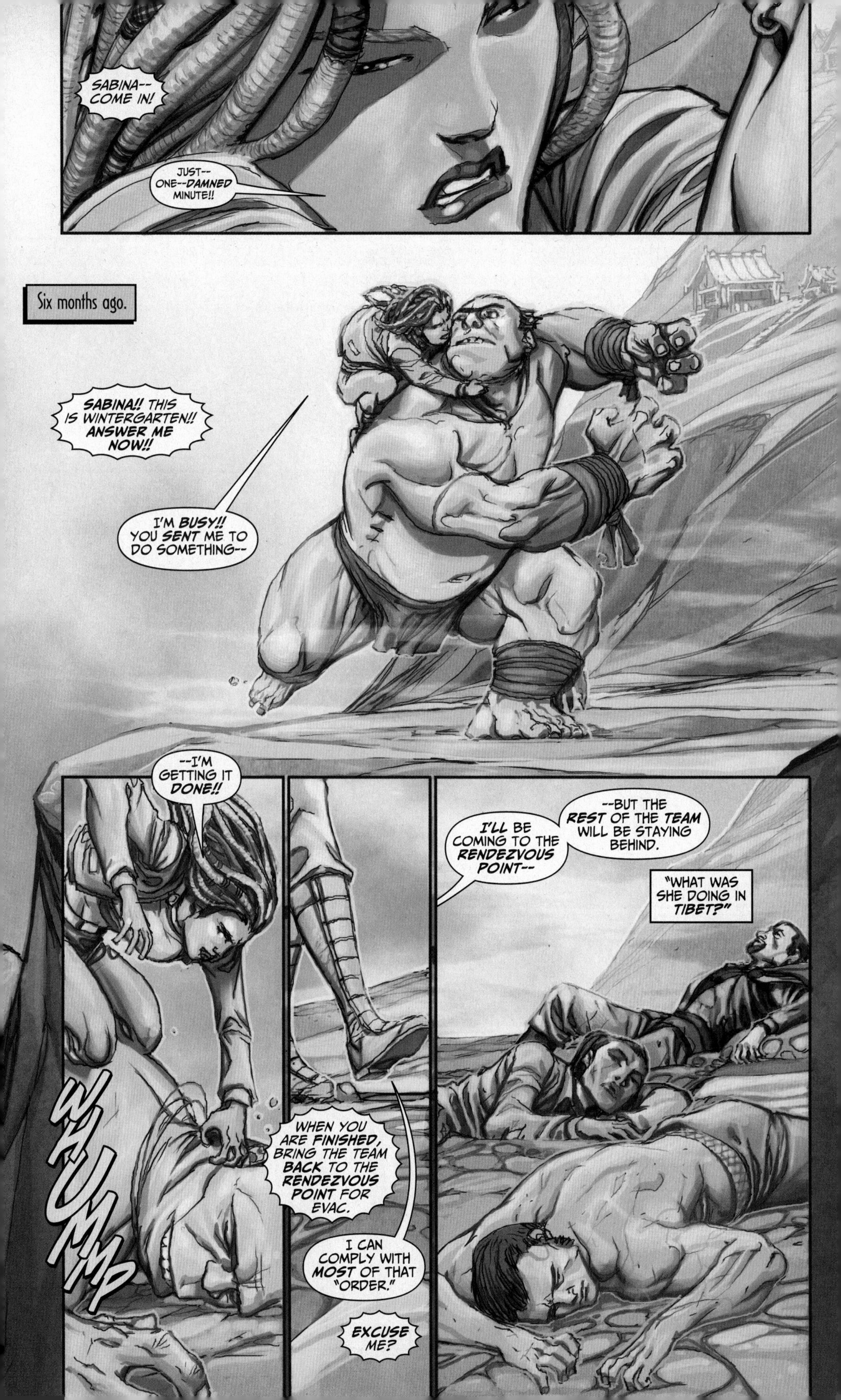

SABINA-- COME IN!
JUST-- ONE--DAMNED MINUTE!!
Six months ago.
SABINA!! THIS IS WINTERGARTEN!! ANSWER ME NOW!!
I'M BUSY!! YOU SENT ME TO DO SOMETHING--
--I'M GETTING IT DONE!!
WHUMMP
WHEN YOU ARE FINISHED, BRING THE TEAM BACK TO THE RENDEZVOUS POINT FOR EVAC.
I CAN COMPLY WITH MOST OF THAT "ORDER."
EXCUSE ME?
I'LL BE COMING TO THE RENDEZVOUS POINT--
--BUT THE REST OF THE TEAM WILL BE STAYING BEHIND.
"WHAT WAS SHE DOING IN TIBET?"

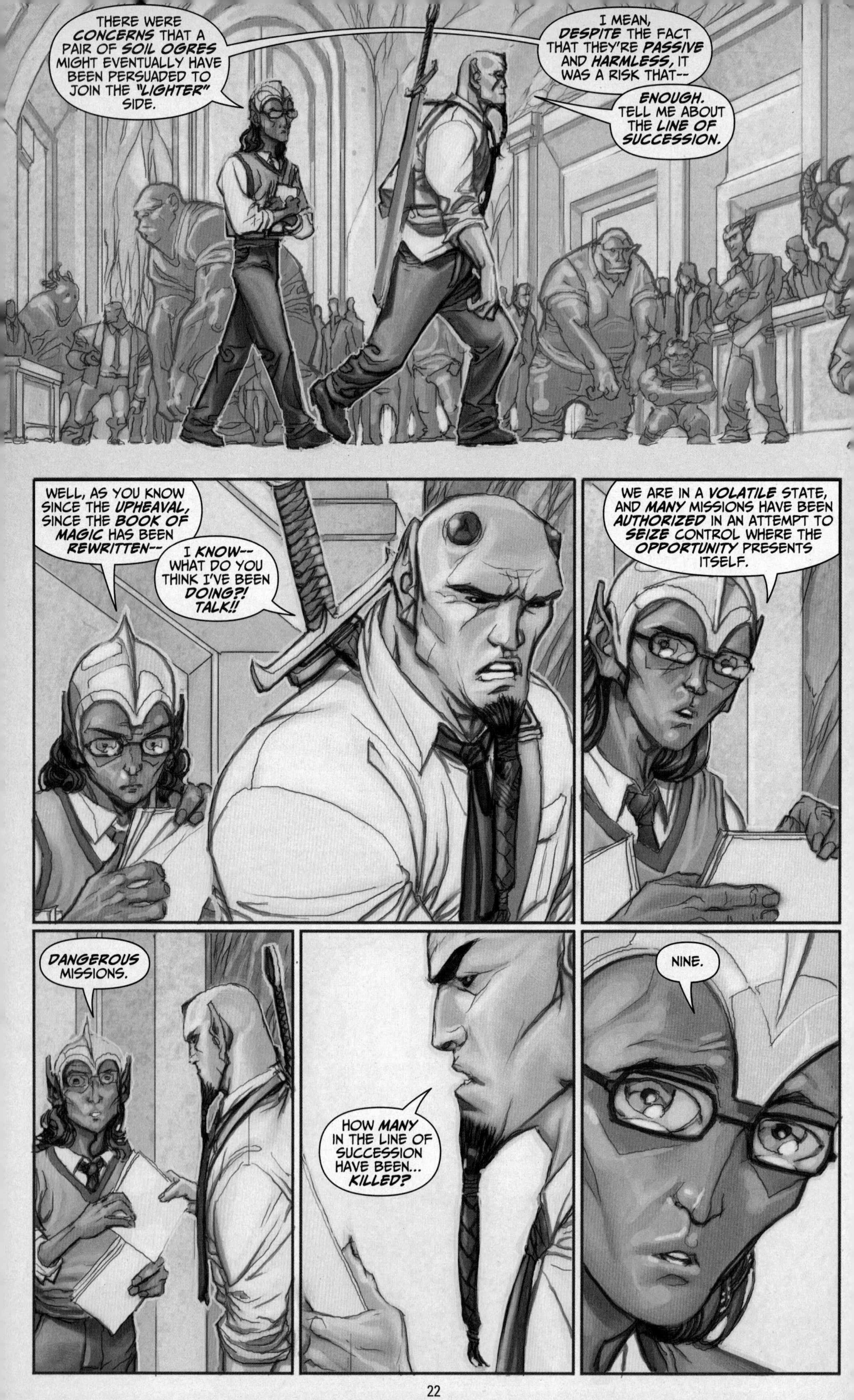
THERE WERE CONCERNS THAT A PAIR OF SOIL OGRES MIGHT EVENTUALLY HAVE BEEN PERSUADED TO JOIN THE "LIGHTER" SIDE.
I MEAN, DESPITE THE FACT THAT THEY'RE PASSIVE AND HARMLESS, IT WAS A RISK THAT--
ENOUGH. TELL ME ABOUT THE LINE OF SUCCESSION.
WELL, AS YOU KNOW SINCE THE UPHEAVAL, SINCE THE BOOK OF MAGIC HAS BEEN REWRITTEN--
I KNOW-- WHAT DO YOU THINK I'VE BEEN DOING?! TALK!!
WE ARE IN A VOLATILE STATE, AND MANY MISSIONS HAVE BEEN AUTHORIZED IN AN ATTEMPT TO SEIZE CONTROL WHERE THE OPPORTUNITY PRESENTS ITSELF.
DANGEROUS MISSIONS.
HOW MANY IN THE LINE OF SUCCESSION HAVE BEEN... KILLED?
NINE.

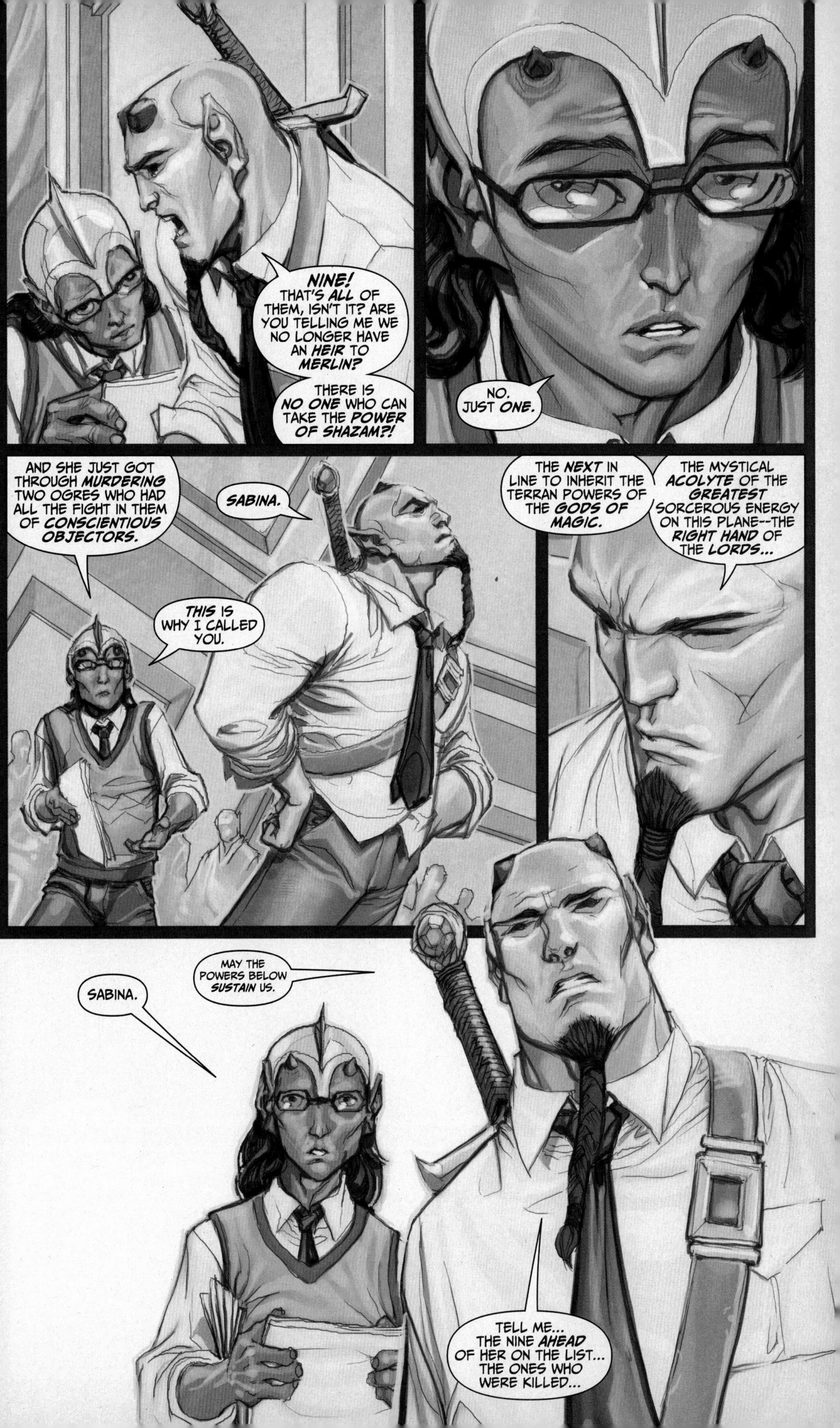
NINE! THAT'S ALL OF THEM, ISN'T IT? ARE YOU TELLING ME WE NO LONGER HAVE AN HEIR TO MERLIN?
THERE IS NO ONE WHO CAN TAKE THE POWER OF SHAZAM?!
NO. JUST ONE.
AND SHE JUST GOT THROUGH MURDERING TWO OGRES WHO HAD ALL THE FIGHT IN THEM OF CONSCIENTIOUS OBJECTORS.
SABINA.
THIS IS WHY I CALLED YOU.
THE NEXT IN LINE TO INHERIT THE TERRAN POWERS OF THE GODS OF MAGIC.
THE MYSTICAL ACOLYTE OF THE GREATEST SORCEROUS ENERGY ON THIS PLANE--THE RIGHT HAND OF THE LORDS...
SABINA.
MAY THE POWERS BELOW SUSTAIN US.
TELL ME... THE NINE AHEAD OF HER ON THE LIST... THE ONES WHO WERE KILLED...

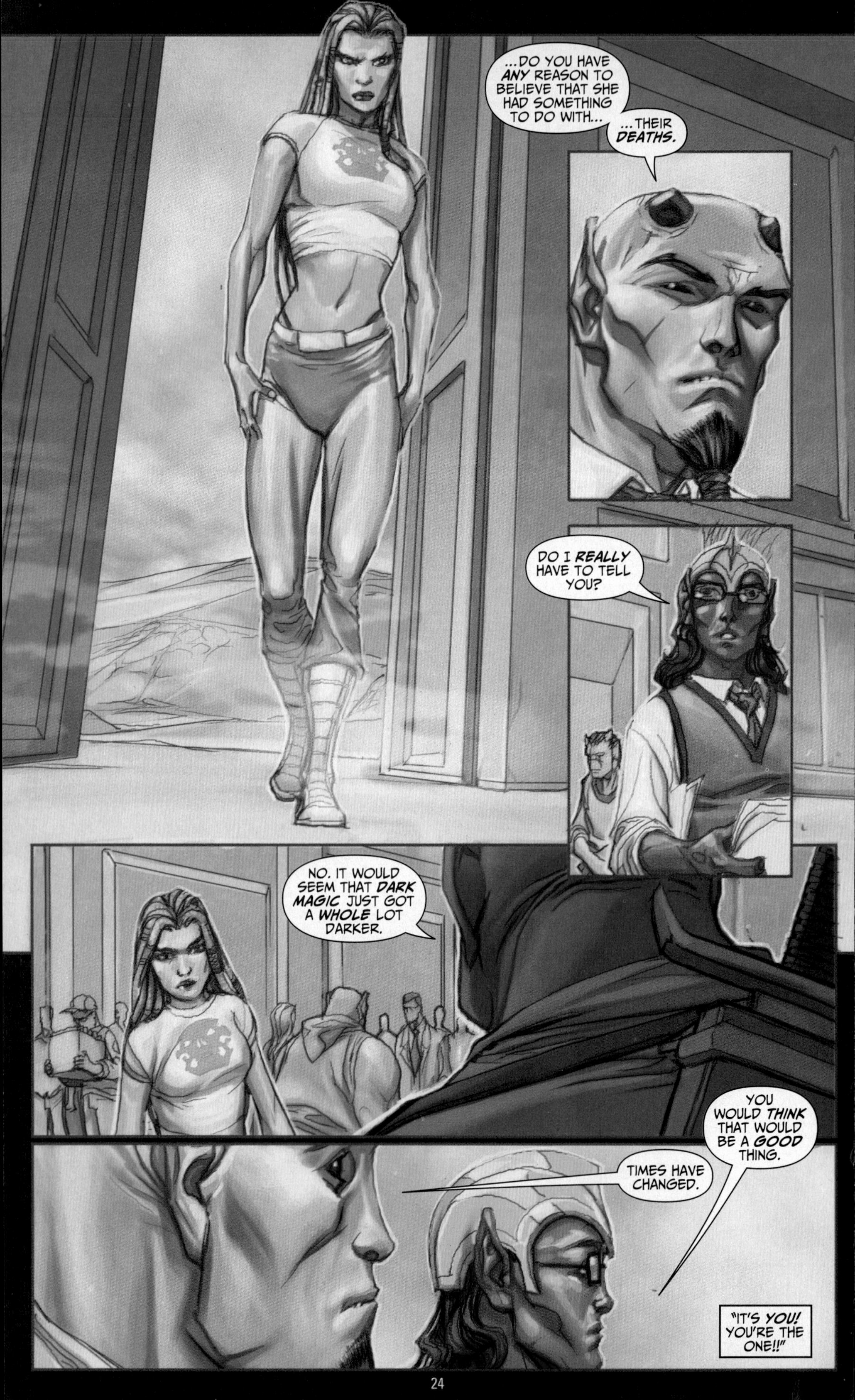

...DO YOU HAVE ANY REASON TO BELIEVE THAT SHE HAD SOMETHING TO DO WITH...
...THEIR DEATHS.
DO I REALLY HAVE TO TELL YOU?
NO. IT WOULD SEEM THAT DARK MAGIC JUST GOT A WHOLE LOT DARKER.
YOU WOULD THINK THAT WOULD BE A GOOD THING.
TIMES HAVE CHANGED.
"IT'S YOU! YOU'RE THE ONE!!"

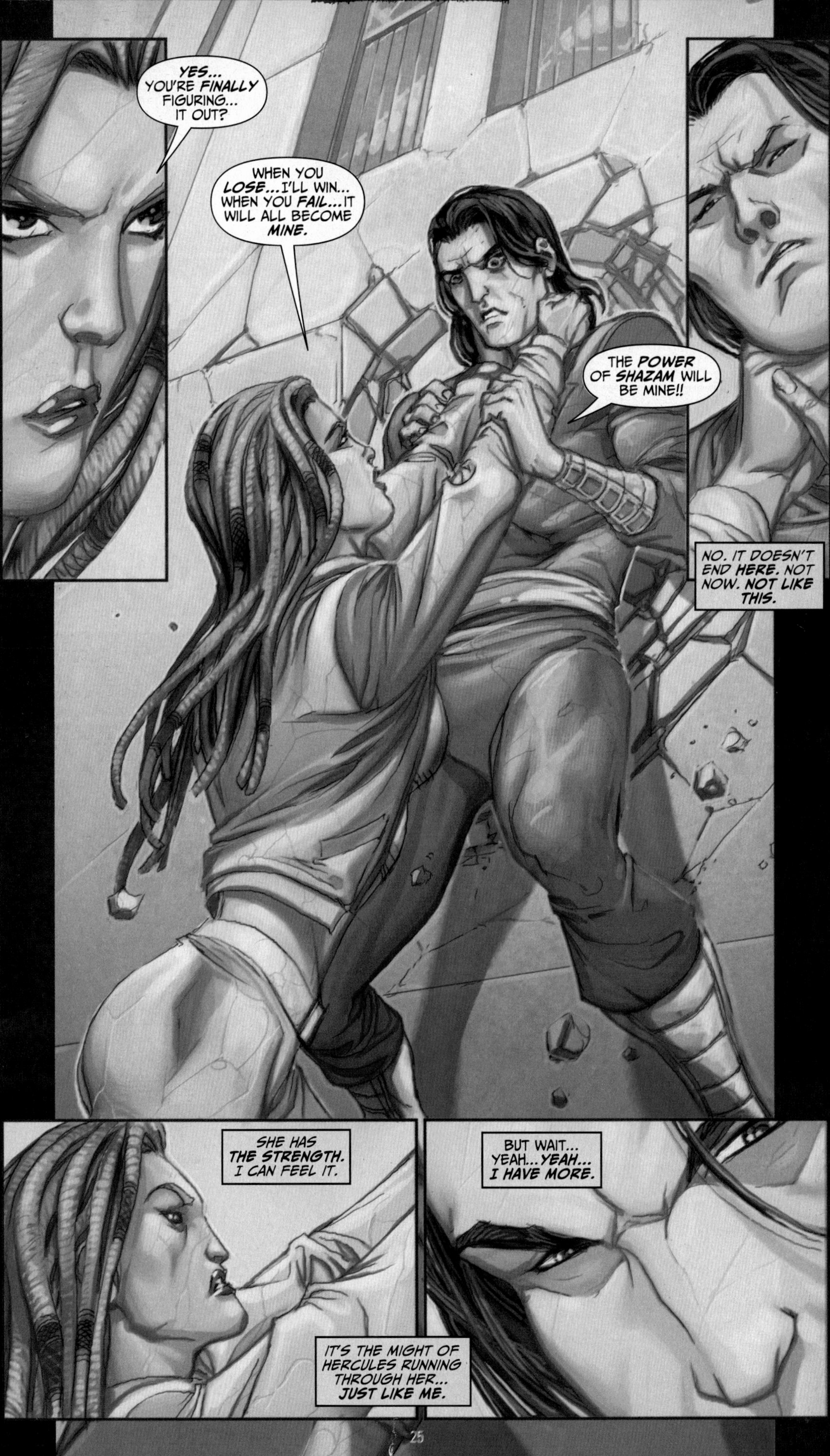
YES... YOU'RE FINALLY FIGURING... IT OUT?
WHEN YOU LOSE...I'LL WIN... WHEN YOU FAIL...IT WILL ALL BECOME MINE.
THE POWER OF SHAZAM WILL BE MINE!!
NO. IT DOESN'T END HERE. NOT NOW. NOT LIKE THIS.
SHE HAS THE STRENGTH. I CAN FEEL IT.
BUT WAIT... YEAH...YEAH... I HAVE MORE.
IT'S THE MIGHT OF HERCULES RUNNING THROUGH HER... JUST LIKE ME.

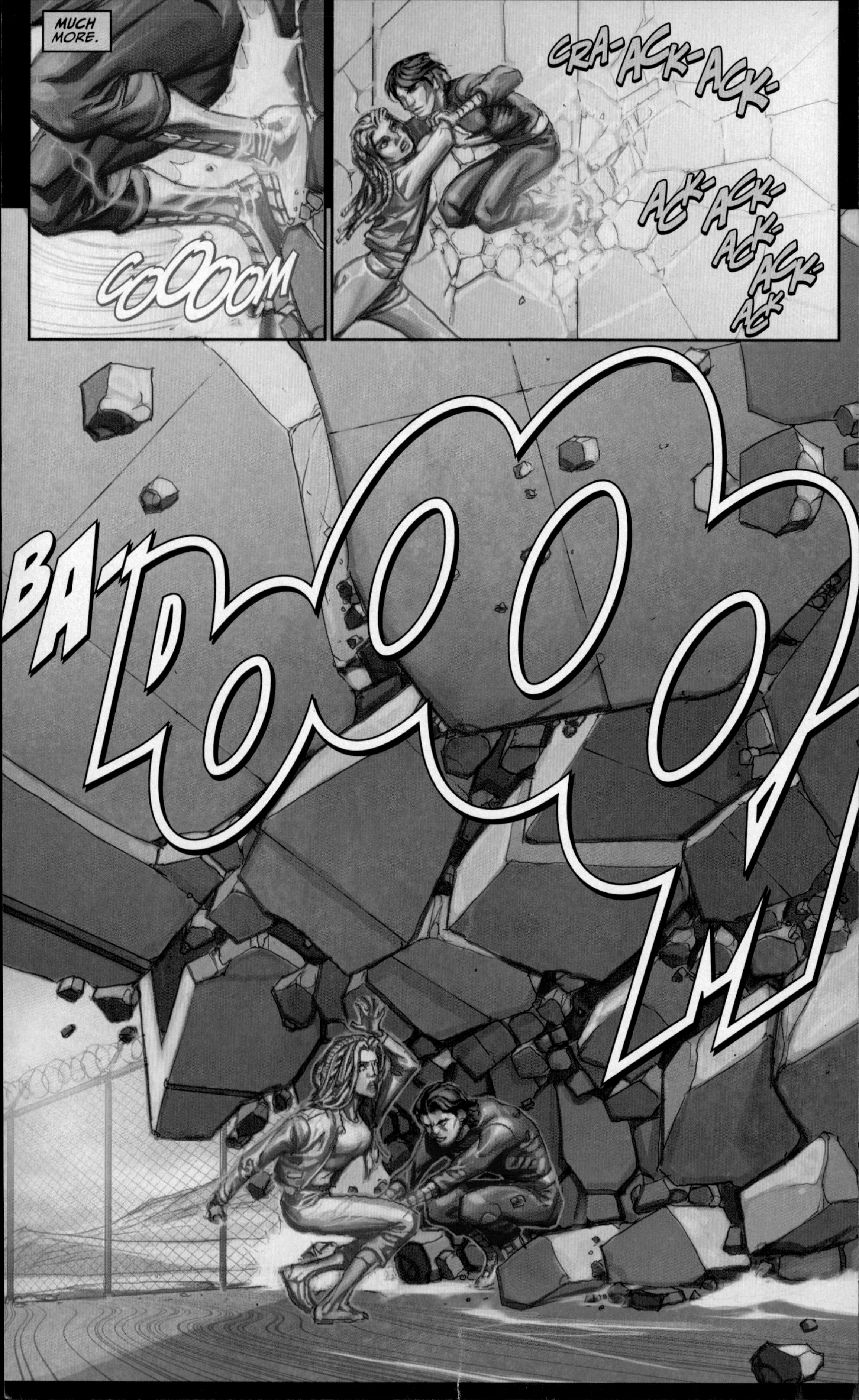
MUCH MORE.
COOOOOM
CRA-ACK-ACK
ACK-ACK-ACK-ACK-ACK
BA-DOOOOM

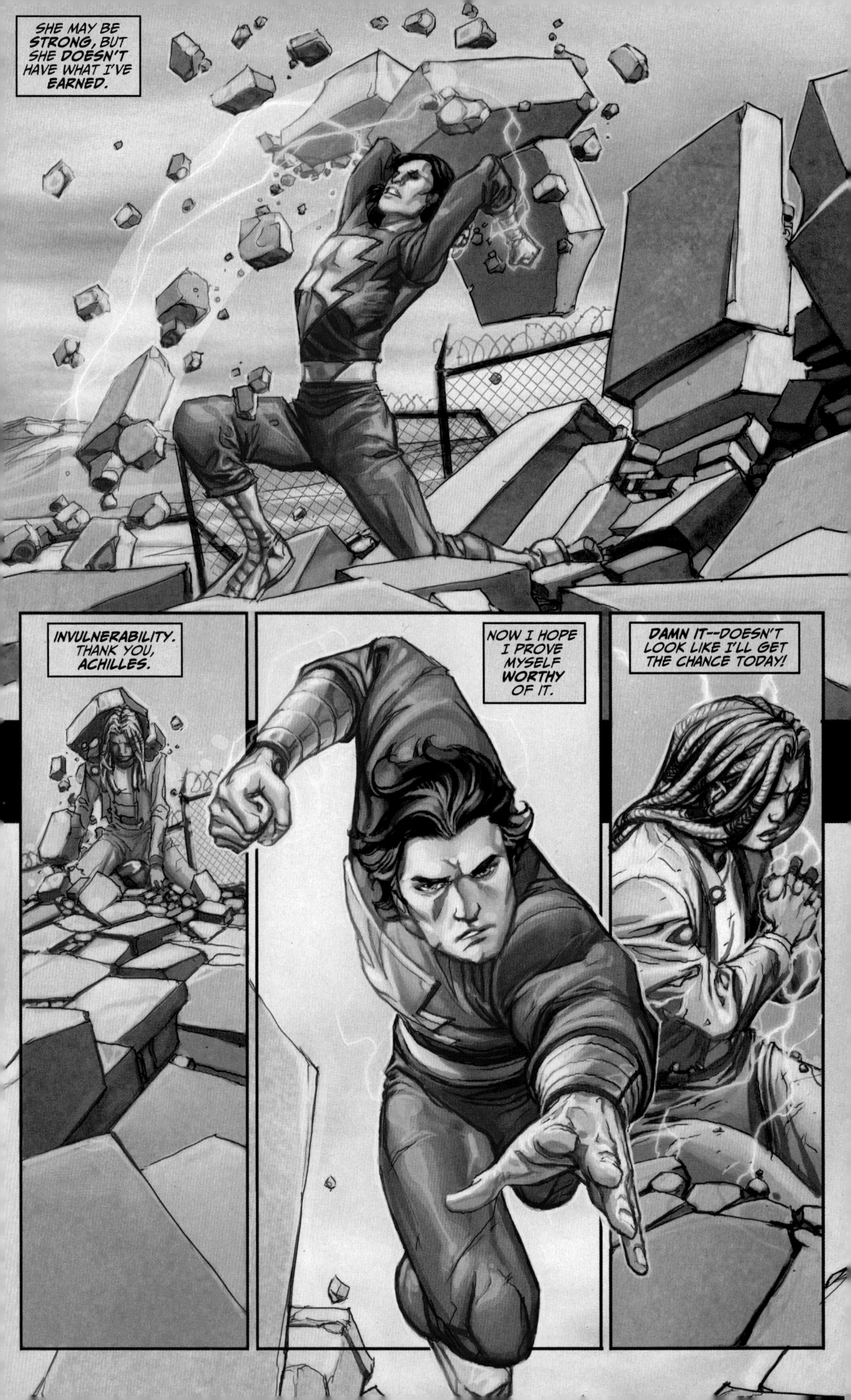
SHE MAY BE STRONG, BUT SHE DOESN'T HAVE WHAT I'VE EARNED.
INVULNERABILITY. THANK YOU, ACHILLES.
NOW I HOPE I PROVE MYSELF WORTHY OF IT.
DAMN IT--DOESN'T LOOK LIKE I'LL GET THE CHANCE TODAY!

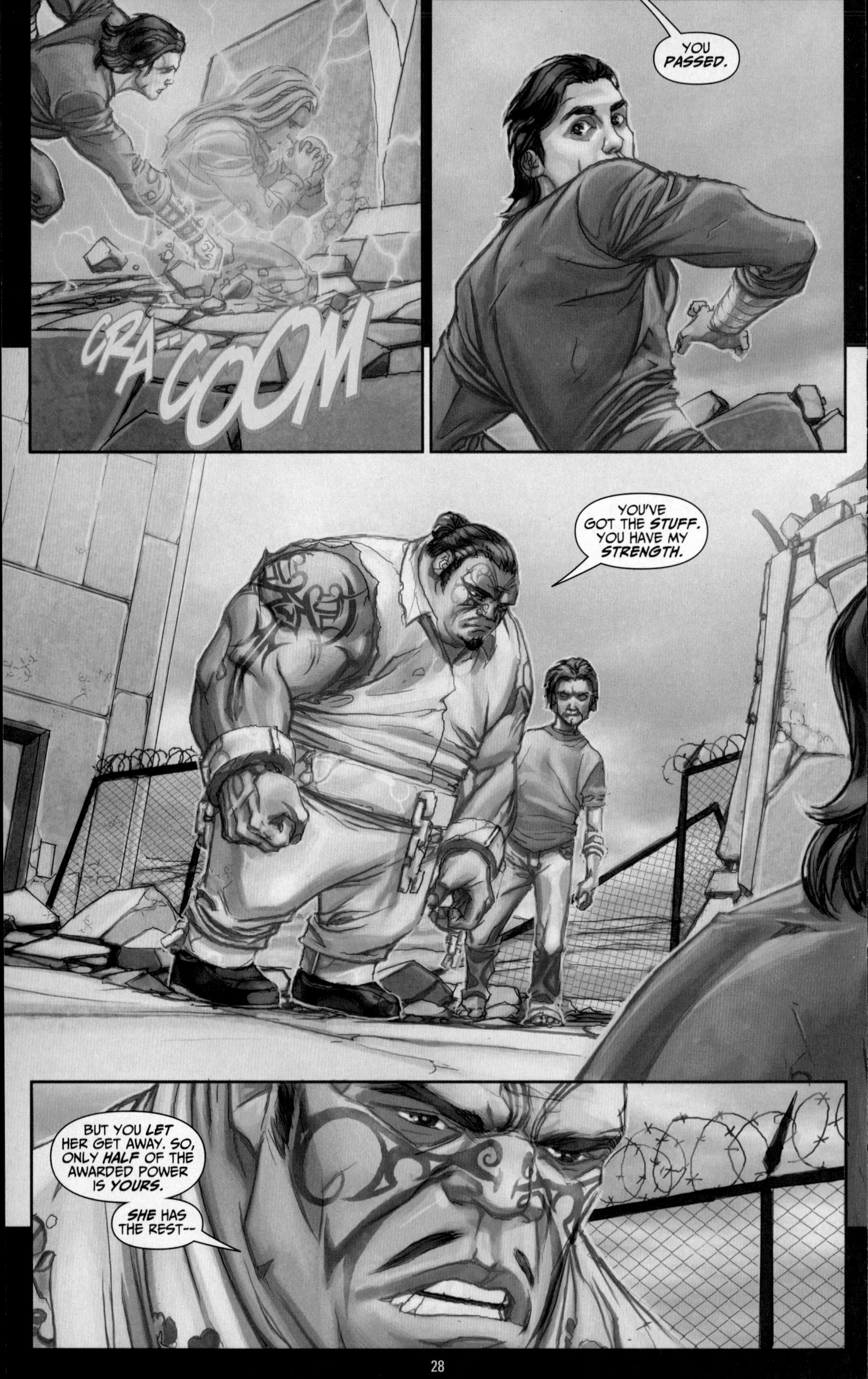
CRA-COOM
YOU PASSED.
YOU'VE GOT THE STUFF. YOU HAVE MY STRENGTH.
BUT YOU LET HER GET AWAY. SO, ONLY HALF OF THE AWARDED POWER IS YOURS.
SHE HAS THE REST--

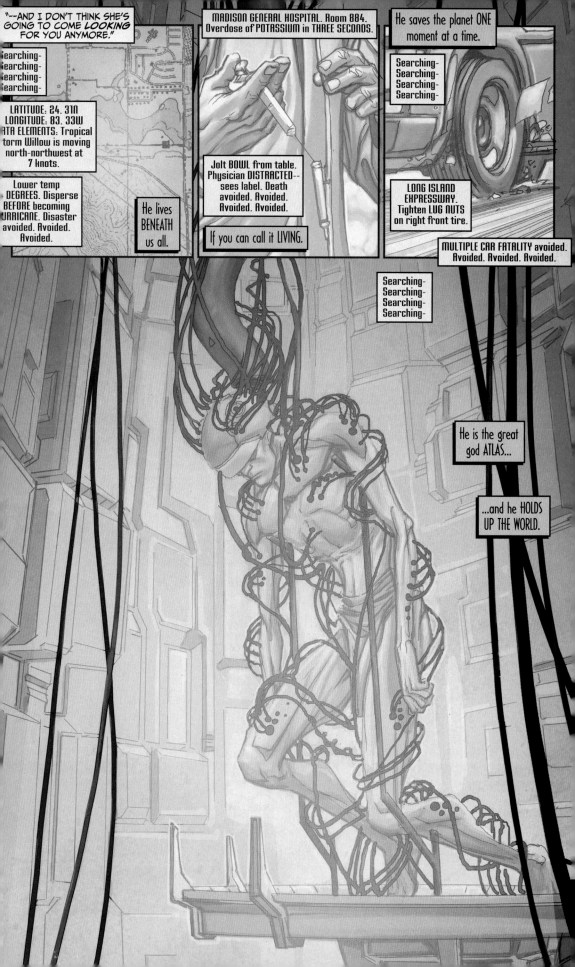

"--AND I DON'T THINK SHE'S GOING TO COME *LOOKING* FOR YOU ANYMORE."

Searching-
Searching-
Searching-
Searching-

LATITUDE: 24. 31N
LONGITUDE: 83. 33W
DATA ELEMENTS: Tropical storm Willow is moving north-northwest at 7 knots.

Lower temp # DEGREES. Disperse BEFORE becoming HURRICANE. Disaster avoided. Avoided. Avoided.

He lives BENEATH us all.

MADISON GENERAL HOSPITAL. Room 884. Overdose of POTASSIUM in THREE SECONDS.

Jolt BOWL from table. Physician DISTRACTED-- sees label. Death avoided. Avoided. Avoided.

If you can call it LIVING.

He saves the planet ONE moment at a time.

Searching-
Searching-
Searching-
Searching-

LONG ISLAND EXPRESSWAY. Tighten LUG NUTS on right front tire.

MULTIPLE CAR FATALITY avoided. Avoided. Avoided. Avoided.

Searching-
Searching-
Searching-
Searching-

He is the great god ATLAS...

...and he HOLDS UP THE WORLD.

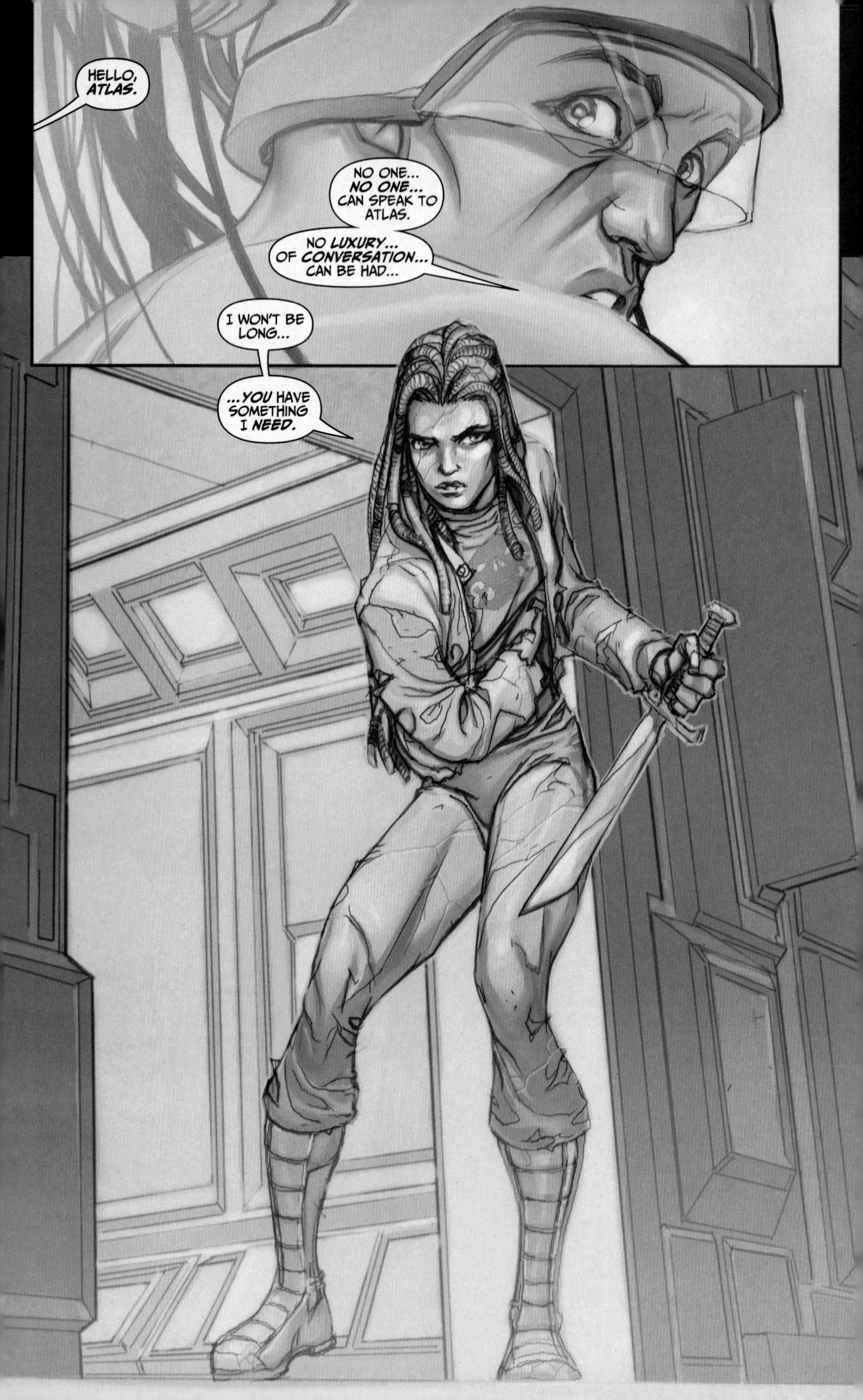
HELLO, ATLAS.
NO ONE... NO ONE... CAN SPEAK TO ATLAS.
NO LUXURY... OF CONVERSATION... CAN BE HAD...
I WON'T BE LONG...
...YOU HAVE SOMETHING I NEED.

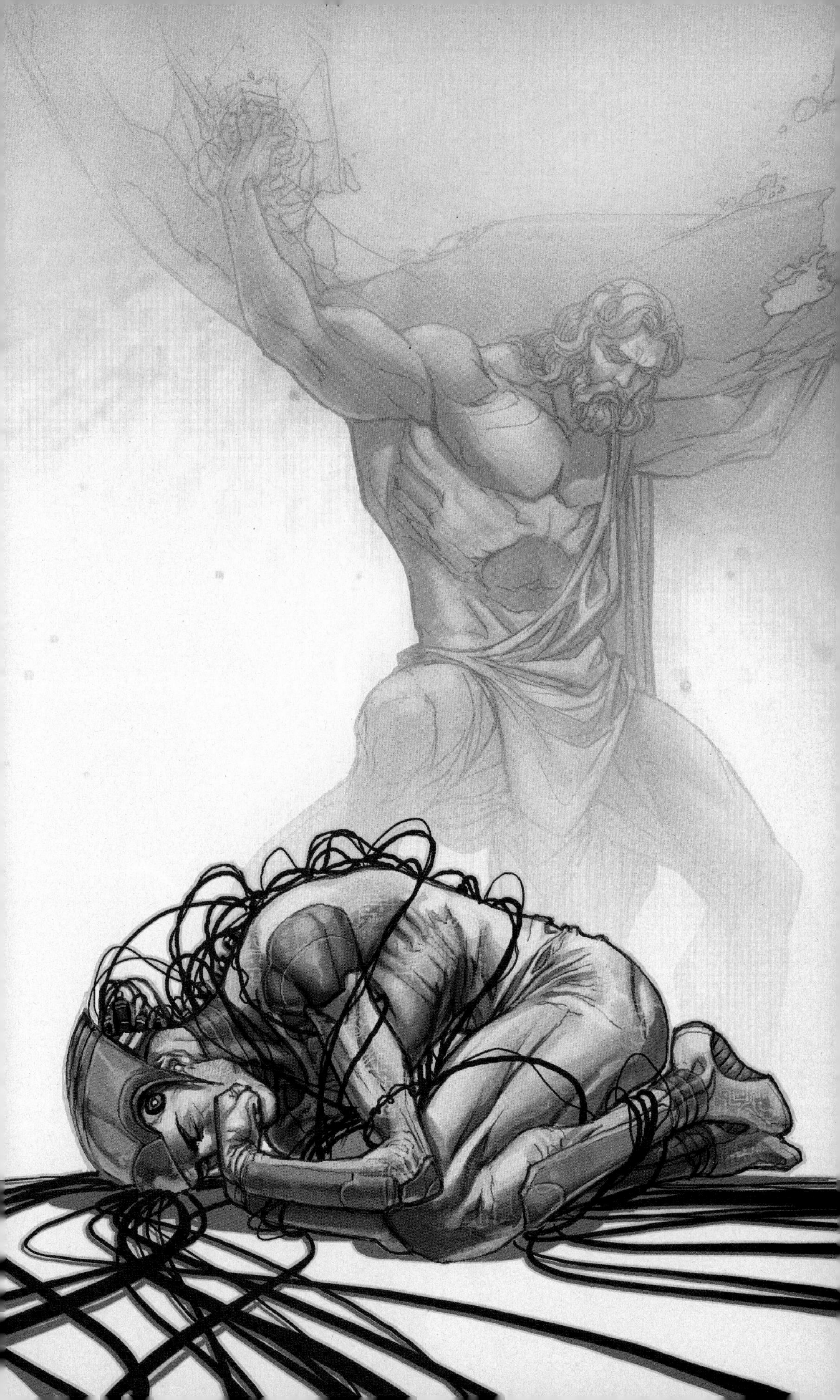

CHAPTER EIGHT:

HE'S GOT THE
WHOLE
WORLD
IN HIS HANDS

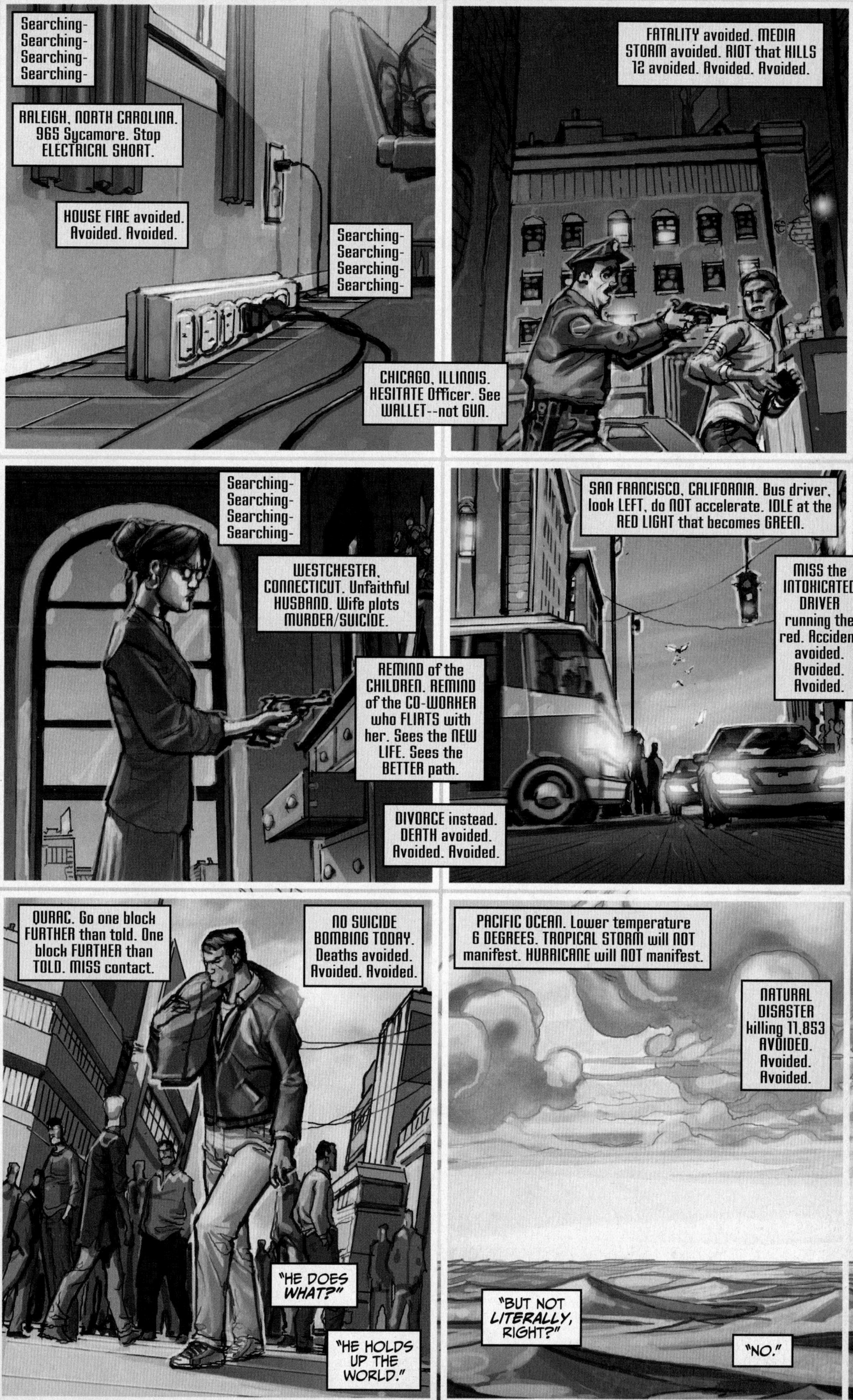
Searching-
Searching-
Searching-
Searching-
RALEIGH, NORTH CAROLINA. 965 Sycamore. Stop ELECTRICAL SHORT.
HOUSE FIRE avoided. Avoided. Avoided.
Searching-
Searching-
Searching-
Searching-
CHICAGO, ILLINOIS. HESITATE Officer. See WALLET--not GUN.
FATALITY avoided. MEDIA STORM avoided. RIOT that KILLS 12 avoided. Avoided. Avoided.
Searching-
Searching-
Searching-
Searching-
WESTCHESTER, CONNECTICUT. Unfaithful HUSBAND. Wife plots MURDER/SUICIDE.
REMIND of the CHILDREN. REMIND of the CO-WORKER who FLIRTS with her. Sees the NEW LIFE. Sees the BETTER path.
DIVORCE instead. DEATH avoided. Avoided. Avoided.
SAN FRANCISCO, CALIFORNIA. Bus driver, look LEFT, do NOT accelerate. IDLE at the RED LIGHT that becomes GREEN.
MISS the INTOXICATED DRIVER running the red. Accident avoided. Avoided. Avoided.
QURAC. Go one block FURTHER than told. One block FURTHER than TOLD. MISS contact.
NO SUICIDE BOMBING TODAY. Deaths avoided. Avoided. Avoided.
"HE DOES *WHAT?*"
"HE HOLDS UP THE WORLD."
PACIFIC OCEAN. Lower temperature 6 DEGREES. TROPICAL STORM will NOT manifest. HURRICANE will NOT manifest.
NATURAL DISASTER killing 11,853 AVOIDED. Avoided. Avoided.
"BUT NOT *LITERALLY*, RIGHT?"
"NO."

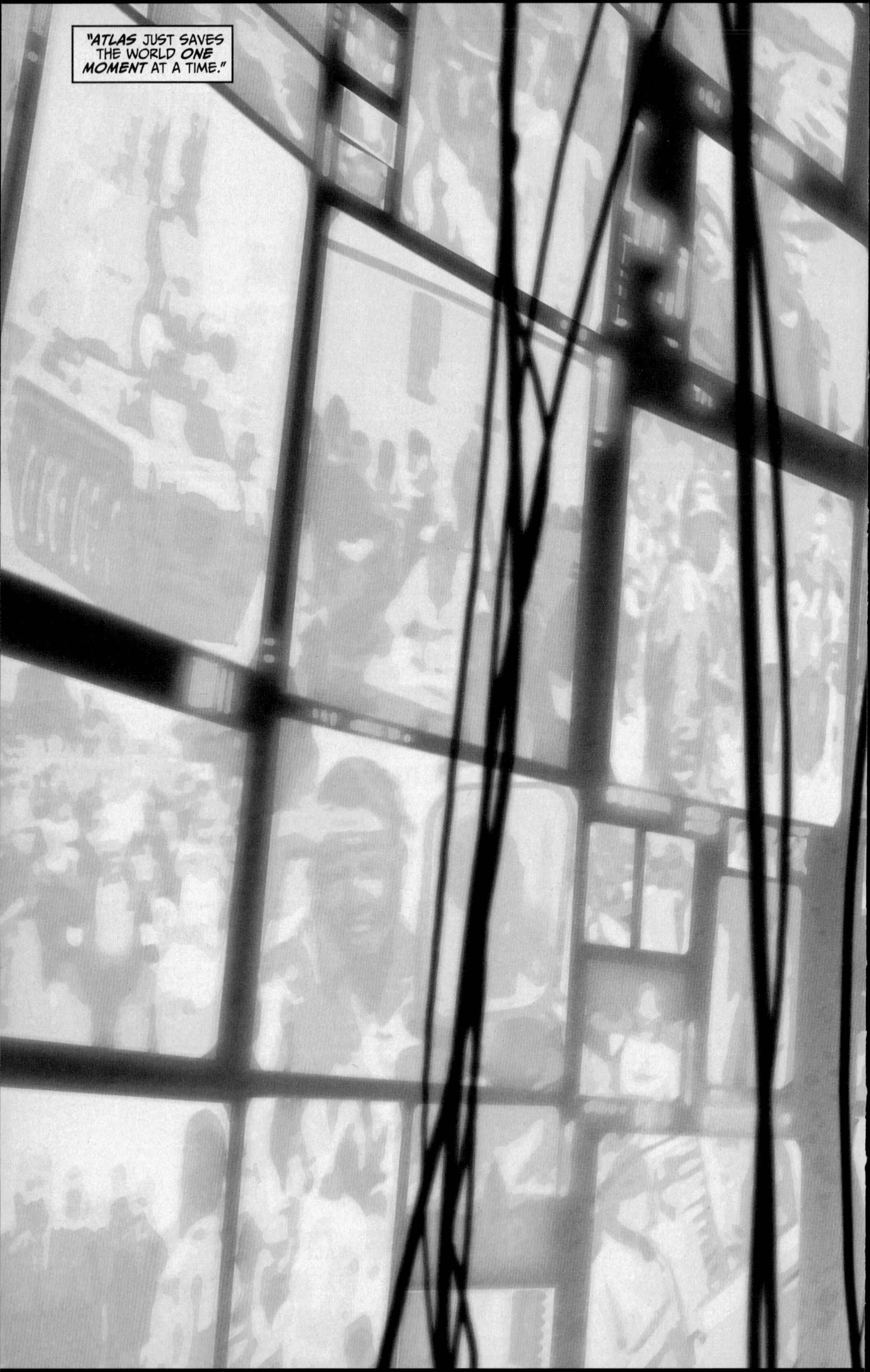
"ATLAS JUST SAVES THE WORLD ONE MOMENT AT A TIME."

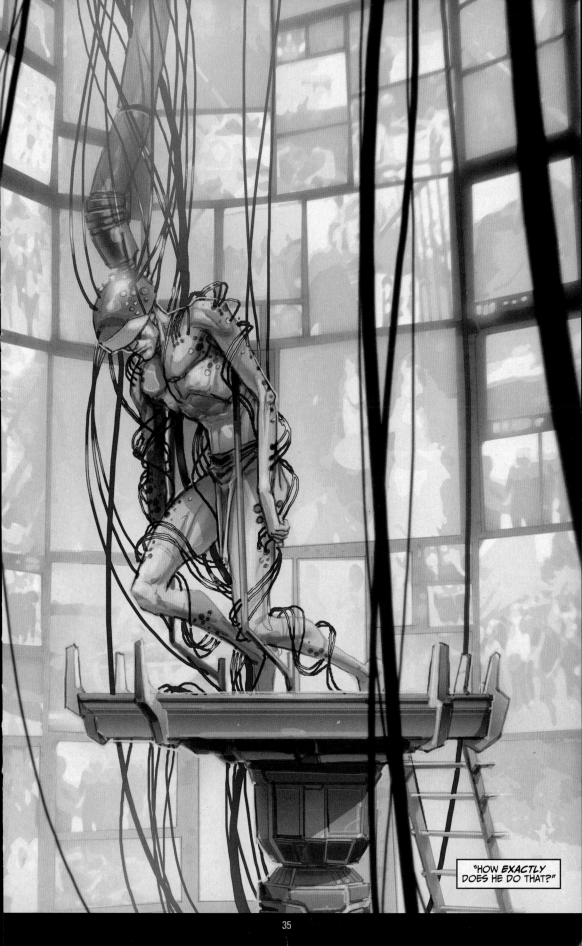

"HOW *EXACTLY* DOES HE DO THAT?"

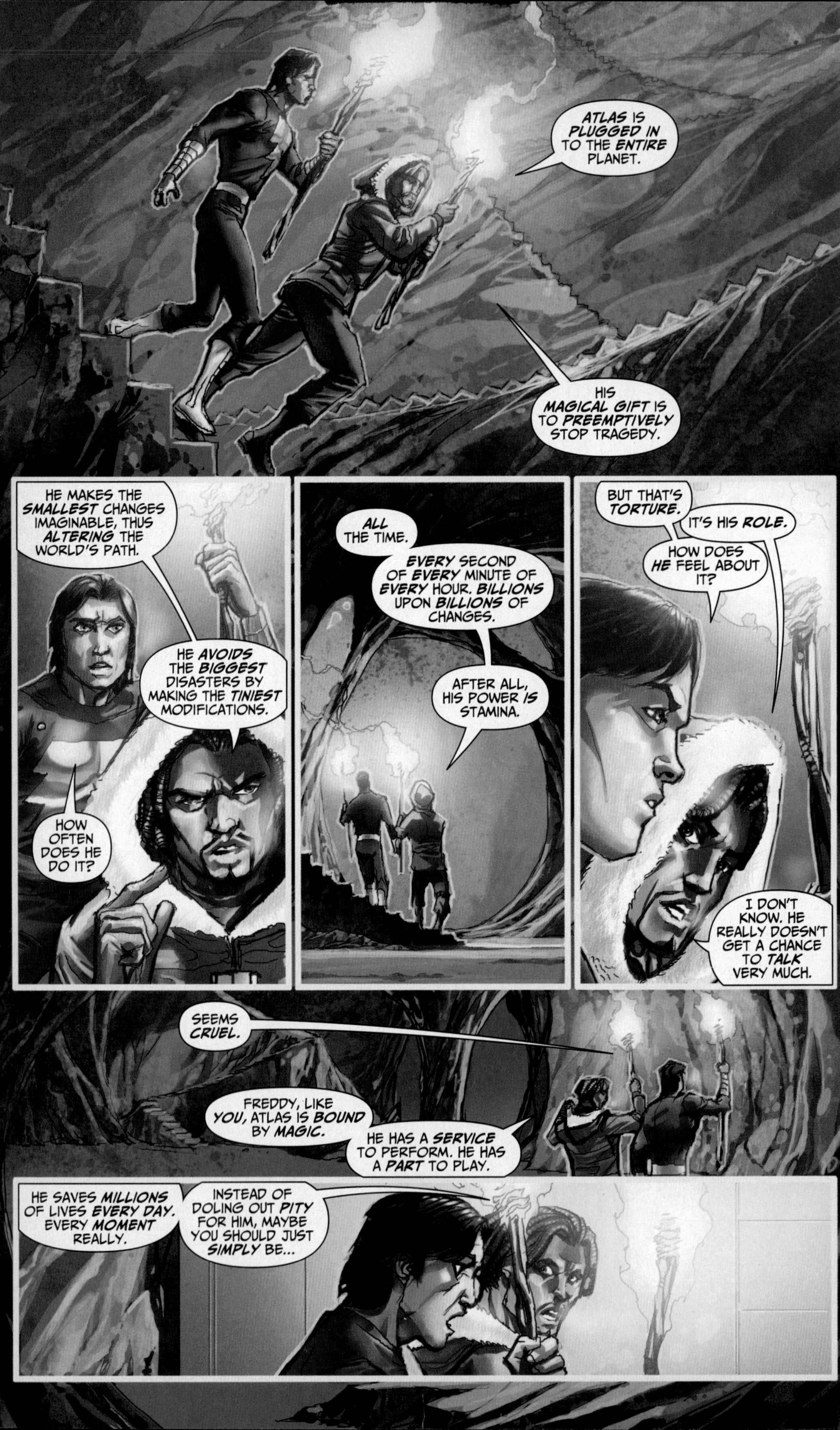
ATLAS IS PLUGGED IN TO THE ENTIRE PLANET.
HIS MAGICAL GIFT IS TO PREEMPTIVELY STOP TRAGEDY.
HE MAKES THE SMALLEST CHANGES IMAGINABLE, THUS ALTERING THE WORLD'S PATH.
HE AVOIDS THE BIGGEST DISASTERS BY MAKING THE TINIEST MODIFICATIONS.
HOW OFTEN DOES HE DO IT?
ALL THE TIME.
EVERY SECOND OF EVERY MINUTE OF EVERY HOUR. BILLIONS UPON BILLIONS OF CHANGES.
AFTER ALL, HIS POWER IS STAMINA.
BUT THAT'S TORTURE.
IT'S HIS ROLE.
HOW DOES HE FEEL ABOUT IT?
I DON'T KNOW. HE REALLY DOESN'T GET A CHANCE TO TALK VERY MUCH.
SEEMS CRUEL.
FREDDY, LIKE YOU, ATLAS IS BOUND BY MAGIC.
HE HAS A SERVICE TO PERFORM. HE HAS A PART TO PLAY.
HE SAVES MILLIONS OF LIVES EVERY DAY. EVERY MOMENT REALLY.
INSTEAD OF DOLING OUT PITY FOR HIM, MAYBE YOU SHOULD JUST SIMPLY BE...

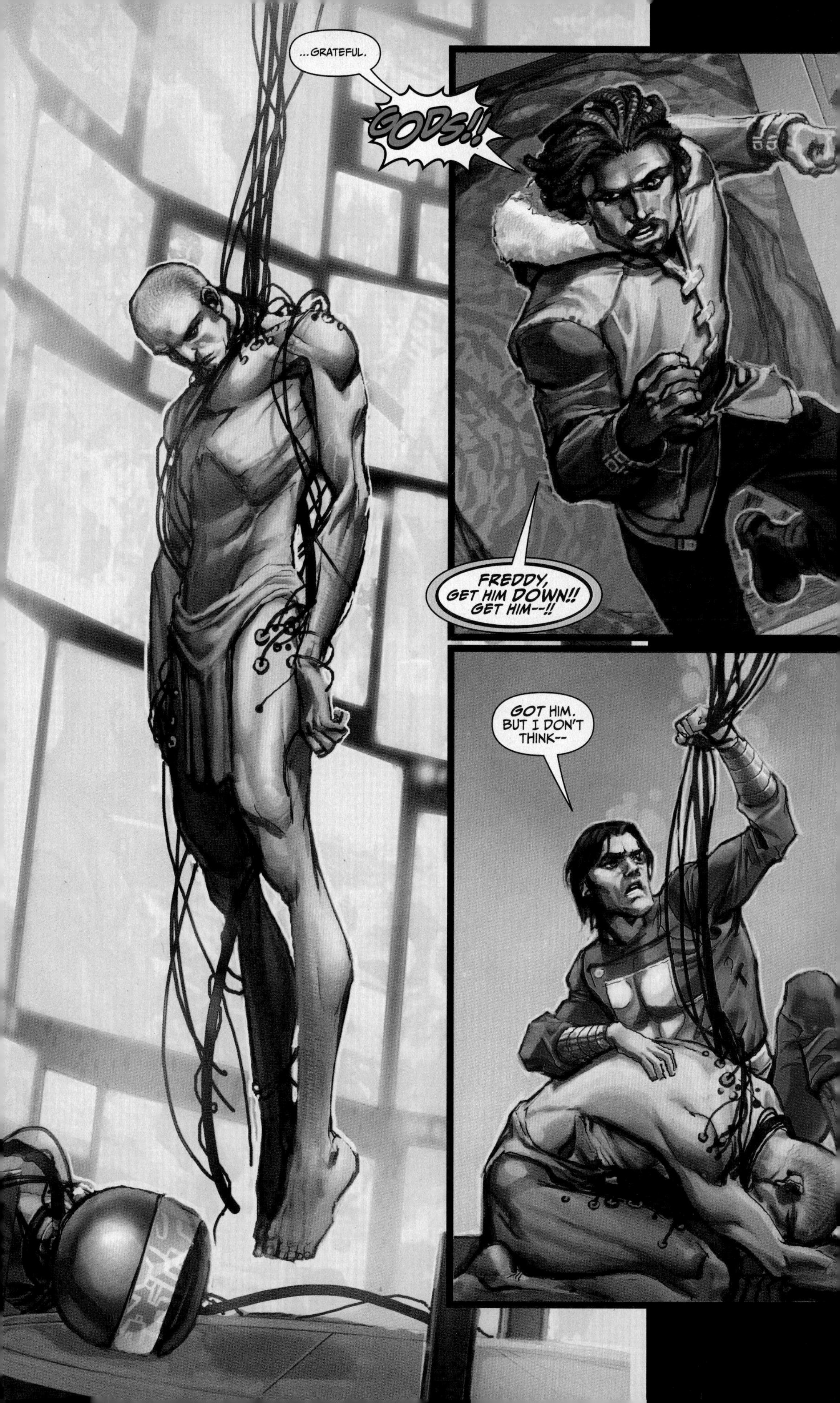
...GRATEFUL.
GODS!!
FREDDY, GET HIM DOWN!! GET HIM--!!
GOT HIM. BUT I DON'T THINK--

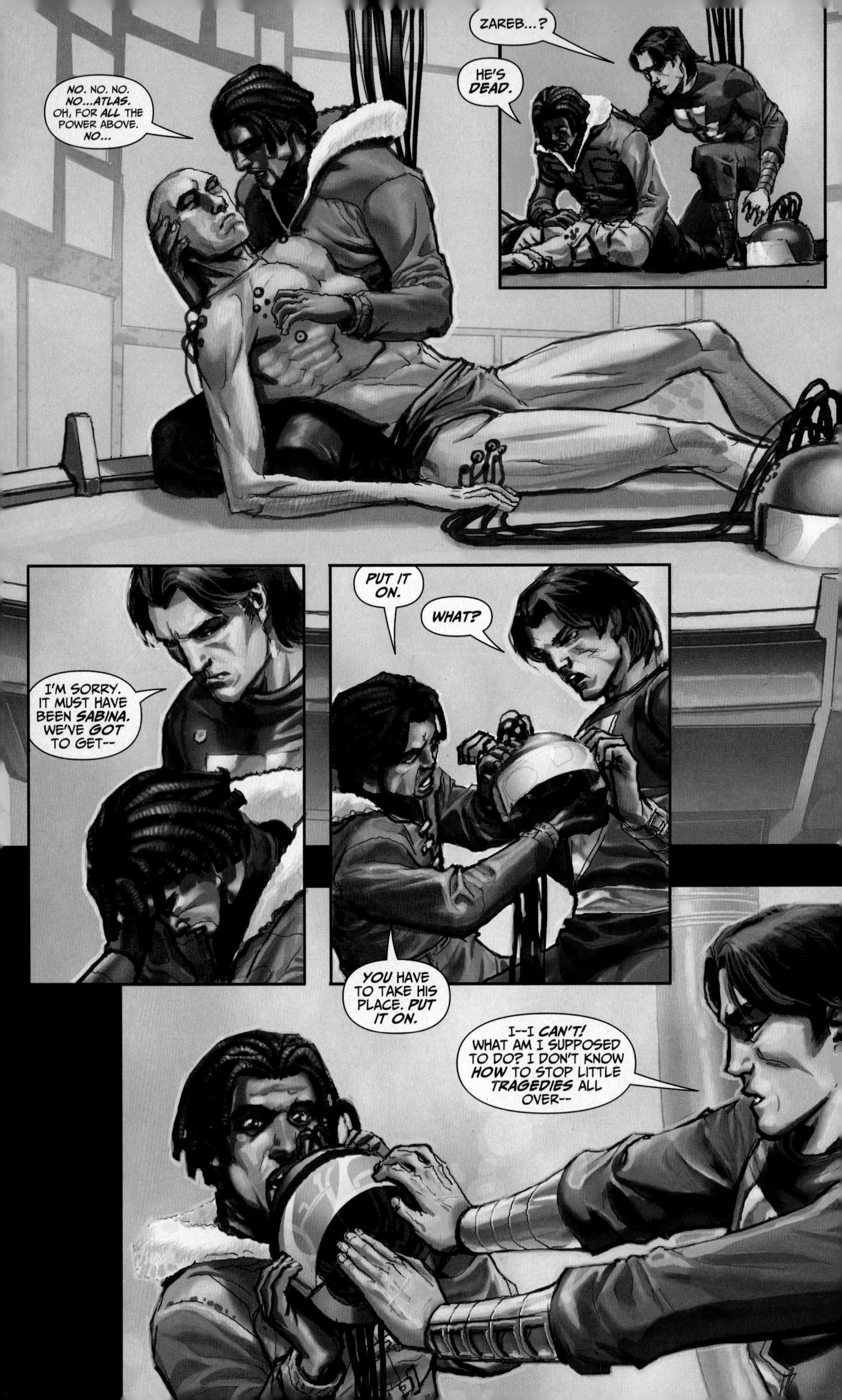
NO. NO. NO. NO...ATLAS. OH, FOR ALL THE POWER ABOVE. NO...
ZAREB...?
HE'S DEAD.
I'M SORRY. IT MUST HAVE BEEN SABINA. WE'VE GOT TO GET--
PUT IT ON.
WHAT?
YOU HAVE TO TAKE HIS PLACE. PUT IT ON.
I--I CAN'T! WHAT AM I SUPPOSED TO DO? I DON'T KNOW HOW TO STOP LITTLE TRAGEDIES ALL OVER--

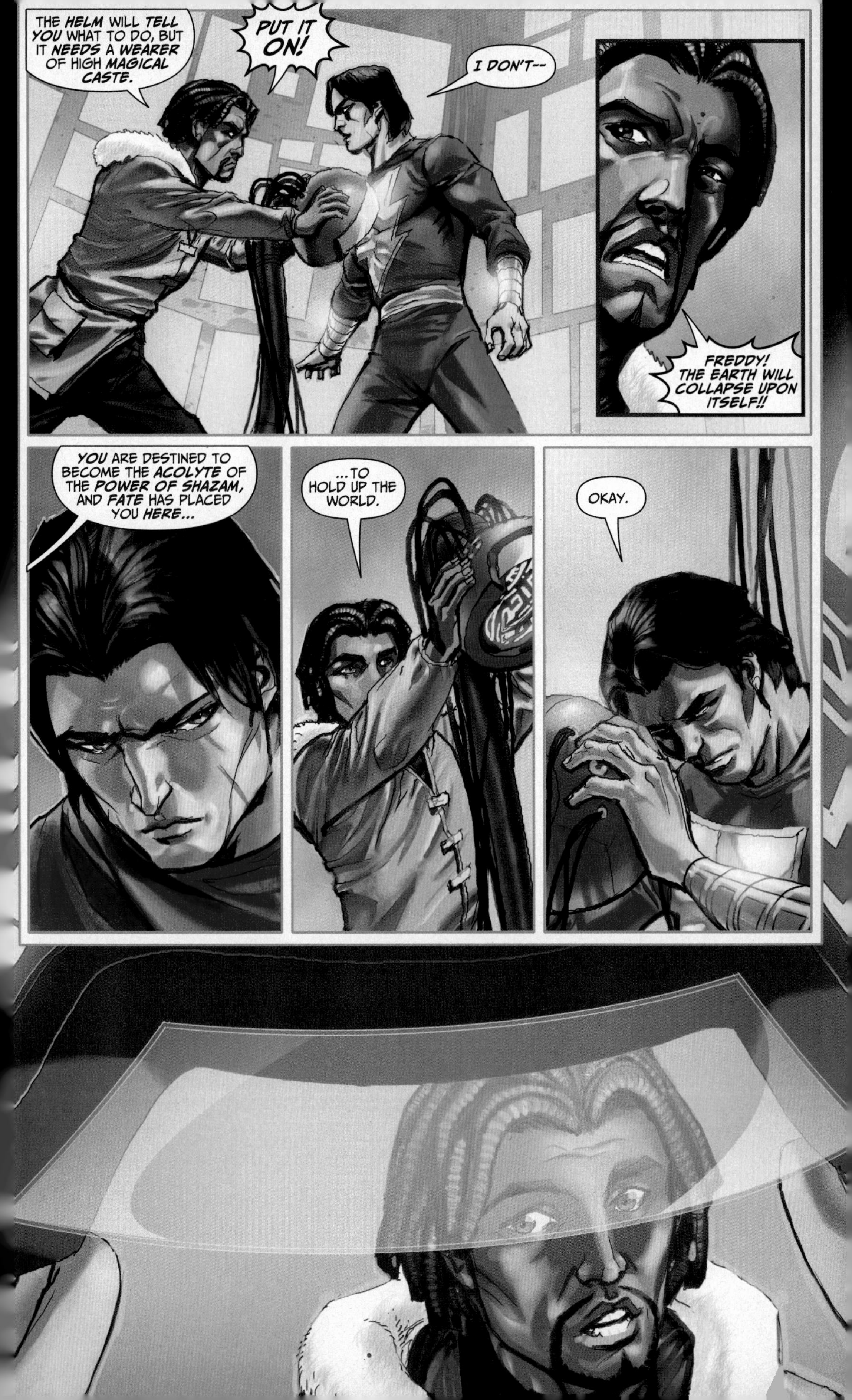
THE HELM WILL TELL YOU WHAT TO DO, BUT IT NEEDS A WEARER OF HIGH MAGICAL CASTE.
PUT IT ON!
I DON'T--
FREDDY! THE EARTH WILL COLLAPSE UPON ITSELF!!
YOU ARE DESTINED TO BECOME THE ACOLYTE OF THE POWER OF SHAZAM, AND FATE HAS PLACED YOU HERE...
...TO HOLD UP THE WORLD.
OKAY.

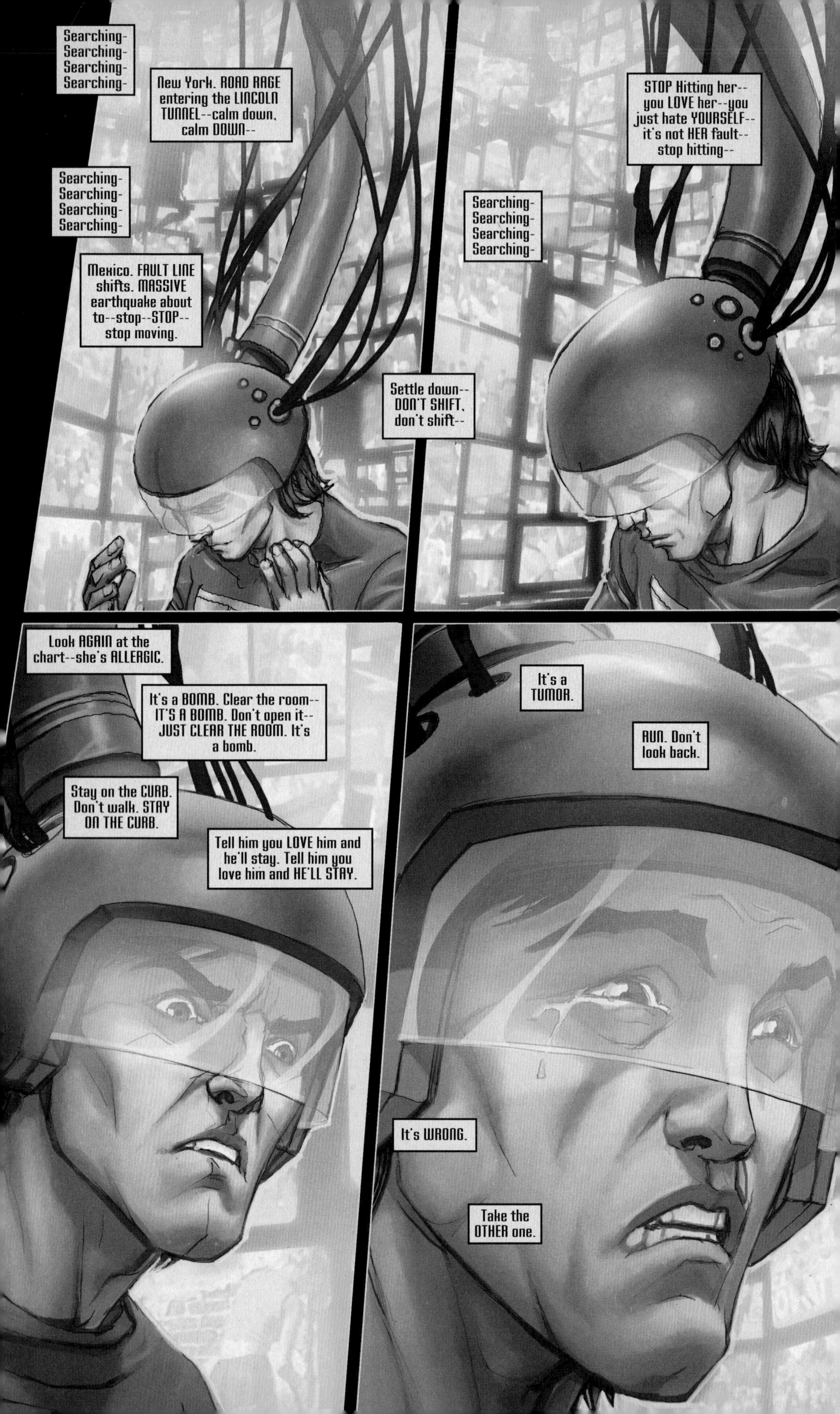
Searching-
Searching-
Searching-
Searching-
New York. ROAD RAGE entering the LINCOLN TUNNEL--calm down, calm DOWN--
Searching-
Searching-
Searching-
Searching-
Mexico. FAULT LINE shifts. MASSIVE earthquake about to--stop--STOP--stop moving.
Settle down--DON'T SHIFT, don't shift--
STOP Hitting her--you LOVE her--you just hate YOURSELF--it's not HER fault--stop hitting--
Searching-
Searching-
Searching-
Searching-
Look AGAIN at the chart--she's ALLERGIC.
It's a BOMB. Clear the room--IT'S A BOMB. Don't open it--JUST CLEAR THE ROOM. It's a bomb.
Stay on the CURB. Don't walk. STAY ON THE CURB.
Tell him you LOVE him and he'll stay. Tell him you love him and HE'LL STAY.
It's a TUMOR.
RUN. Don't look back.
It's WRONG.
Take the OTHER one.

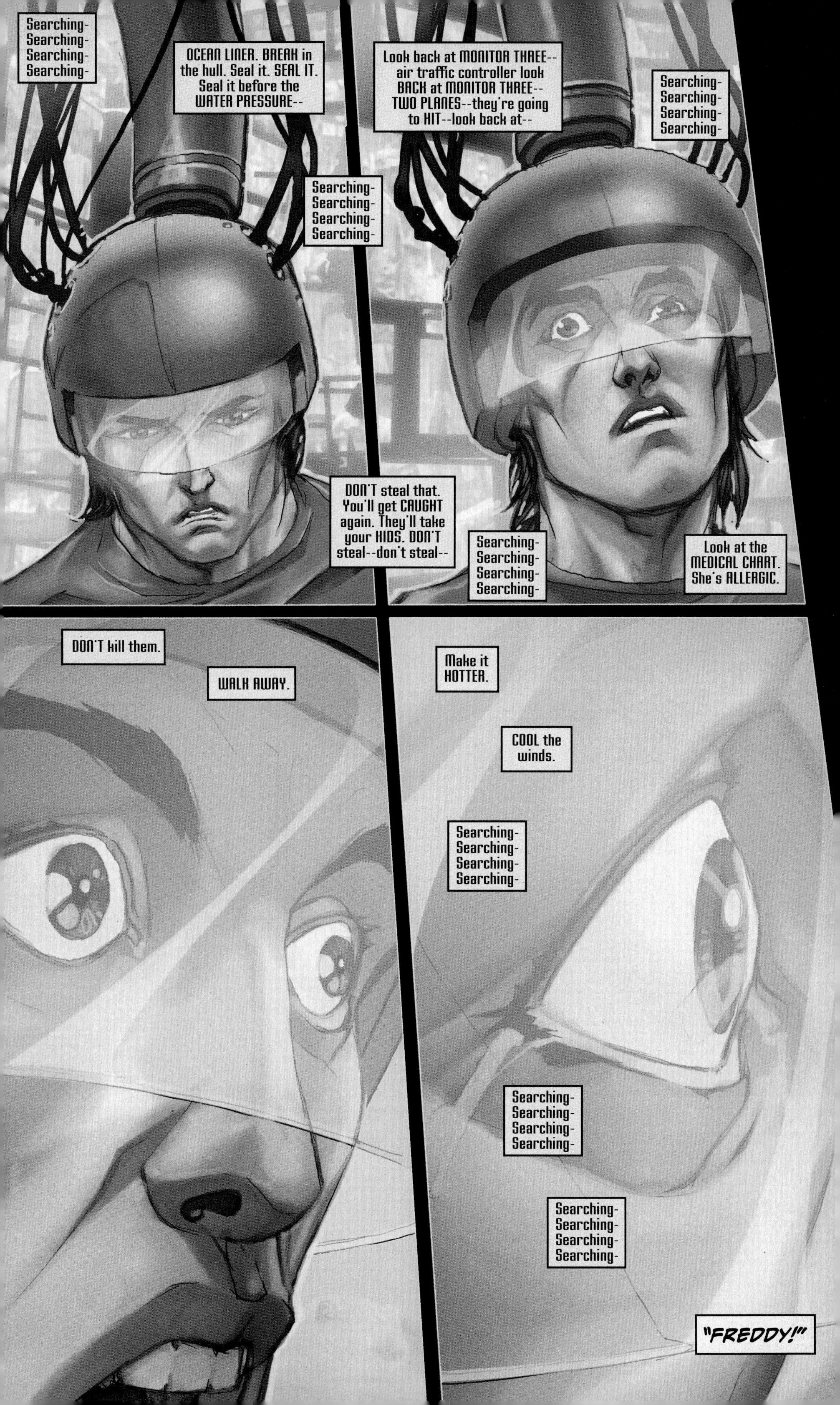

Searching-
Searching-
Searching-
Searching-
OCEAN LINER. BREAK in the hull. Seal it. SEAL IT. Seal it before the WATER PRESSURE--
Searching-
Searching-
Searching-
Searching-
DON'T steal that. You'll get CAUGHT again. They'll take your KIDS. DON'T steal--don't steal--
Look back at MONITOR THREE-- air traffic controller look BACK at MONITOR THREE-- TWO PLANES--they're going to HIT--look back at--
Searching-
Searching-
Searching-
Searching-
Searching-
Searching-
Searching-
Searching-
Look at the MEDICAL CHART. She's ALLERGIC.
DON'T kill them.
WALK AWAY.
Make it HOTTER.
COOL the winds.
Searching-
Searching-
Searching-
Searching-
Searching-
Searching-
Searching-
Searching-
Searching-
Searching-
Searching-
Searching-
"FREDDY!"

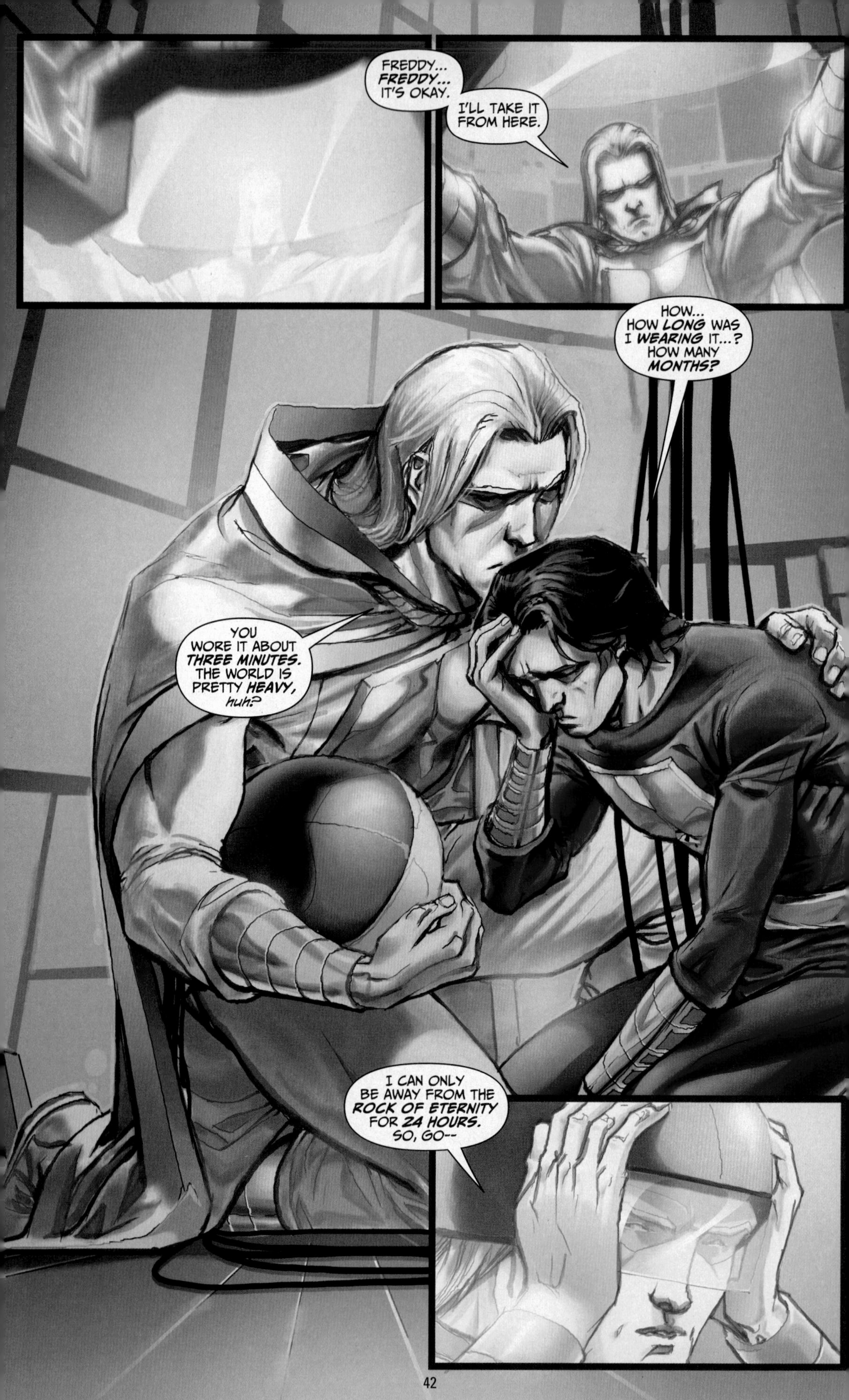

FREDDY... FREDDY... IT'S OKAY.
I'LL TAKE IT FROM HERE.
HOW... HOW LONG WAS I WEARING IT...? HOW MANY MONTHS?
YOU WORE IT ABOUT THREE MINUTES. THE WORLD IS PRETTY HEAVY, huh?
I CAN ONLY BE AWAY FROM THE ROCK OF ETERNITY FOR 24 HOURS. SO, GO--

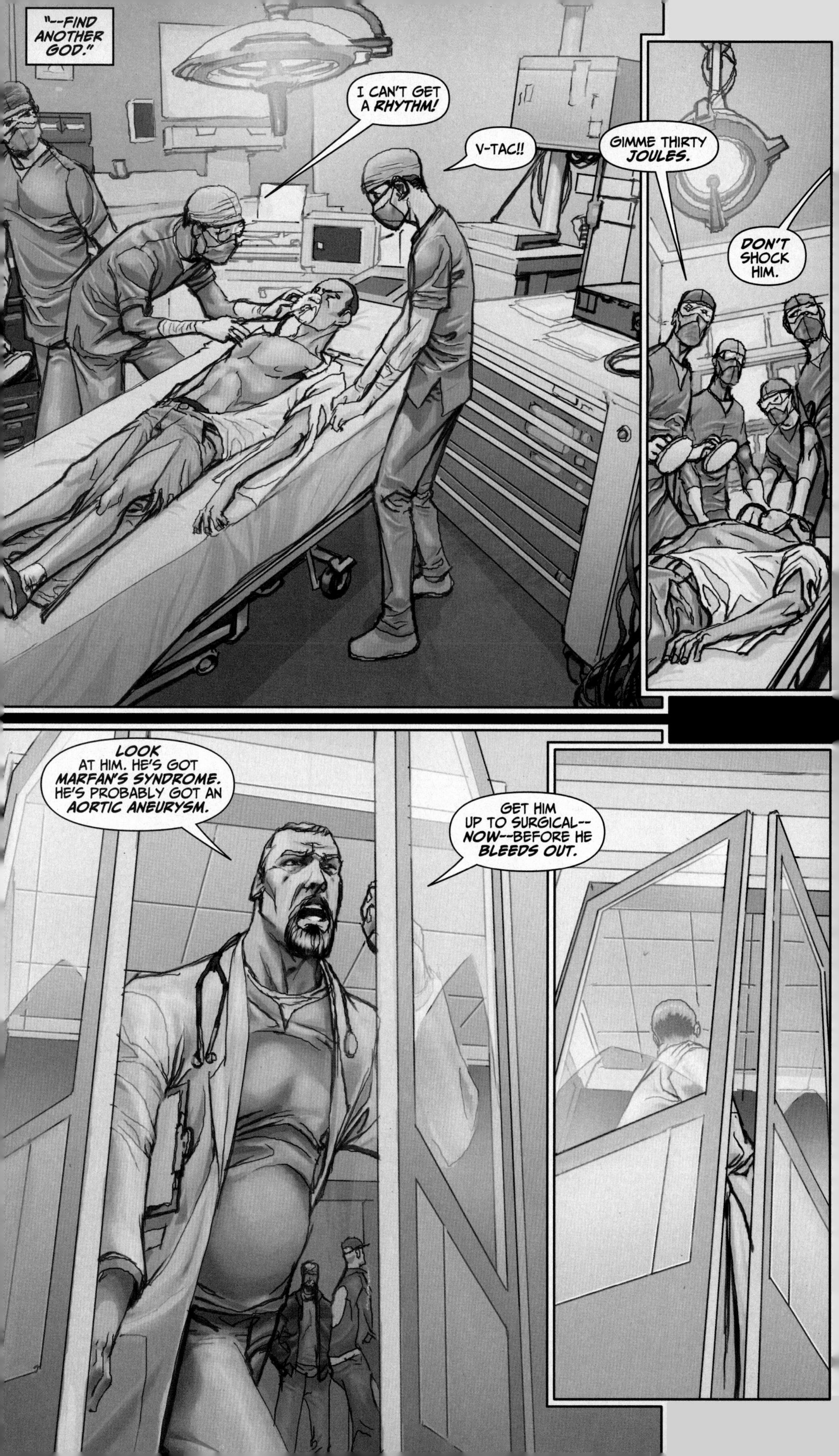
"--FIND ANOTHER GOD."
I CAN'T GET A RHYTHM!
V-TAC!!
GIMME THIRTY JOULES.
DON'T SHOCK HIM.
LOOK AT HIM. HE'S GOT MARFAN'S SYNDROME. HE'S PROBABLY GOT AN AORTIC ANEURYSM.
GET HIM UP TO SURGICAL--NOW--BEFORE HE BLEEDS OUT.

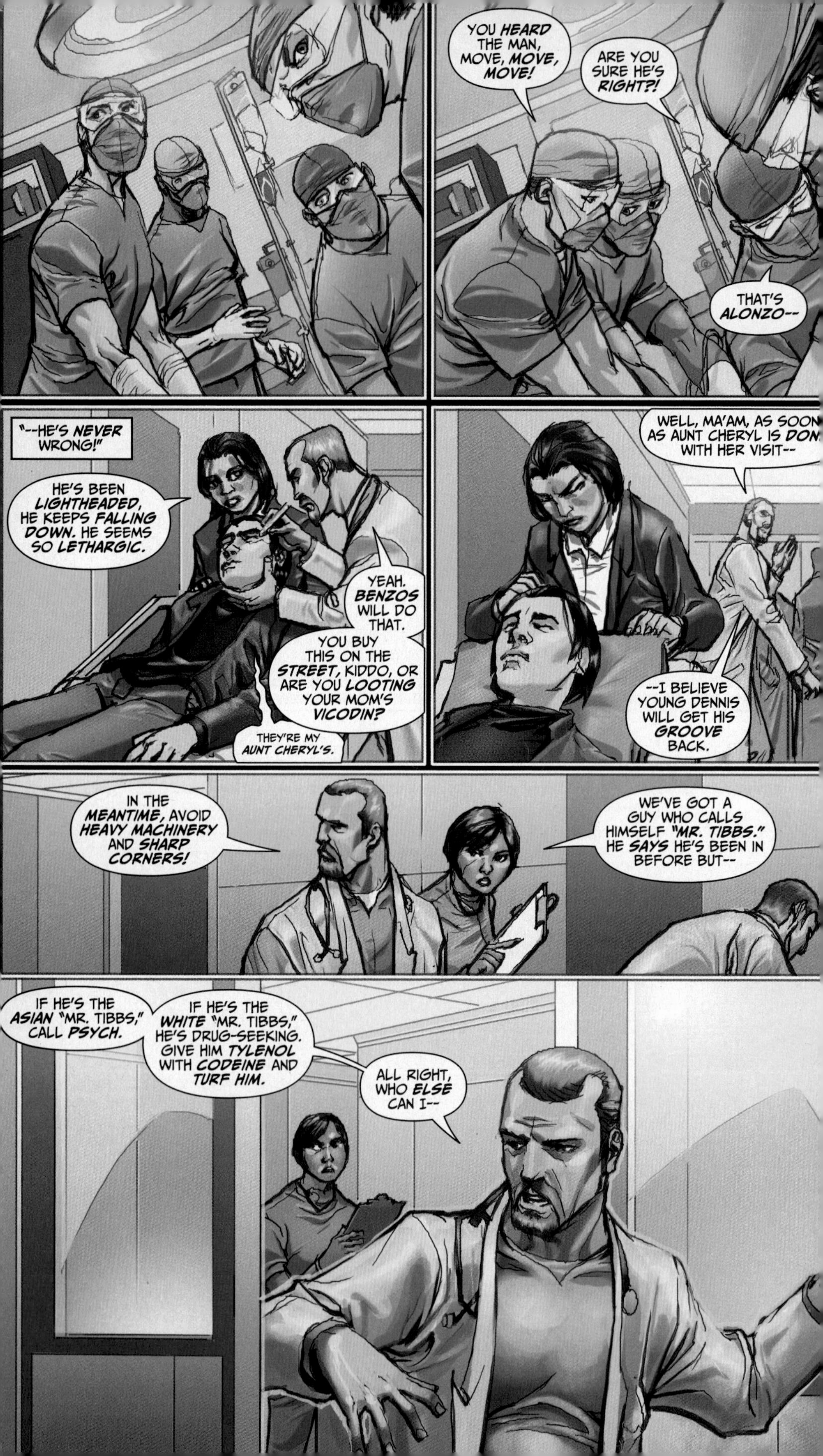
YOU HEARD THE MAN, MOVE, MOVE, MOVE!
ARE YOU SURE HE'S RIGHT?!
THAT'S ALONZO--
"--HE'S NEVER WRONG!"
HE'S BEEN LIGHTHEADED, HE KEEPS FALLING DOWN. HE SEEMS SO LETHARGIC.
YEAH. BENZOS WILL DO THAT.
YOU BUY THIS ON THE STREET, KIDDO, OR ARE YOU LOOTING YOUR MOM'S VICODIN?
THEY'RE MY AUNT CHERYL'S.
WELL, MA'AM, AS SOON AS AUNT CHERYL IS DONE WITH HER VISIT--
--I BELIEVE YOUNG DENNIS WILL GET HIS GROOVE BACK.
IN THE MEANTIME, AVOID HEAVY MACHINERY AND SHARP CORNERS!
WE'VE GOT A GUY WHO CALLS HIMSELF "MR. TIBBS." HE SAYS HE'S BEEN IN BEFORE BUT--
IF HE'S THE ASIAN "MR. TIBBS," CALL PSYCH.
IF HE'S THE WHITE "MR. TIBBS," HE'S DRUG-SEEKING. GIVE HIM TYLENOL WITH CODEINE AND TURF HIM.
ALL RIGHT, WHO ELSE CAN I--

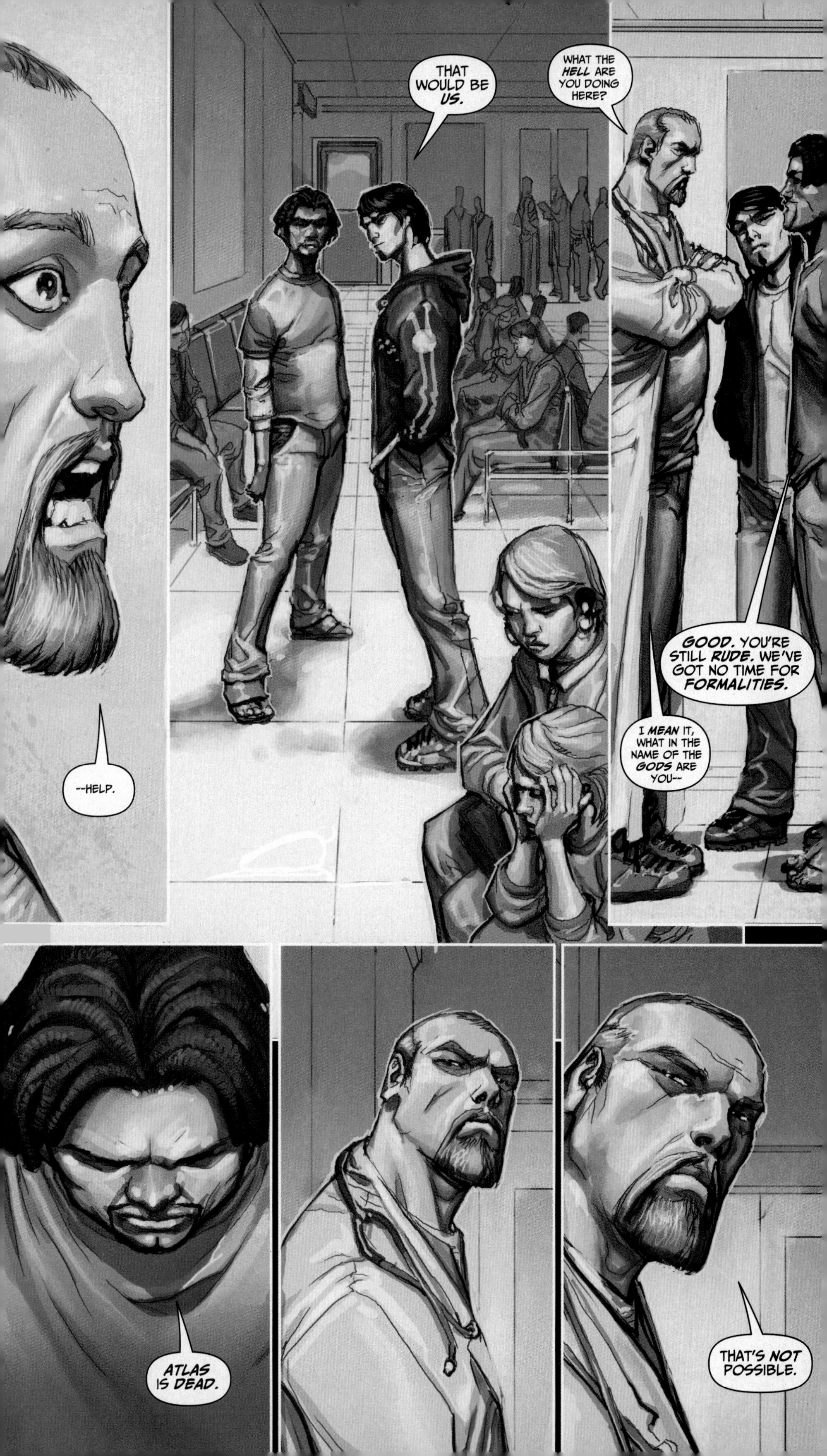
--HELP.
THAT WOULD BE US.
WHAT THE HELL ARE YOU DOING HERE?
GOOD. YOU'RE STILL RUDE. WE'VE GOT NO TIME FOR FORMALITIES.
I MEAN IT, WHAT IN THE NAME OF THE GODS ARE YOU--
ATLAS IS DEAD.
THAT'S NOT POSSIBLE.

IT *IS*. IT'S HAPPENED.

WE'RE IN THE MIDST OF THE *TRIALS*, SO WEAKNESSES ARE ALL--

NO. IT'S NOT *POSSIBLE. BRING ME TO HIM. I CAN FIX HIM.*

YOU *CAN'T.* NOT EVEN *YOU.* HE'S GONE.

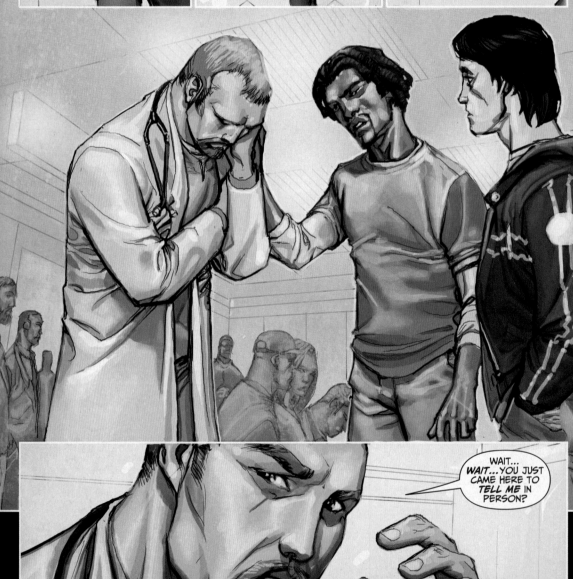

WAIT... *WAIT*...YOU JUST CAME HERE TO *TELL* ME IN PERSON?

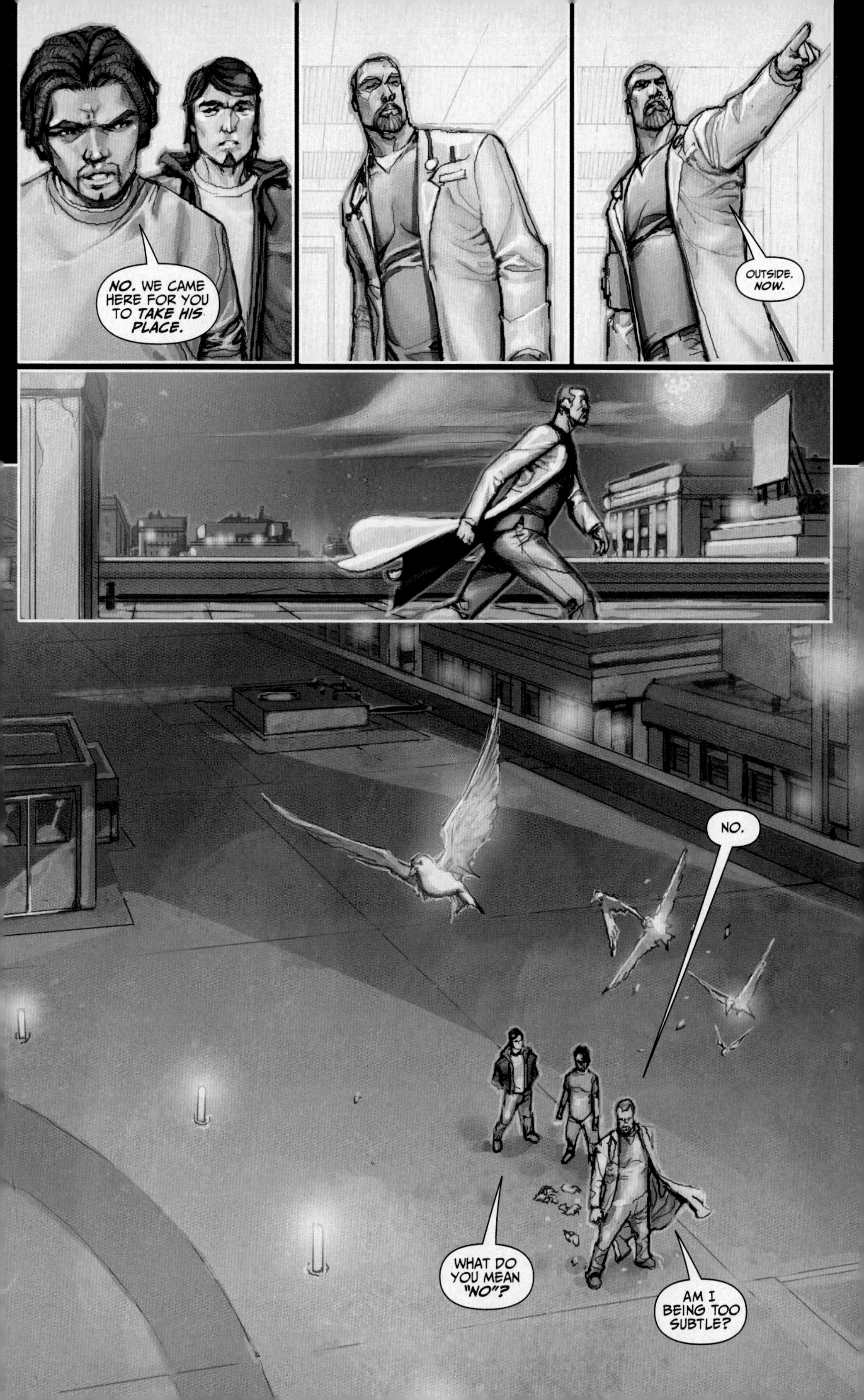
NO. WE CAME HERE FOR YOU TO TAKE HIS PLACE.
OUTSIDE. NOW.
NO.
WHAT DO YOU MEAN "NO"?
AM I BEING TOO SUBTLE?

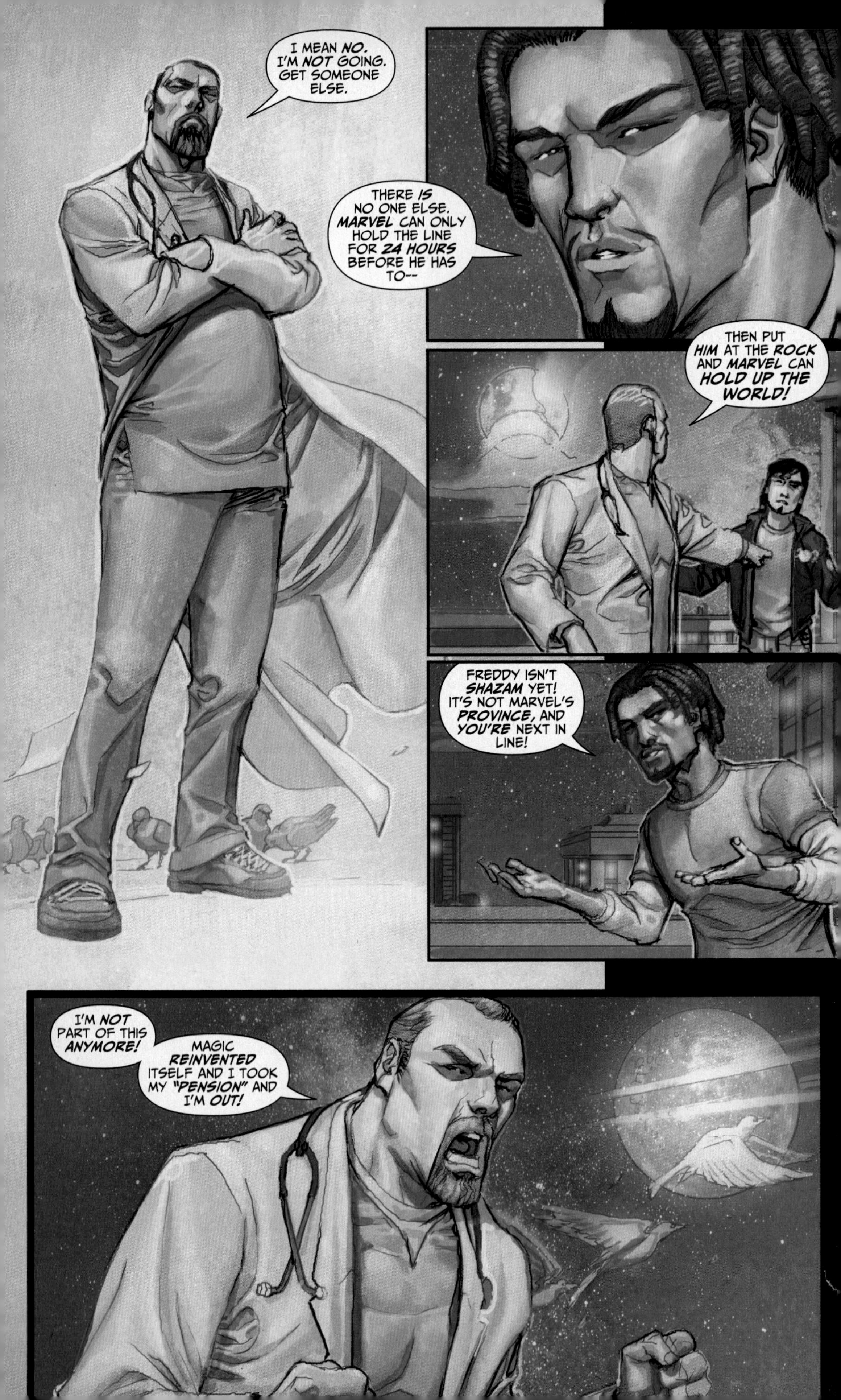
I MEAN NO. I'M NOT GOING. GET SOMEONE ELSE.
THERE IS NO ONE ELSE. MARVEL CAN ONLY HOLD THE LINE FOR 24 HOURS BEFORE HE HAS TO--
THEN PUT HIM AT THE ROCK AND MARVEL CAN HOLD UP THE WORLD!
FREDDY ISN'T SHAZAM YET! IT'S NOT MARVEL'S PROVINCE, AND YOU'RE NEXT IN LINE!
I'M NOT PART OF THIS ANYMORE!
MAGIC REINVENTED ITSELF AND I TOOK MY "PENSION" AND I'M OUT!

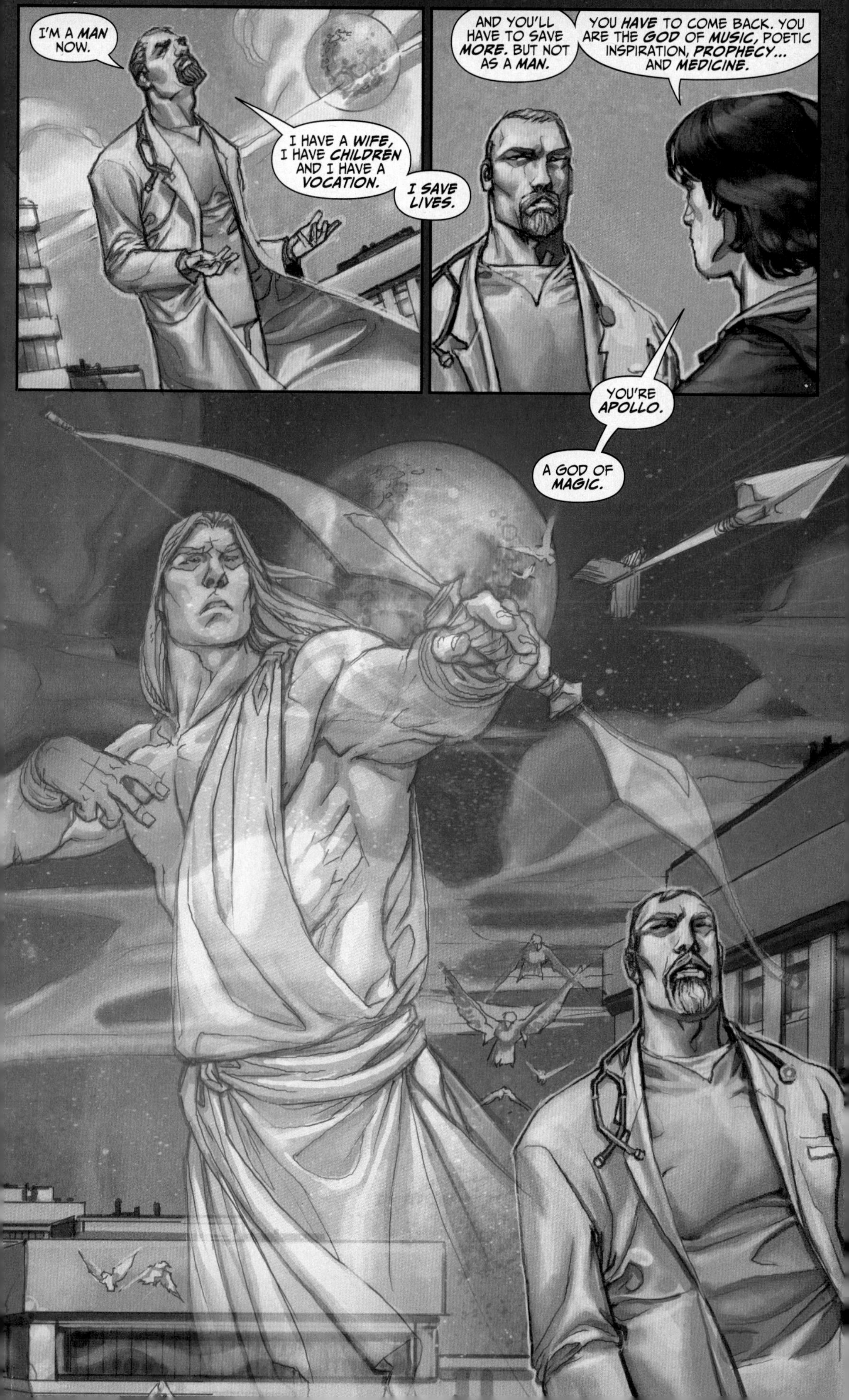

I'M A MAN NOW.
I HAVE A WIFE, I HAVE CHILDREN AND I HAVE A VOCATION.
I SAVE LIVES.
AND YOU'LL HAVE TO SAVE MORE. BUT NOT AS A MAN.
YOU HAVE TO COME BACK. YOU ARE THE GOD OF MUSIC, POETIC INSPIRATION, PROPHECY... AND MEDICINE.
YOU'RE APOLLO.
A GOD OF MAGIC.

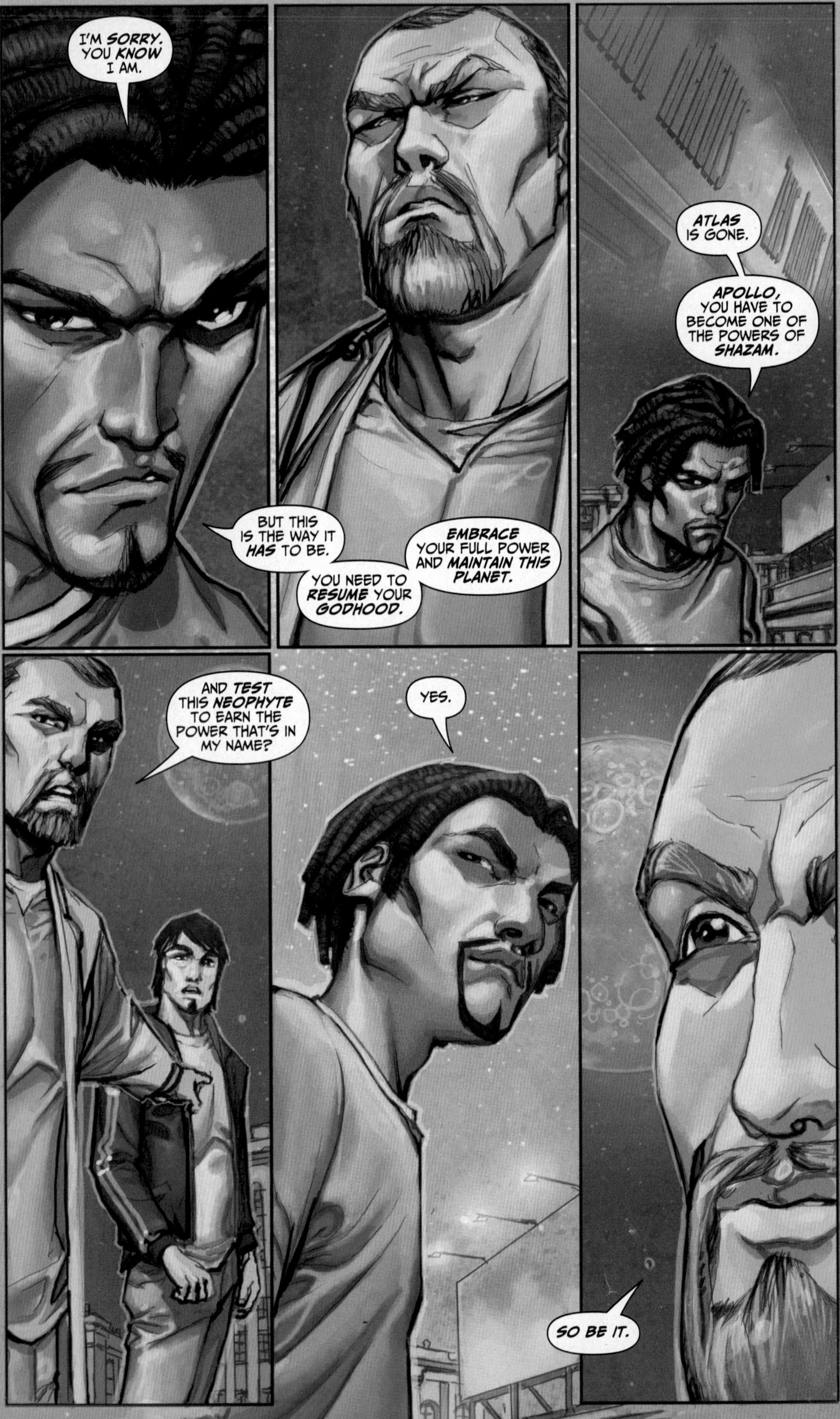
I'M SORRY. YOU KNOW I AM.
BUT THIS IS THE WAY IT HAS TO BE.
YOU NEED TO RESUME YOUR GODHOOD.
EMBRACE YOUR FULL POWER AND MAINTAIN THIS PLANET.
ATLAS IS GONE.
APOLLO, YOU HAVE TO BECOME ONE OF THE POWERS OF SHAZAM.
AND TEST THIS NEOPHYTE TO EARN THE POWER THAT'S IN MY NAME?
YES.
SO BE IT.

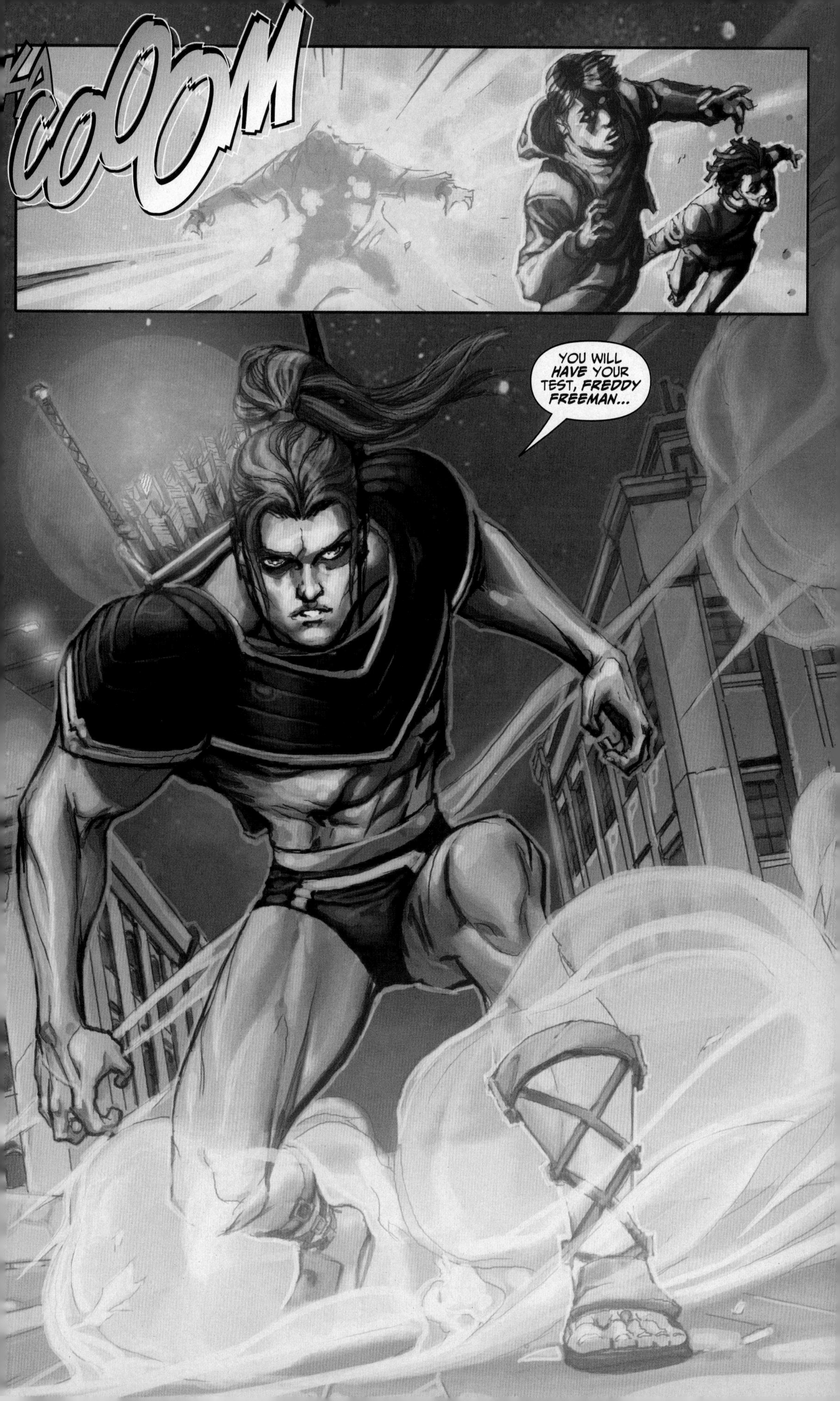
KA-COOOM
YOU WILL HAVE YOUR TEST, FREDDY FREEMAN...

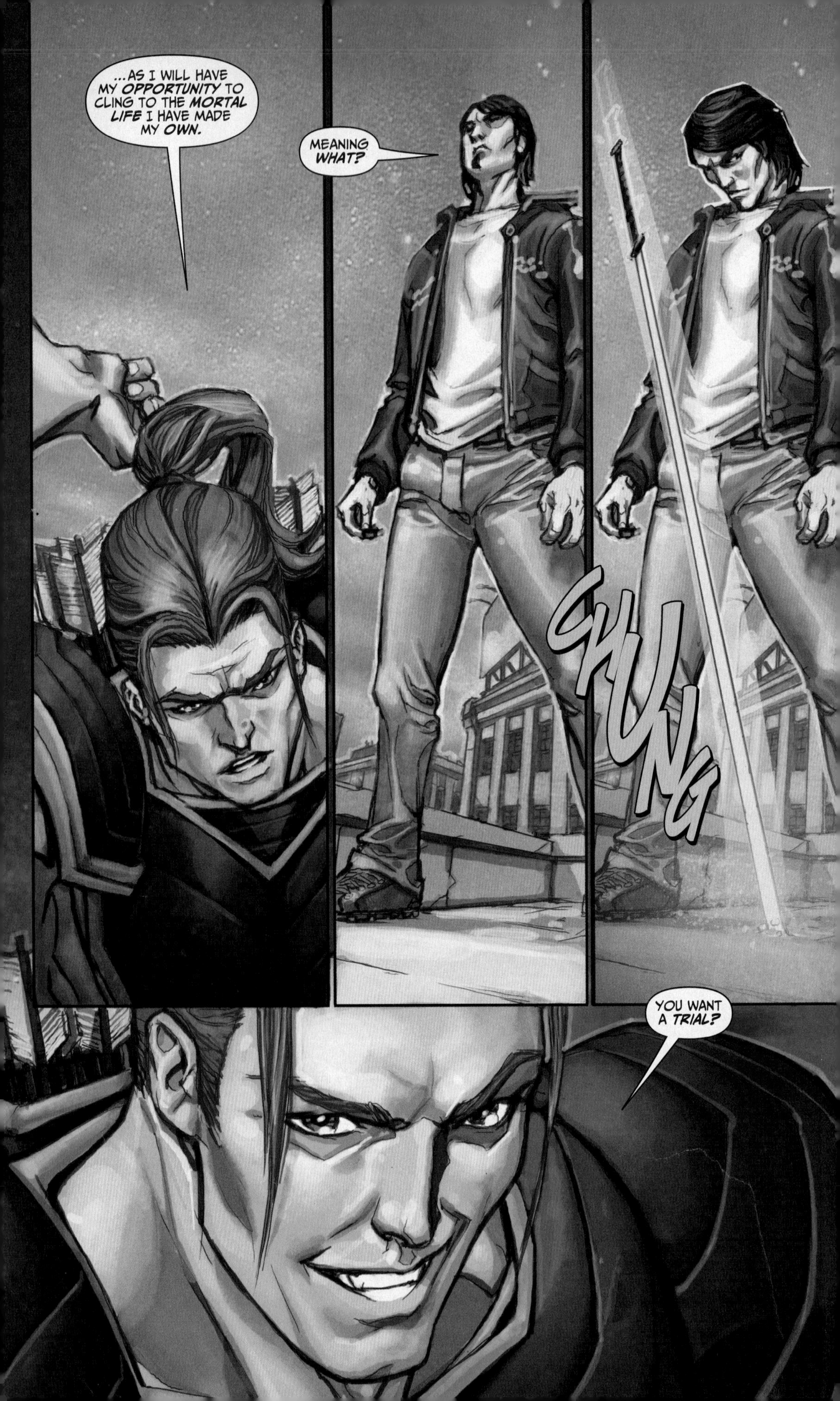
...AS I WILL HAVE MY OPPORTUNITY TO CLING TO THE MORTAL LIFE I HAVE MADE MY OWN.
MEANING WHAT?
CHUNG
YOU WANT A TRIAL?

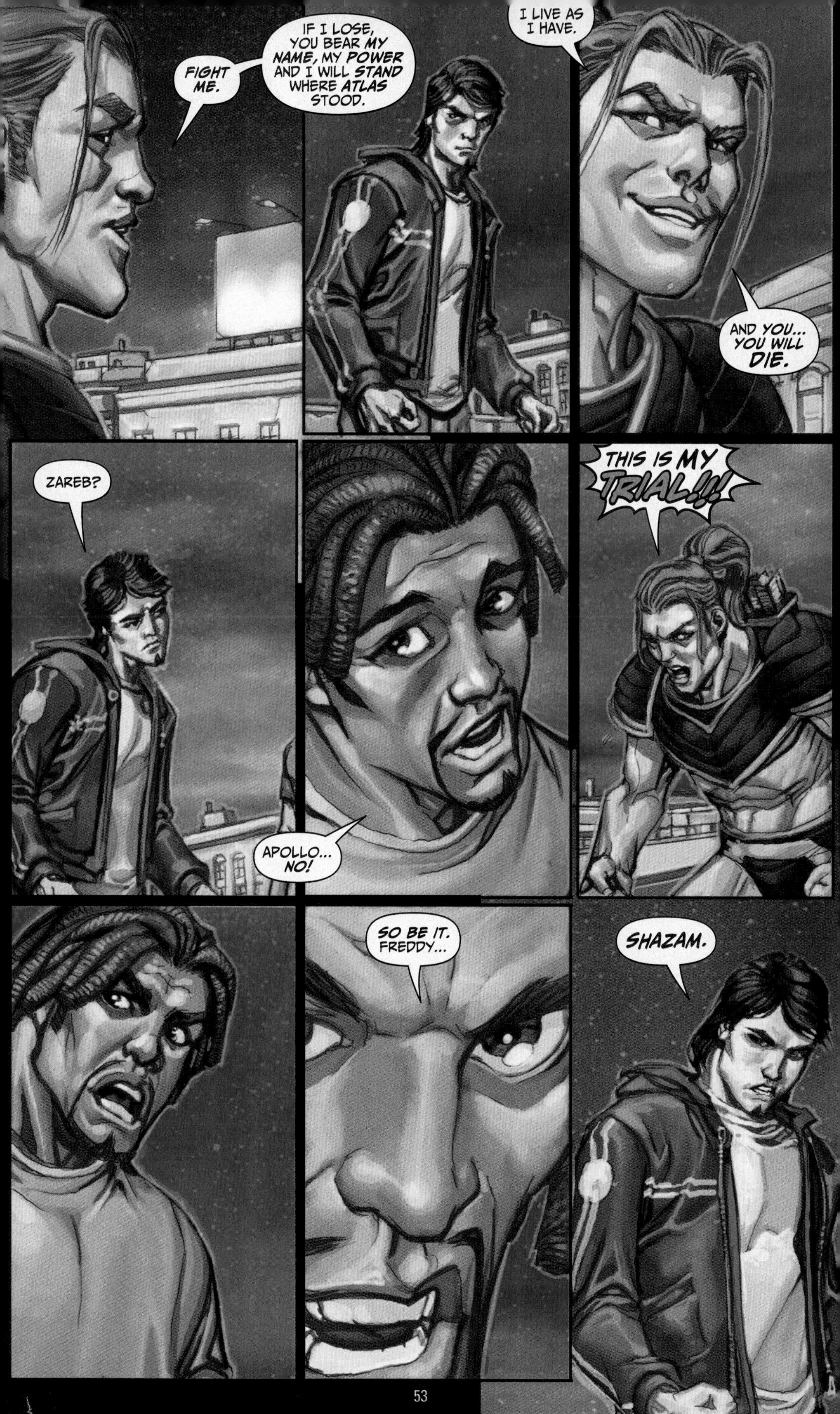
FIGHT ME.
IF I LOSE, YOU BEAR MY NAME, MY POWER AND I WILL STAND WHERE ATLAS STOOD.
I LIVE AS I HAVE.
AND YOU... YOU WILL DIE.
ZAREB?
APOLLO... NO!
THIS IS MY TRIAL!!!
SO BE IT. FREDDY...
SHAZAM.

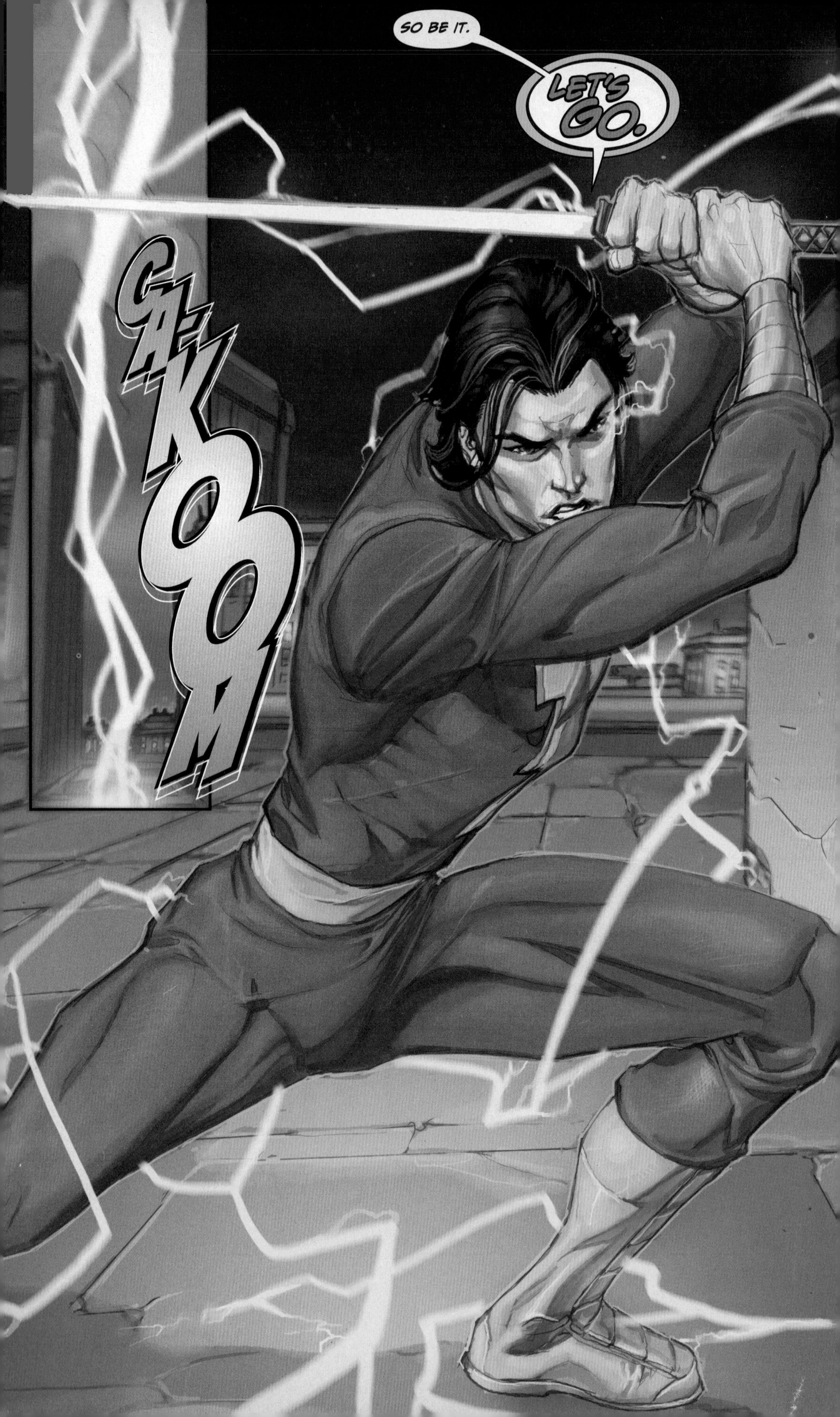
SO BE IT.
LET'S GO.
CA-KOOM

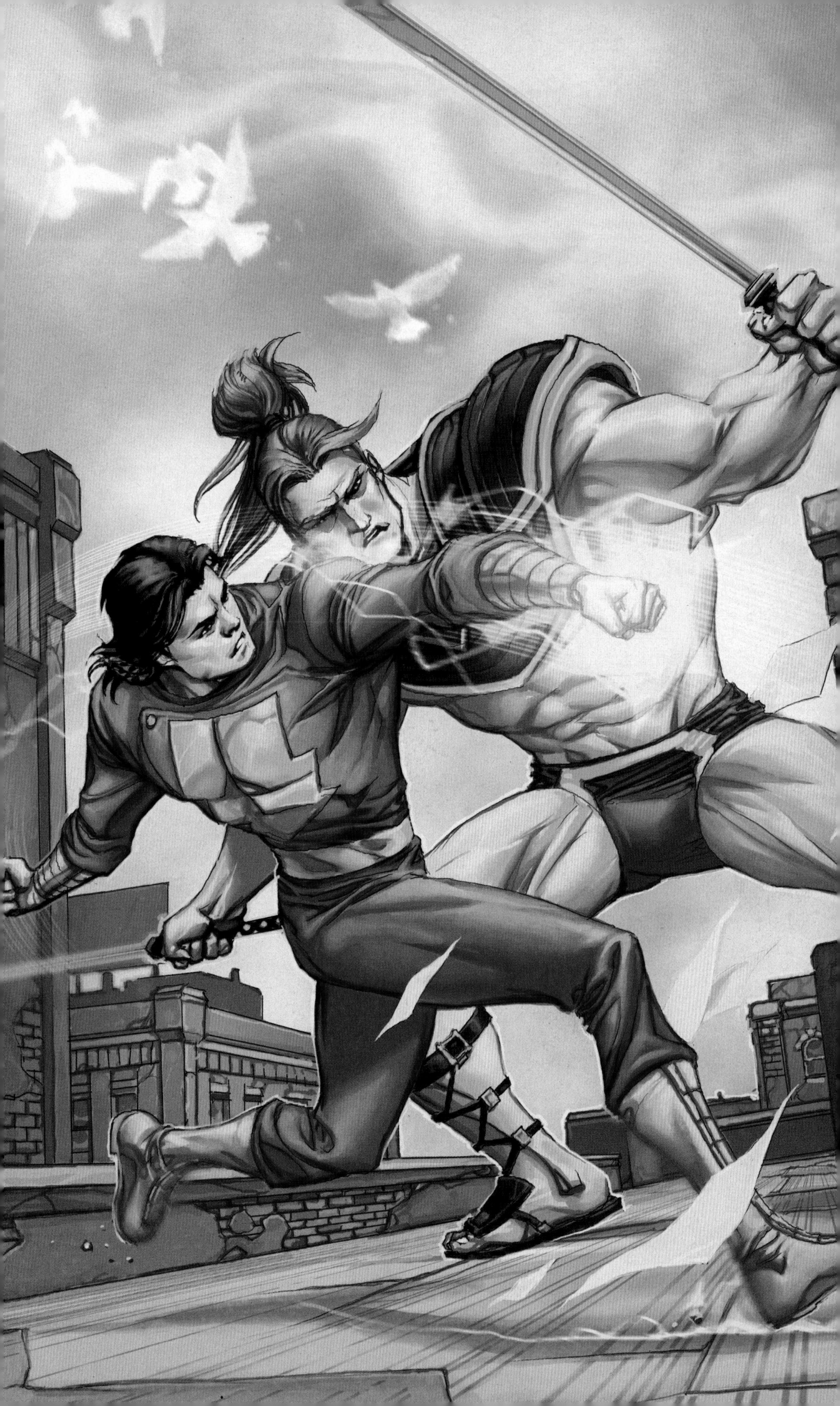

CHAPTER NINE:

THE GODS MUST BE
CRAZY

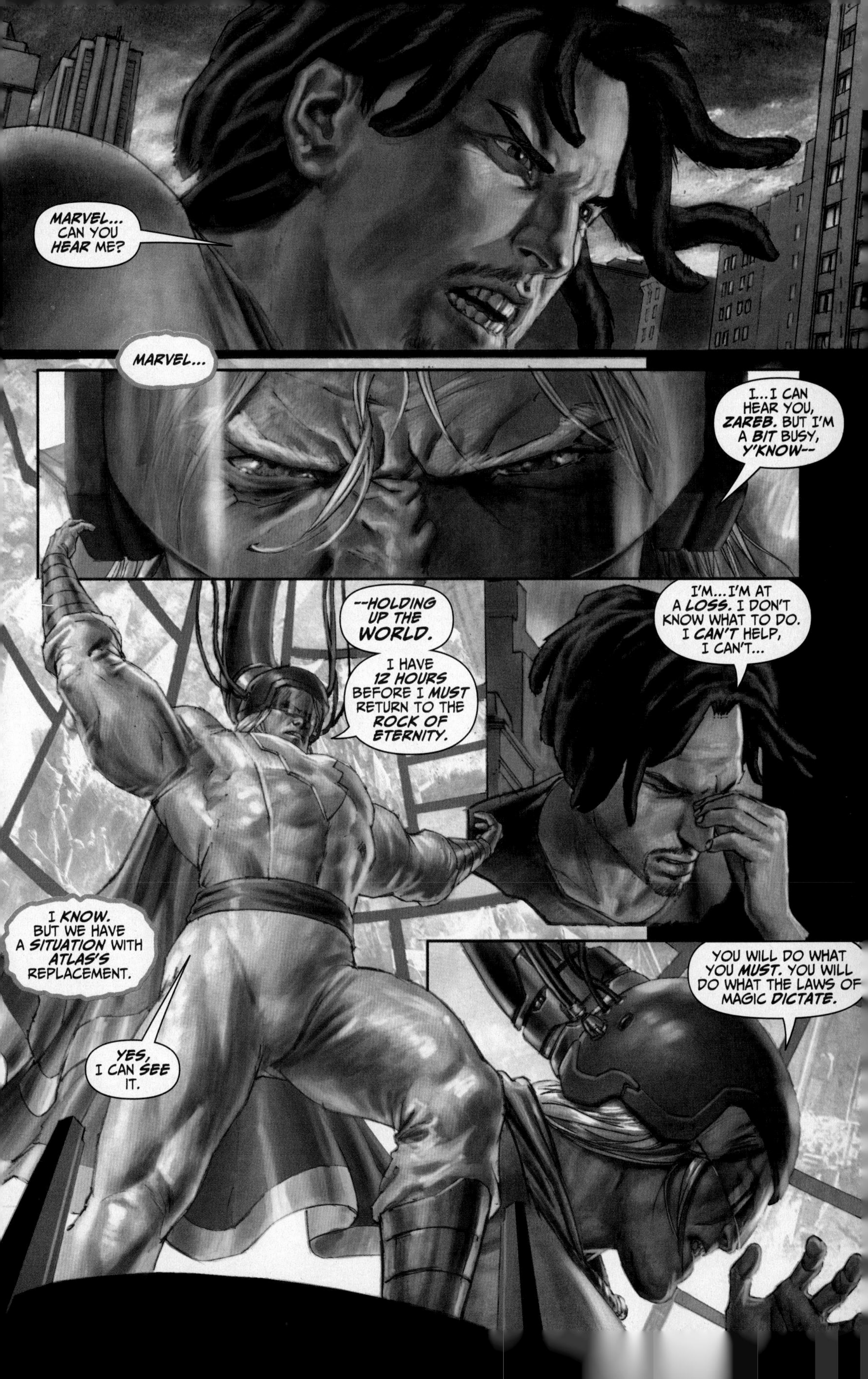
MARVEL... CAN YOU HEAR ME?
MARVEL...
I...I CAN HEAR YOU, ZAREB. BUT I'M A BIT BUSY, Y'KNOW--
--HOLDING UP THE WORLD.
I HAVE 12 HOURS BEFORE I MUST RETURN TO THE ROCK OF ETERNITY.
I'M...I'M AT A LOSS. I DON'T KNOW WHAT TO DO. I CAN'T HELP, I CAN'T...
I KNOW. BUT WE HAVE A SITUATION WITH ATLAS'S REPLACEMENT.
YOU WILL DO WHAT YOU MUST. YOU WILL DO WHAT THE LAWS OF MAGIC DICTATE.
YES, I CAN SEE IT.

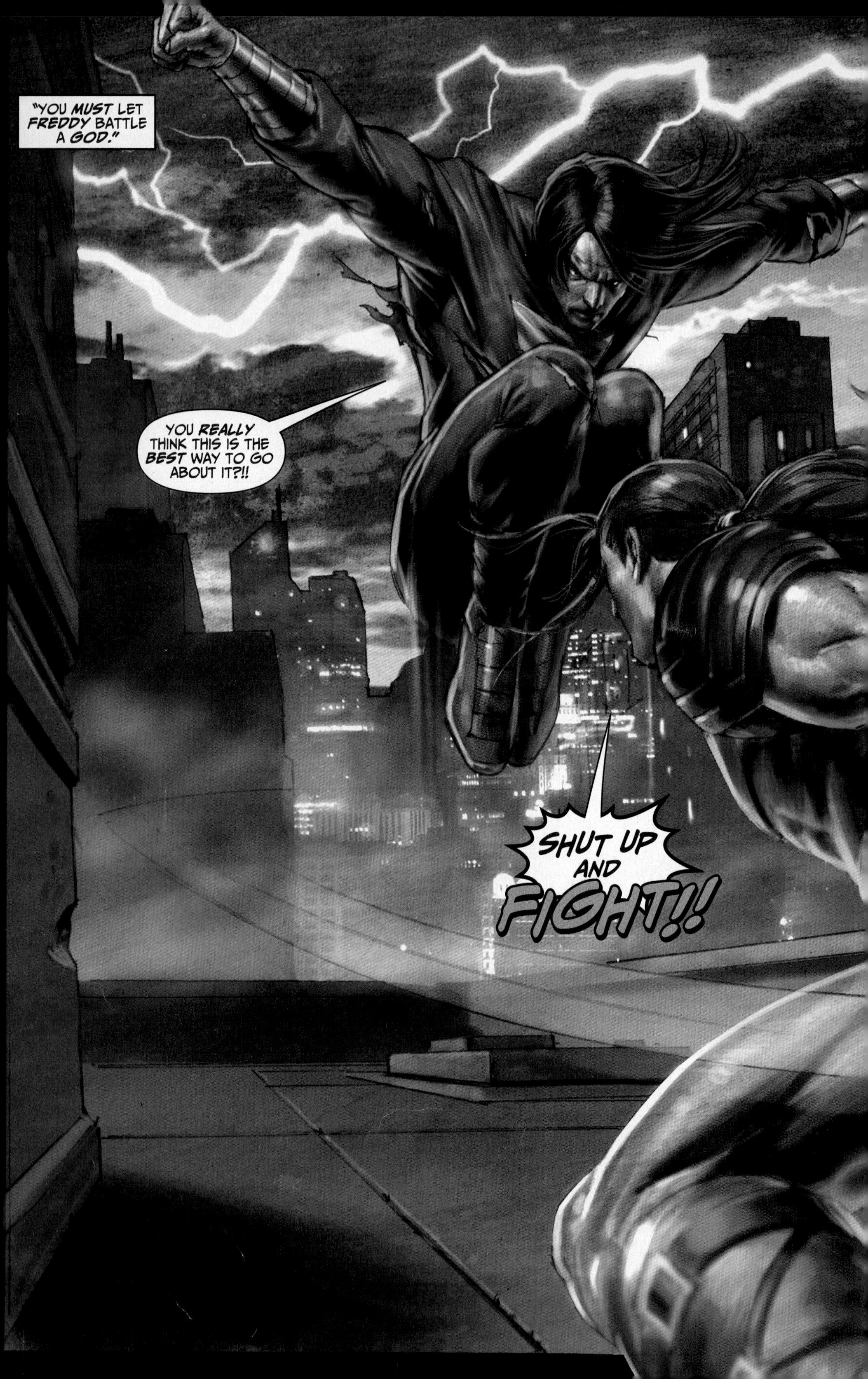
"YOU MUST LET FREDDY BATTLE A GOD."
YOU REALLY THINK THIS IS THE BEST WAY TO GO ABOUT IT?!!
SHUT UP AND FIGHT!!

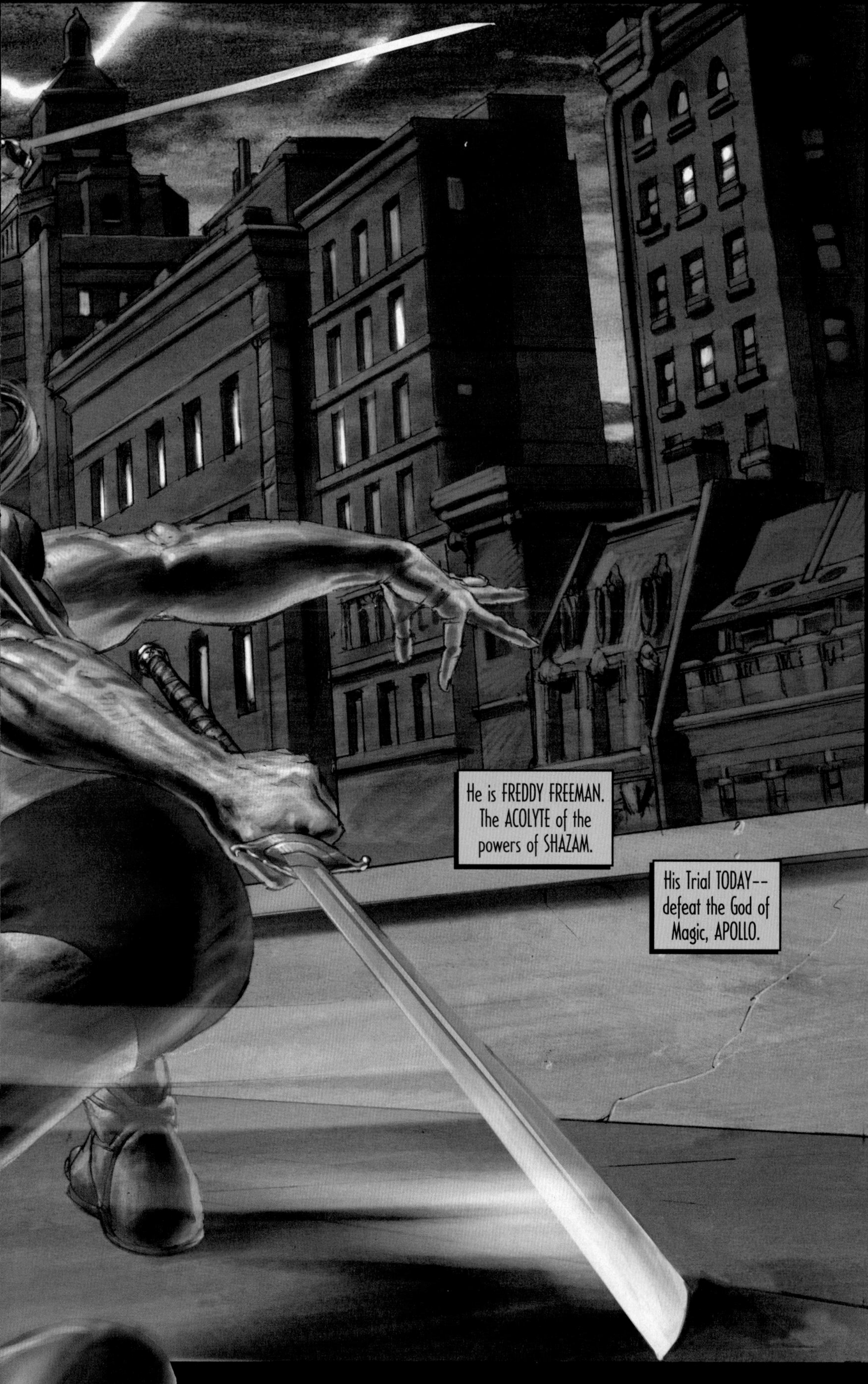
He is FREDDY FREEMAN. The ACOLYTE of the powers of SHAZAM.
His Trial TODAY-- defeat the God of Magic, APOLLO.

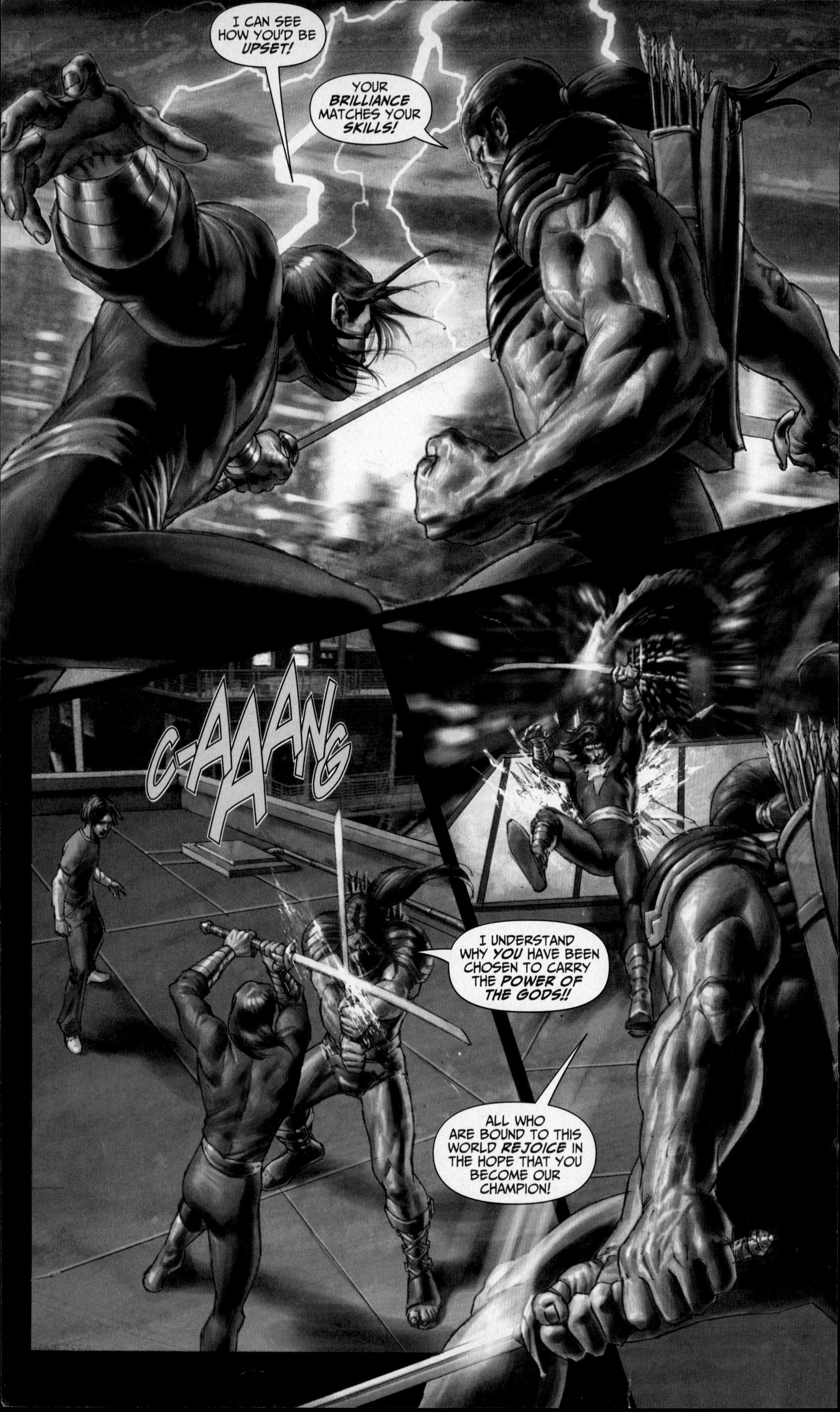
I CAN SEE HOW YOU'D BE UPSET!
YOUR BRILLIANCE MATCHES YOUR SKILLS!
C-AAAANG
I UNDERSTAND WHY YOU HAVE BEEN CHOSEN TO CARRY THE POWER OF THE GODS!!
ALL WHO ARE BOUND TO THIS WORLD REJOICE IN THE HOPE THAT YOU BECOME OUR CHAMPION!

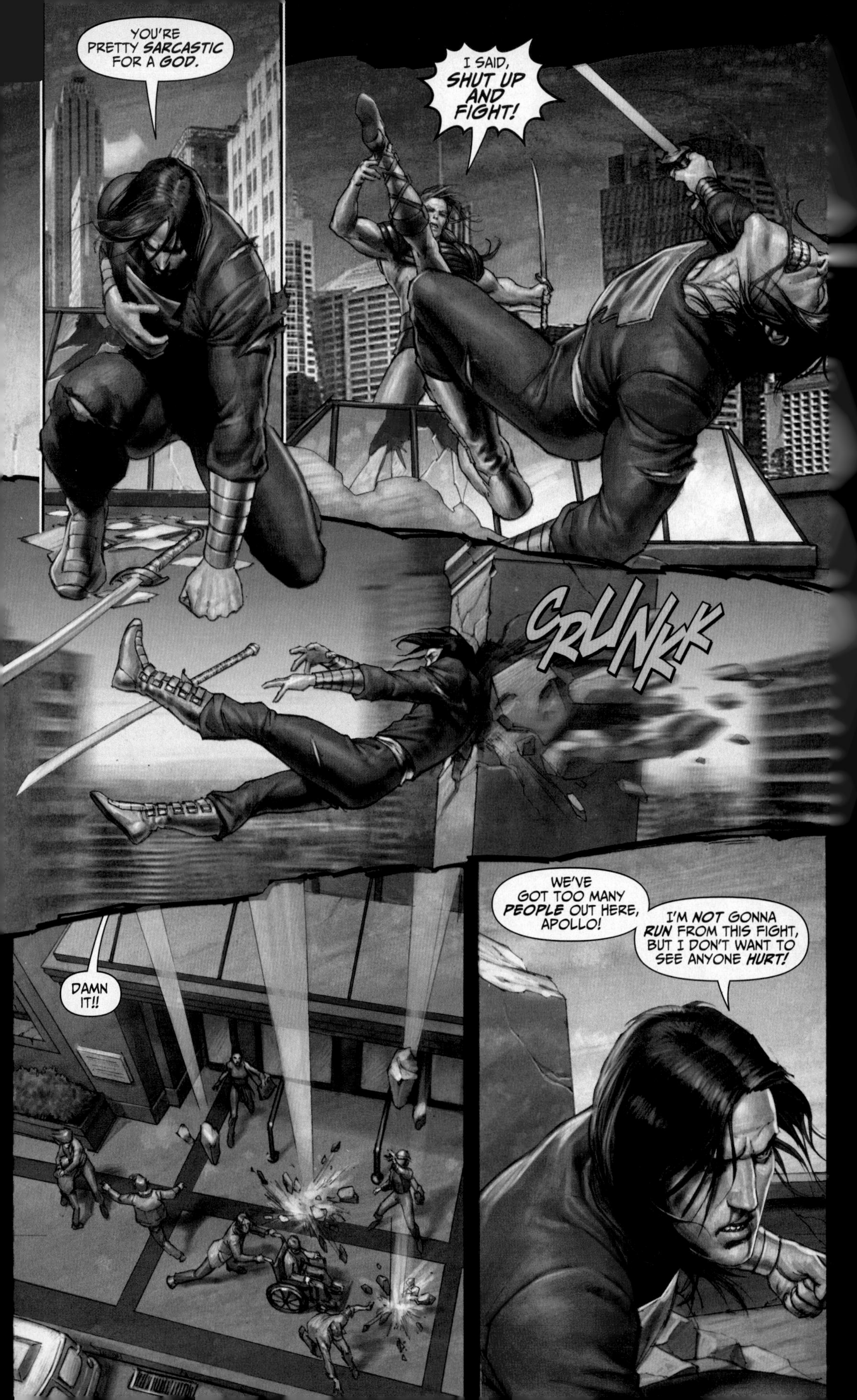
YOU'RE PRETTY SARCASTIC FOR A GOD.
I SAID, SHUT UP AND FIGHT!
CRUNKK
DAMN IT!!
WE'VE GOT TOO MANY PEOPLE OUT HERE, APOLLO!
I'M NOT GONNA RUN FROM THIS FIGHT, BUT I DON'T WANT TO SEE ANYONE HURT!

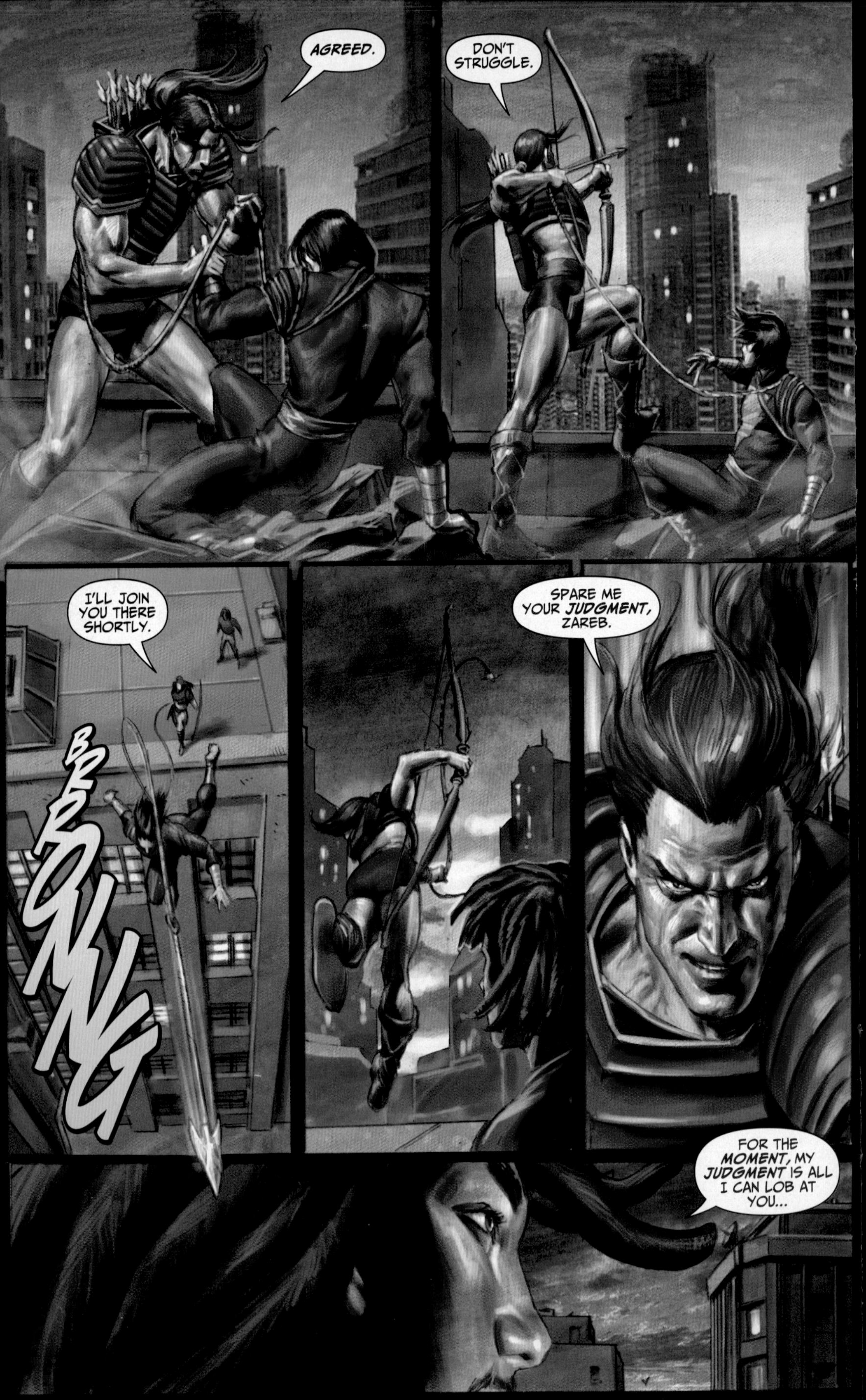
AGREED.
DON'T STRUGGLE.
I'LL JOIN YOU THERE SHORTLY.
BRRONNG
SPARE ME YOUR JUDGMENT, ZAREB.
FOR THE MOMENT, MY JUDGMENT IS ALL I CAN LOB AT YOU...

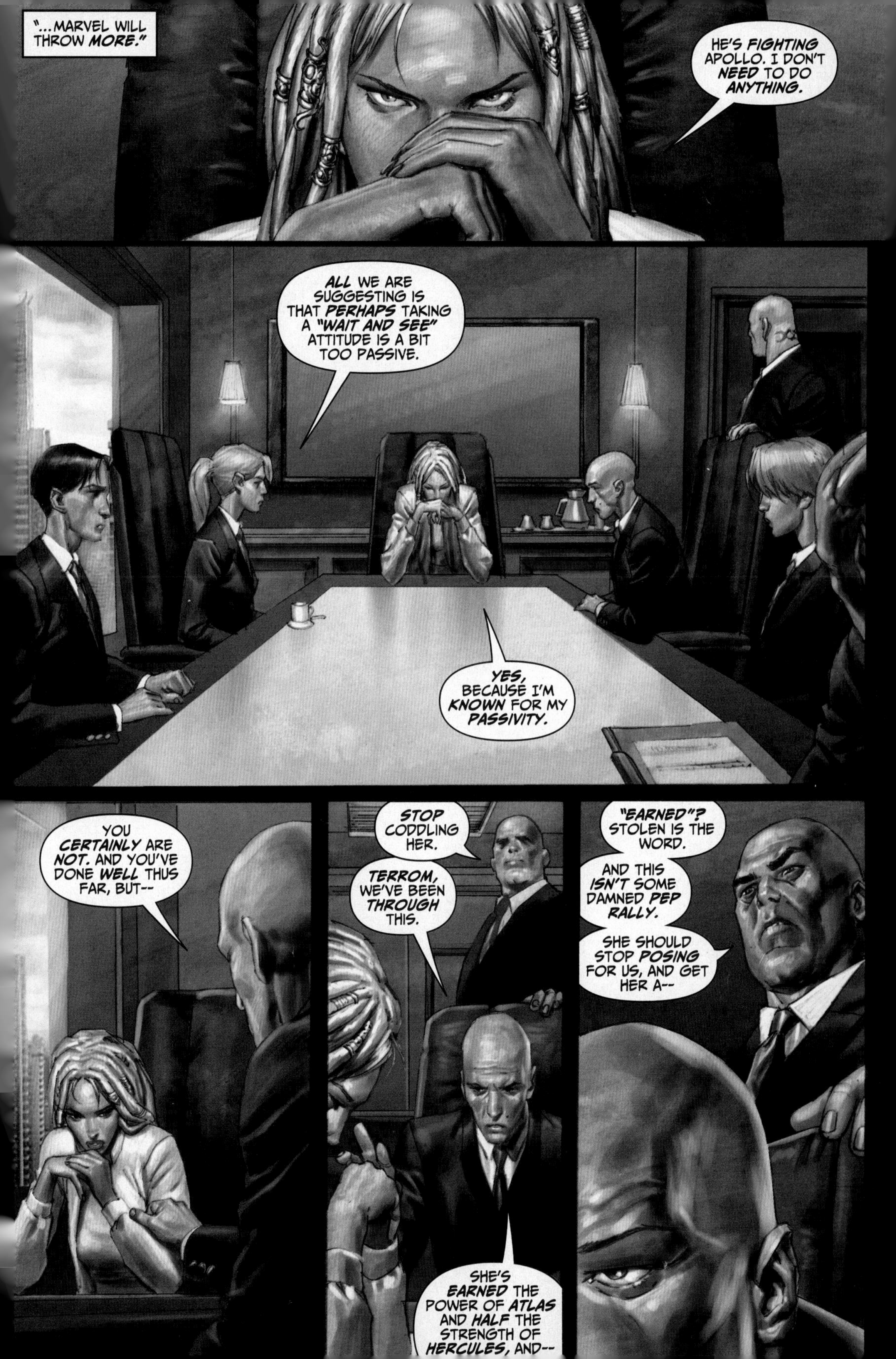
"...MARVEL WILL THROW MORE."
HE'S FIGHTING APOLLO. I DON'T NEED TO DO ANYTHING.
ALL WE ARE SUGGESTING IS THAT PERHAPS TAKING A "WAIT AND SEE" ATTITUDE IS A BIT TOO PASSIVE.
YES, BECAUSE I'M KNOWN FOR MY PASSIVITY.
YOU CERTAINLY ARE NOT. AND YOU'VE DONE WELL THUS FAR, BUT--
STOP CODDLING HER.
TERROM, WE'VE BEEN THROUGH THIS.
SHE'S EARNED THE POWER OF ATLAS AND HALF THE STRENGTH OF HERCULES, AND--
"EARNED"? STOLEN IS THE WORD.
AND THIS ISN'T SOME DAMNED PEP RALLY.
SHE SHOULD STOP POSING FOR US, AND GET HER A--

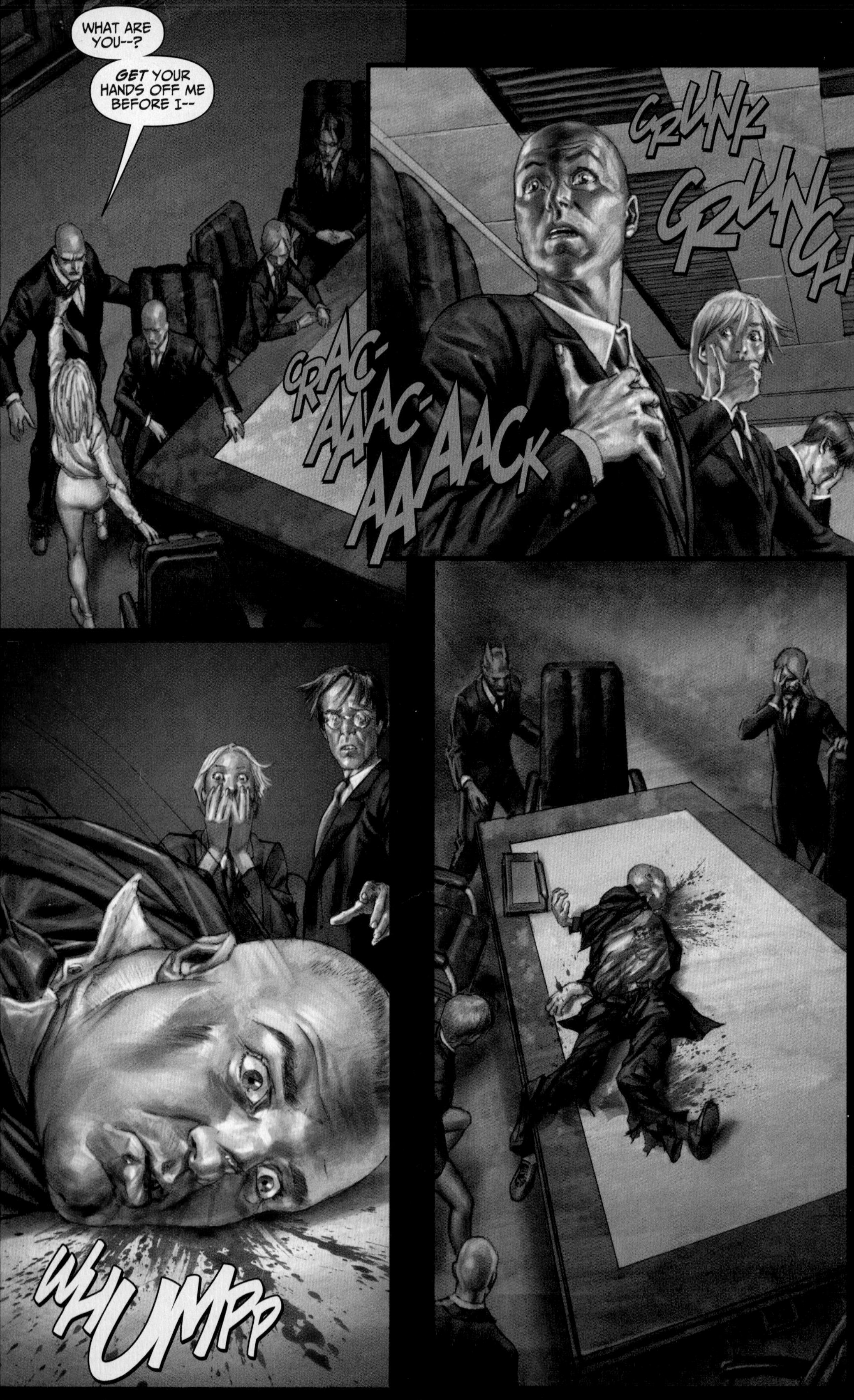
WHAT ARE YOU--?
GET YOUR HANDS OFF ME BEFORE I--
CRAC-AAAC-AAAACK
CRUNK
CRUNCH
WHUMPP

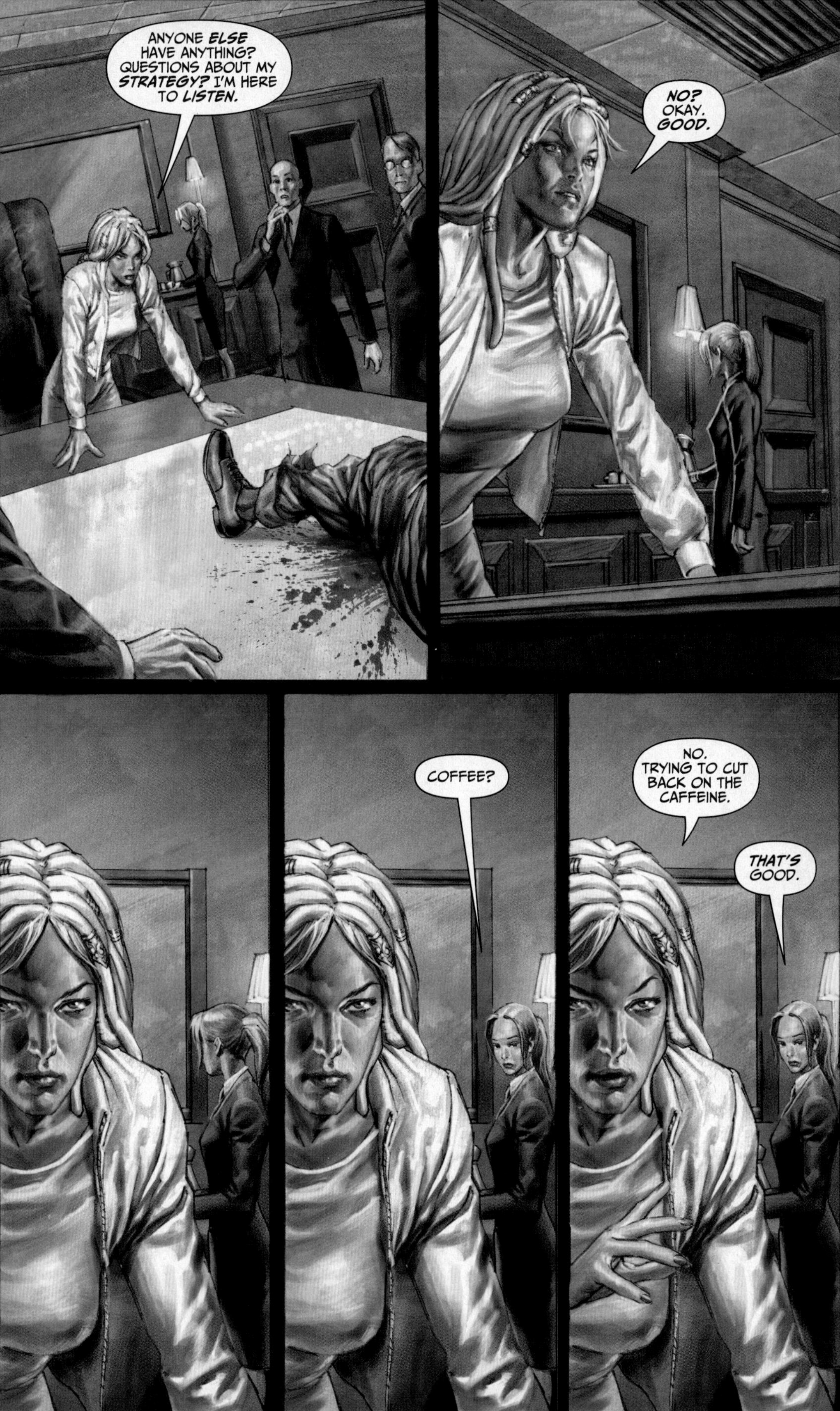
ANYONE ELSE HAVE ANYTHING? QUESTIONS ABOUT MY STRATEGY? I'M HERE TO LISTEN.
NO? OKAY. GOOD.
COFFEE?
NO. TRYING TO CUT BACK ON THE CAFFEINE.
THAT'S GOOD.

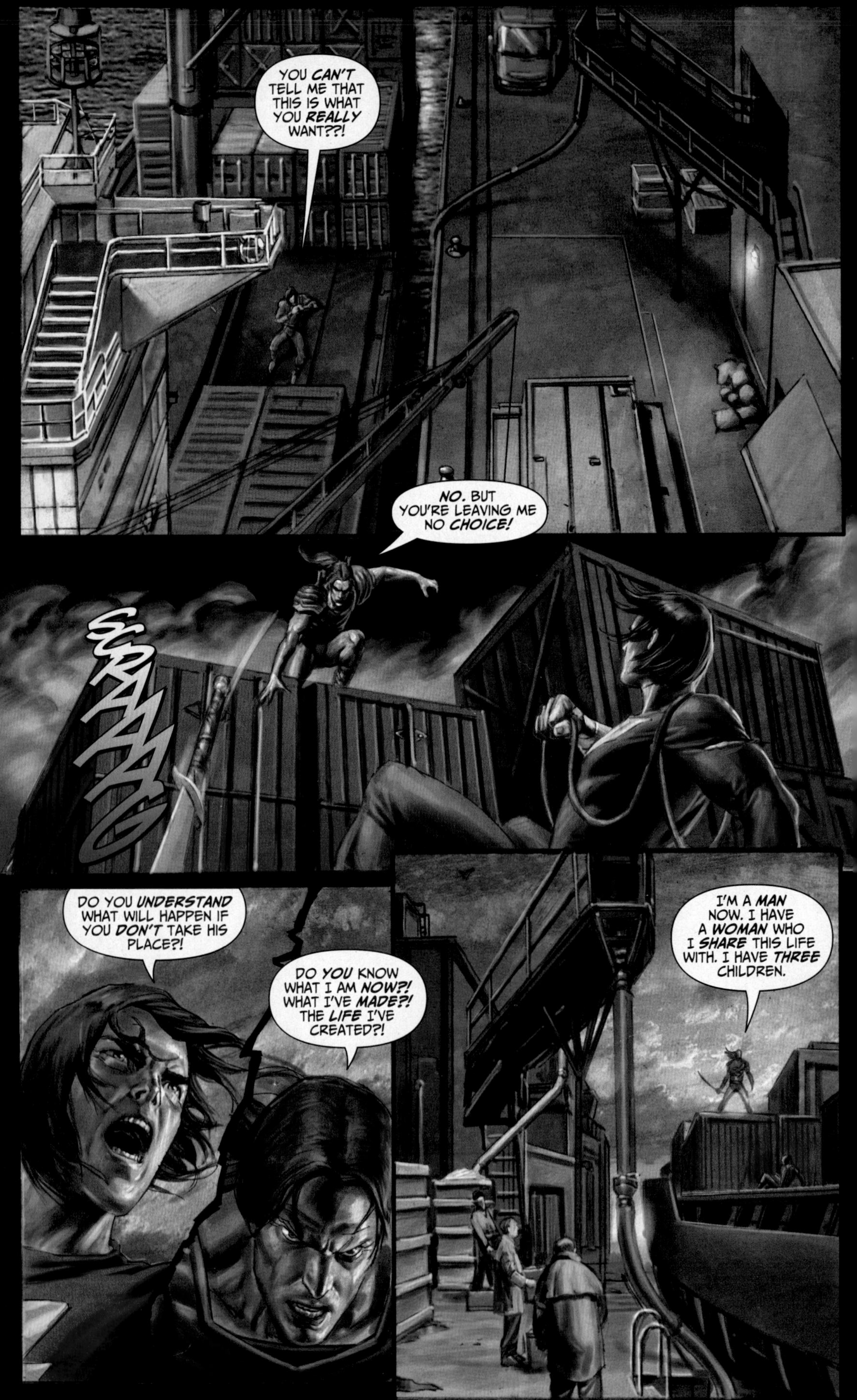

YOU CAN'T TELL ME THAT THIS IS WHAT YOU REALLY WANT??!
NO. BUT YOU'RE LEAVING ME NO CHOICE!
DO YOU UNDERSTAND WHAT WILL HAPPEN IF YOU DON'T TAKE HIS PLACE?!
DO YOU KNOW WHAT I AM NOW?! WHAT I'VE MADE?! THE LIFE I'VE CREATED?!
I'M A MAN NOW. I HAVE A WOMAN WHO I SHARE THIS LIFE WITH. I HAVE THREE CHILDREN.

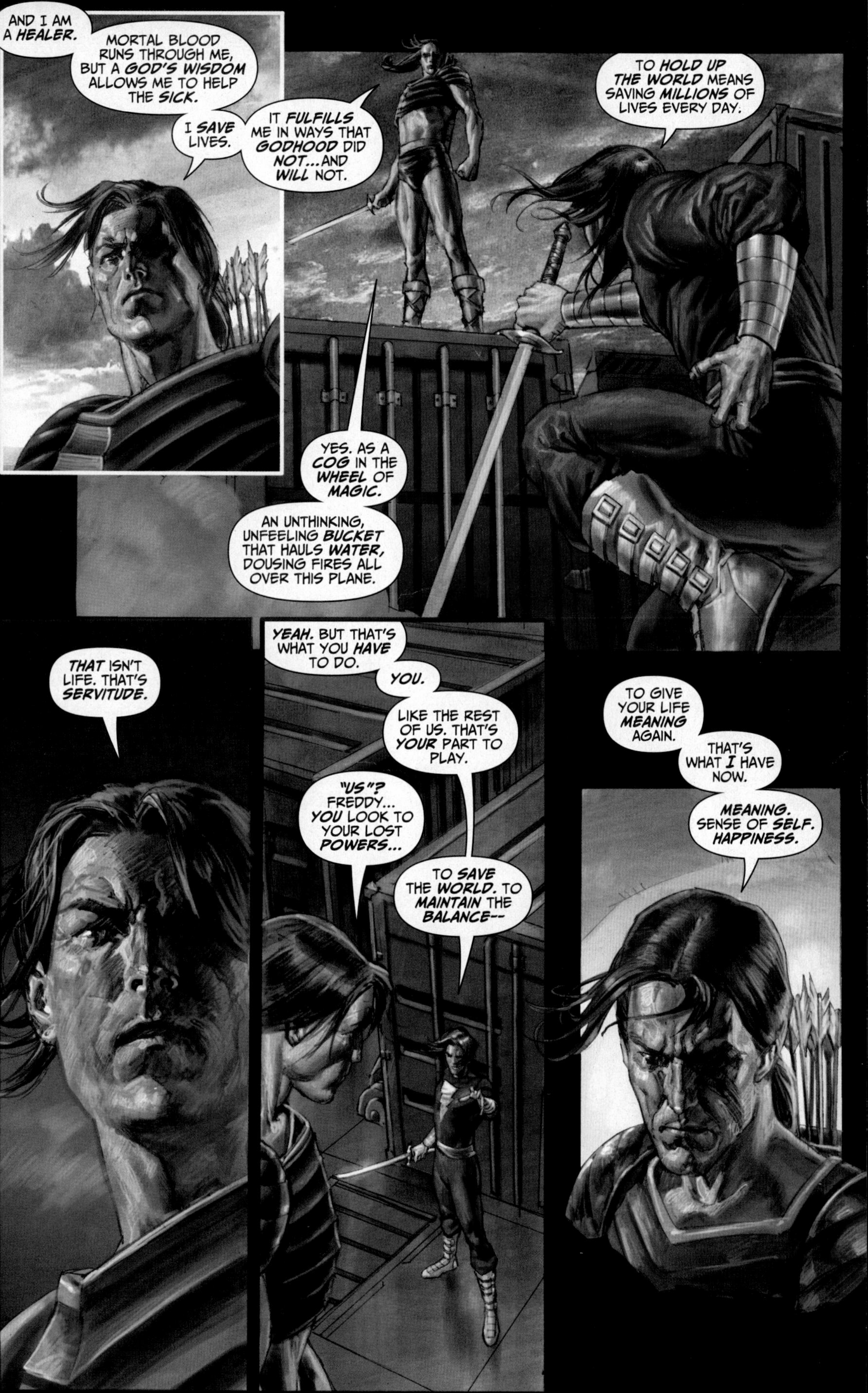
AND I AM A HEALER.
MORTAL BLOOD RUNS THROUGH ME, BUT A GOD'S WISDOM ALLOWS ME TO HELP THE SICK.
I SAVE LIVES.
IT FULFILLS ME IN WAYS THAT GODHOOD DID NOT...AND WILL NOT.
TO HOLD UP THE WORLD MEANS SAVING MILLIONS OF LIVES EVERY DAY.
YES. AS A COG IN THE WHEEL OF MAGIC.
AN UNTHINKING, UNFEELING BUCKET THAT HAULS WATER, DOUSING FIRES ALL OVER THIS PLANE.
THAT ISN'T LIFE. THAT'S SERVITUDE.
YEAH. BUT THAT'S WHAT YOU HAVE TO DO.
YOU.
LIKE THE REST OF US. THAT'S YOUR PART TO PLAY.
"US"? FREDDY... YOU LOOK TO YOUR LOST POWERS...
TO SAVE THE WORLD. TO MAINTAIN THE BALANCE--
TO GIVE YOUR LIFE MEANING AGAIN.
THAT'S WHAT I HAVE NOW.
MEANING. SENSE OF SELF. HAPPINESS.

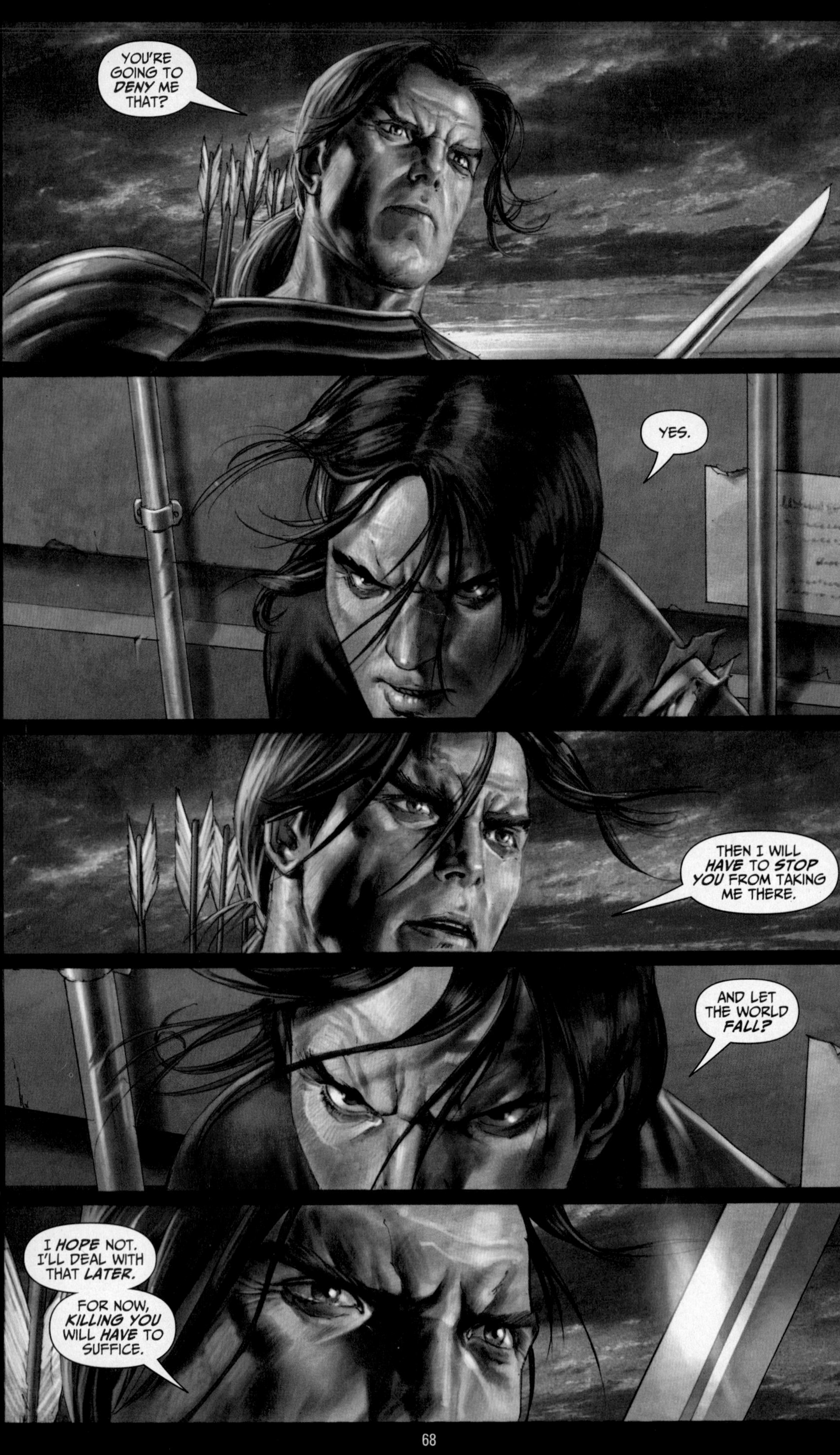
YOU'RE GOING TO DENY ME THAT?
YES.
THEN I WILL HAVE TO STOP YOU FROM TAKING ME THERE.
AND LET THE WORLD FALL?
I HOPE NOT. I'LL DEAL WITH THAT LATER.
FOR NOW, KILLING YOU WILL HAVE TO SUFFICE.

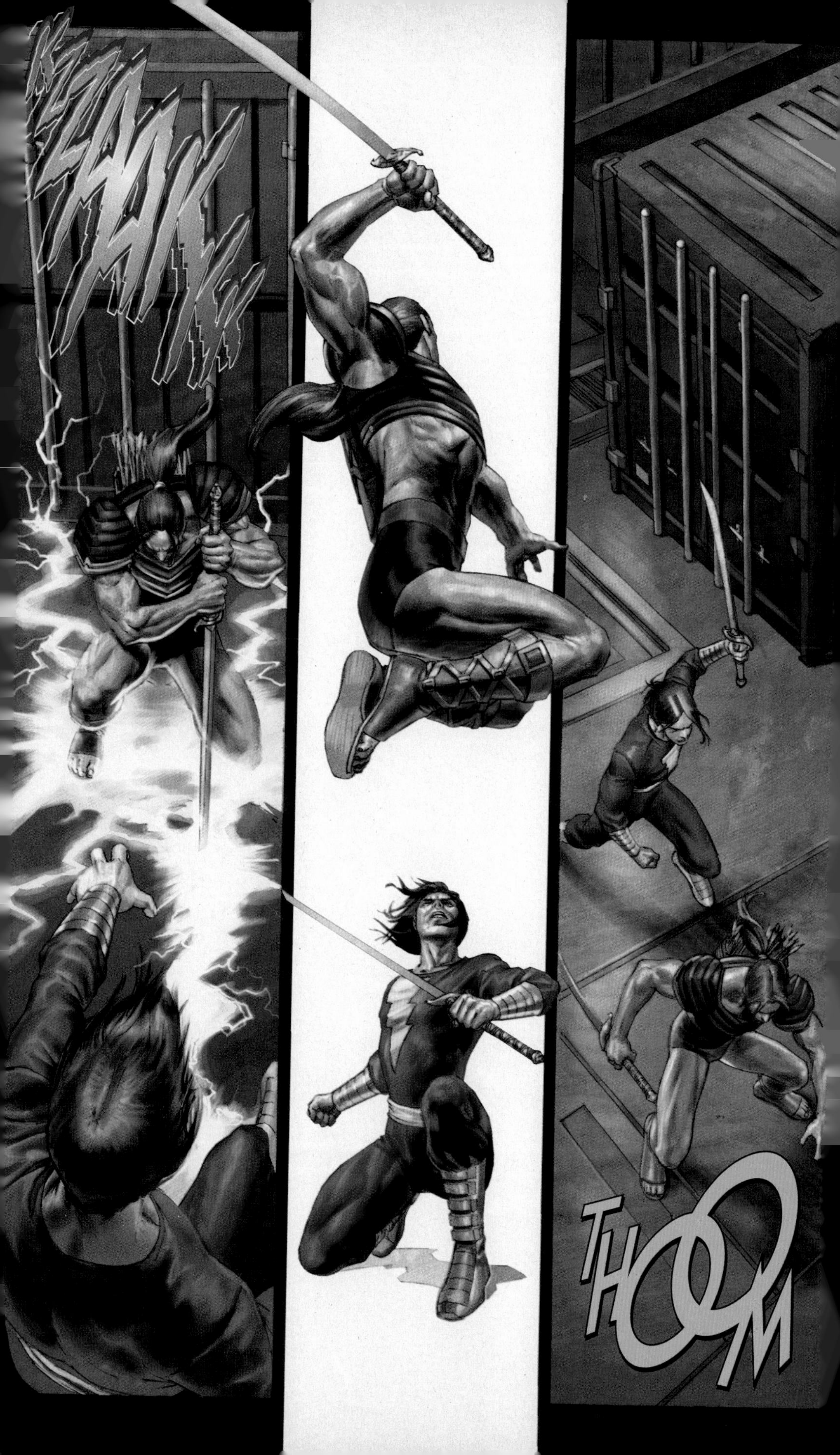
THOOM

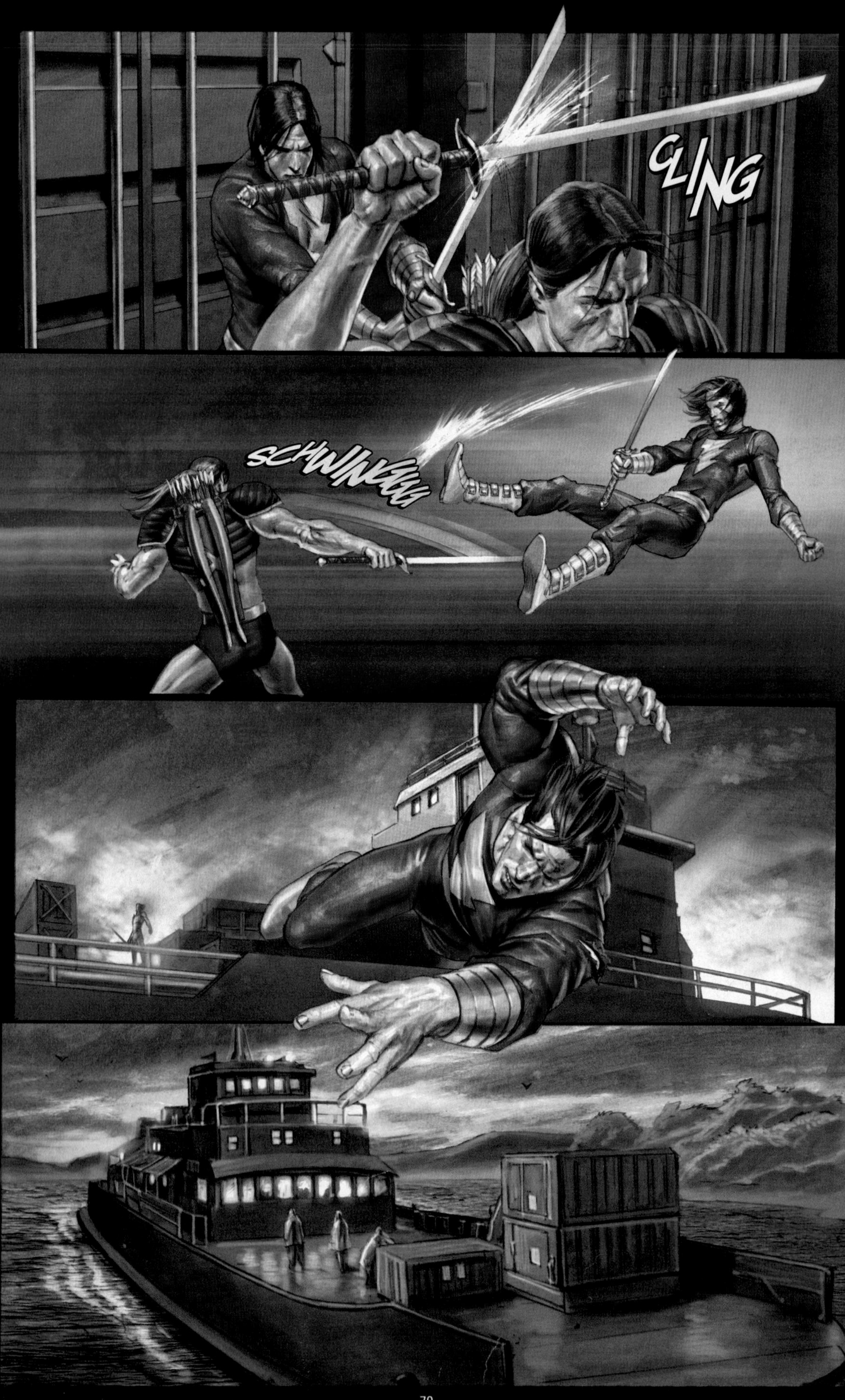
CLING
SCHWINGGG

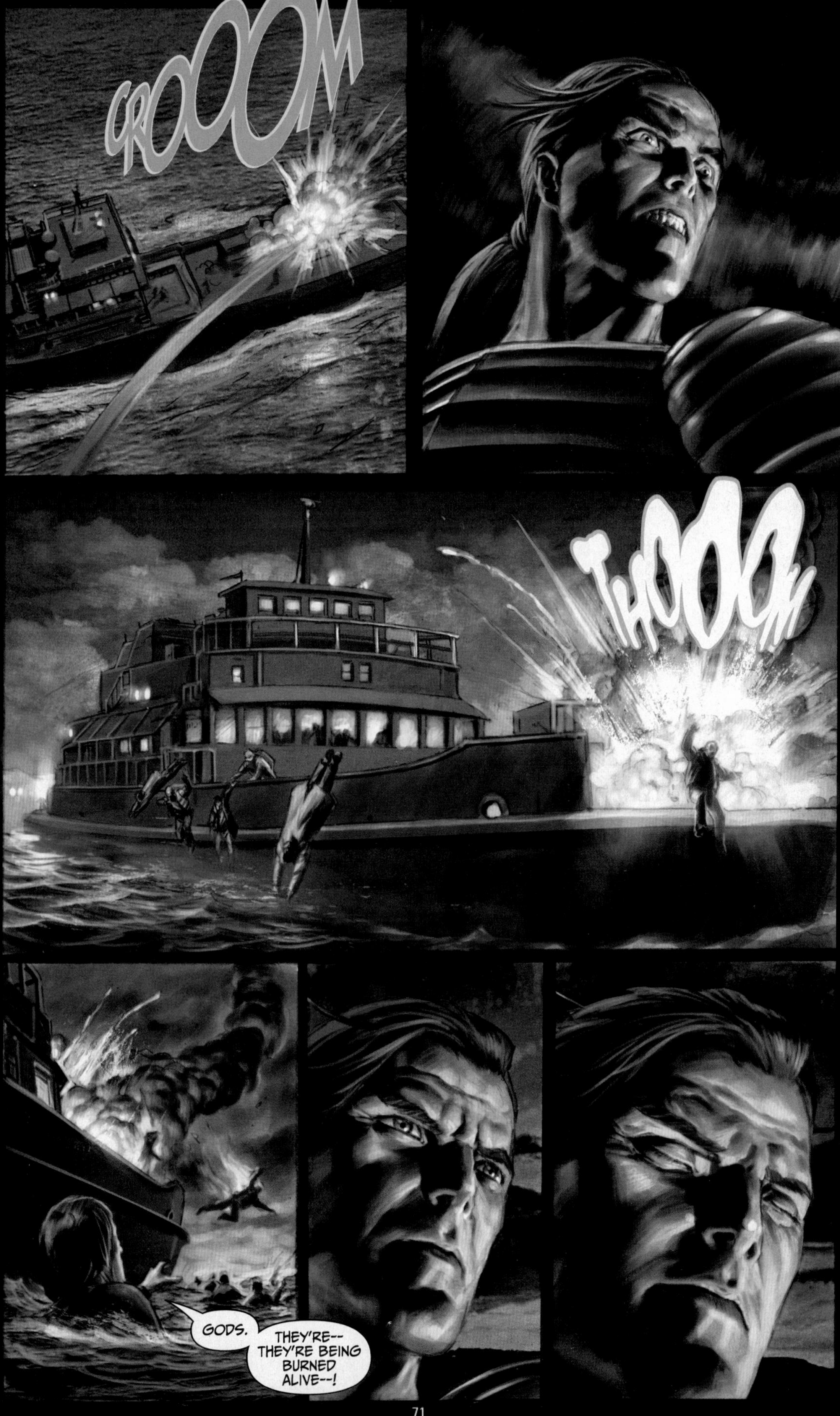
CROOOM
THOOOM
GODS.
THEY'RE-- THEY'RE BEING BURNED ALIVE--!

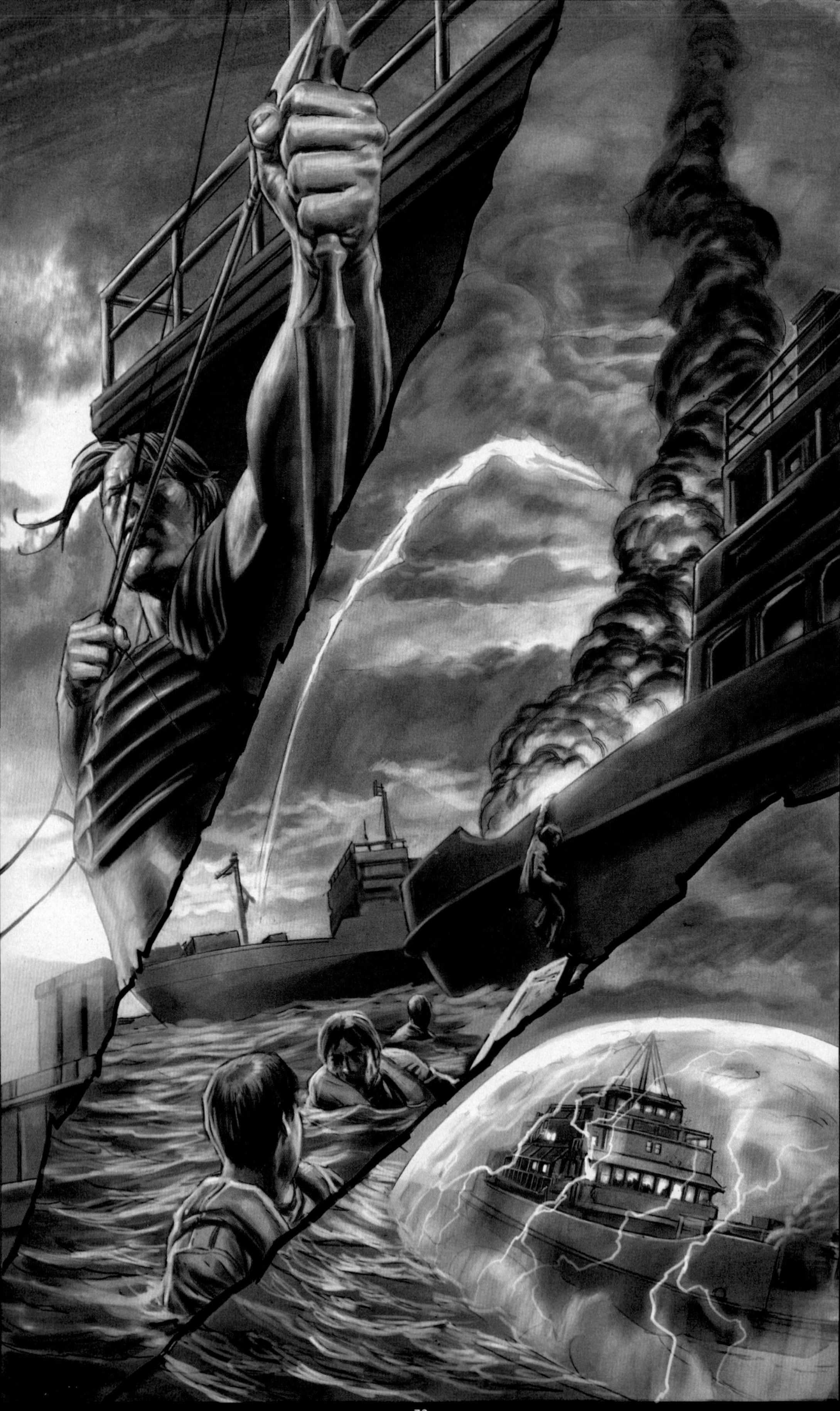

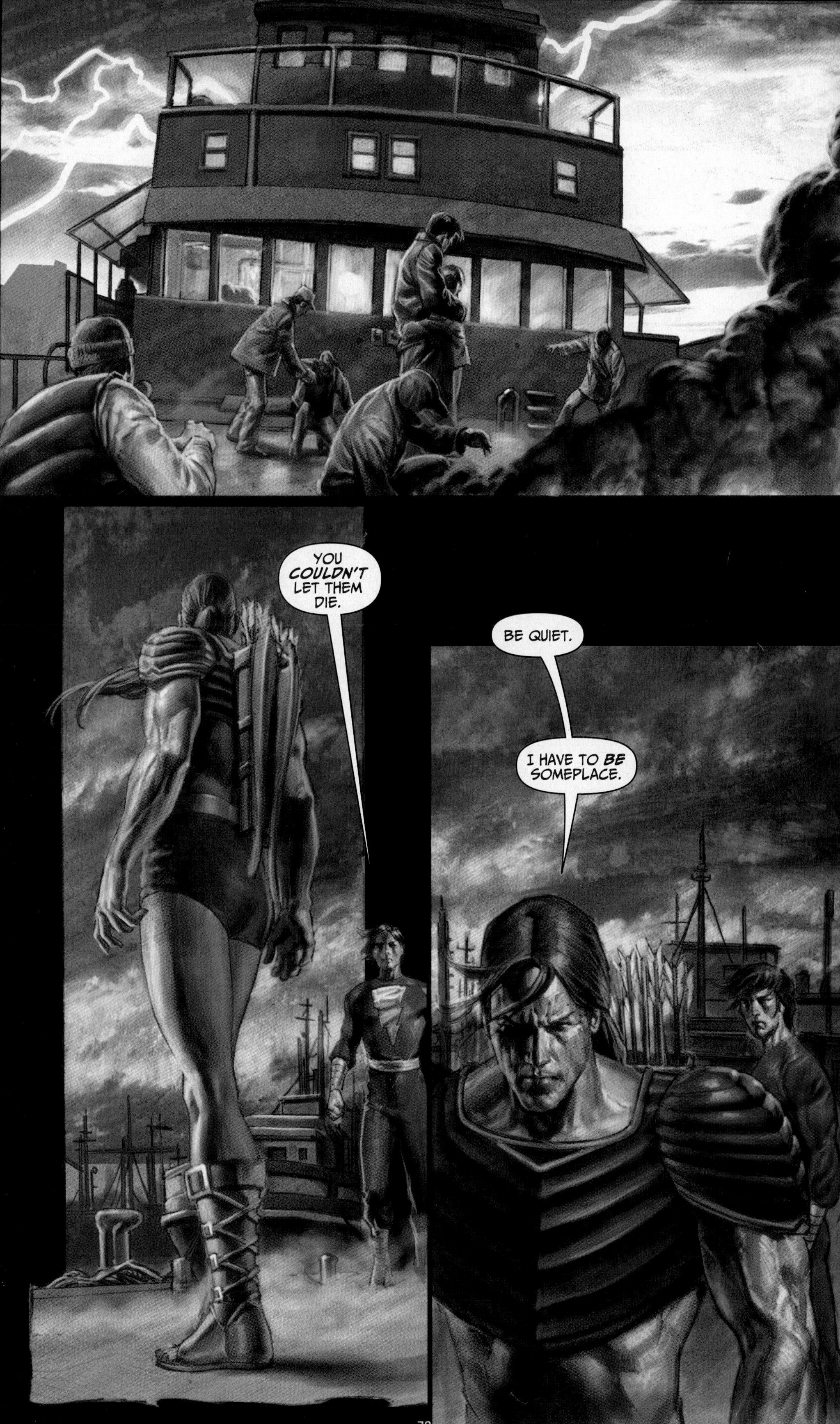
YOU *COULDN'T* LET THEM DIE.
BE QUIET.
I HAVE TO *BE* SOMEPLACE.

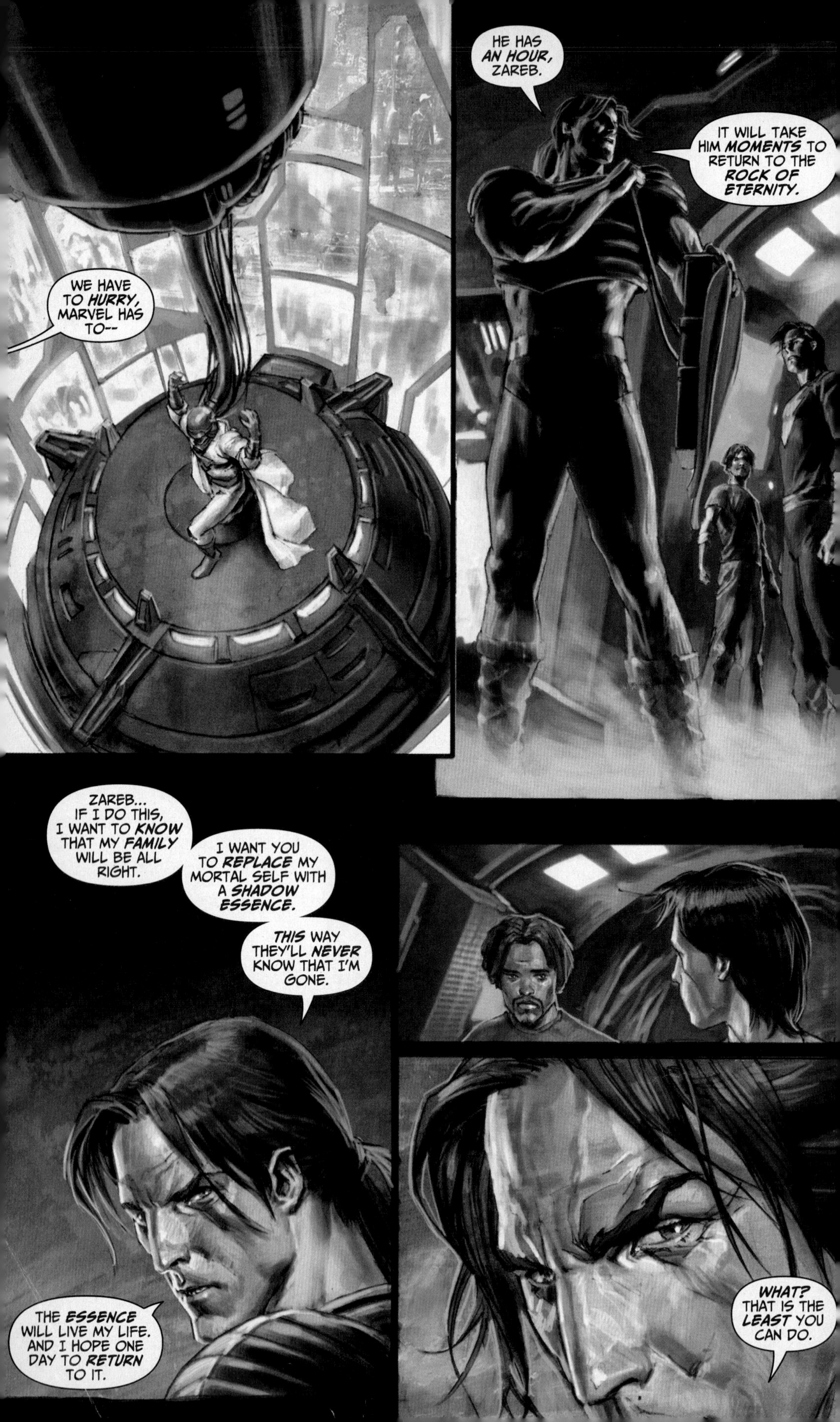
WE HAVE TO HURRY, MARVEL HAS TO--
HE HAS AN HOUR, ZAREB.
IT WILL TAKE HIM MOMENTS TO RETURN TO THE ROCK OF ETERNITY.
ZAREB... IF I DO THIS, I WANT TO KNOW THAT MY FAMILY WILL BE ALL RIGHT.
I WANT YOU TO REPLACE MY MORTAL SELF WITH A SHADOW ESSENCE.
THIS WAY THEY'LL NEVER KNOW THAT I'M GONE.
THE ESSENCE WILL LIVE MY LIFE. AND I HOPE ONE DAY TO RETURN TO IT.
WHAT? THAT IS THE LEAST YOU CAN DO.

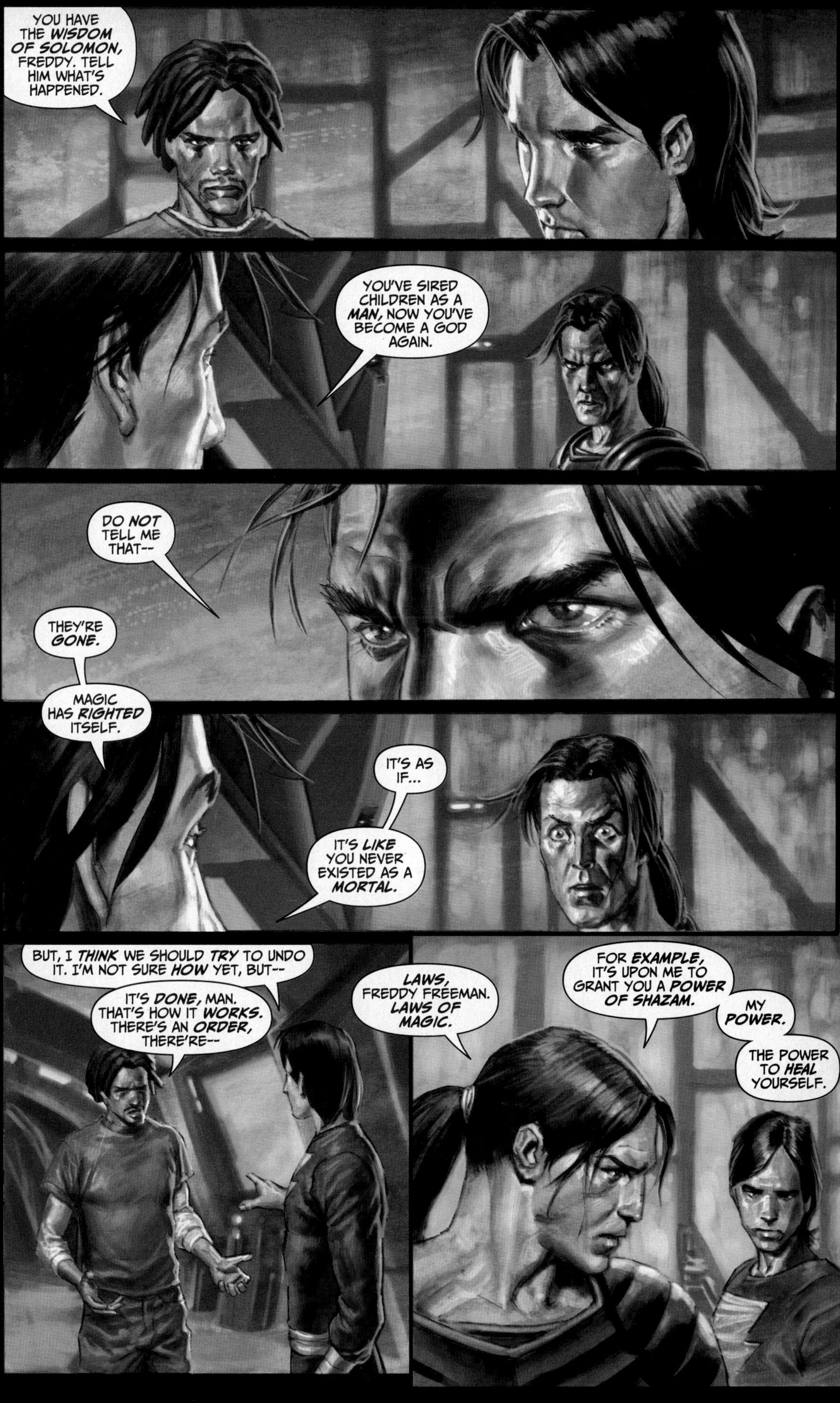
YOU HAVE THE *WISDOM OF SOLOMON,* FREDDY. TELL HIM WHAT'S HAPPENED.
YOU'VE SIRED CHILDREN AS A *MAN,* NOW YOU'VE BECOME A GOD AGAIN.
DO *NOT* TELL ME THAT--
THEY'RE *GONE.*
MAGIC HAS *RIGHTED* ITSELF.
IT'S AS IF...
IT'S *LIKE* YOU NEVER EXISTED AS A *MORTAL.*
BUT, I *THINK* WE SHOULD *TRY* TO UNDO IT. I'M NOT SURE *HOW* YET, BUT--
IT'S *DONE,* MAN. THAT'S HOW IT *WORKS.* THERE'S AN *ORDER,* THERE'RE--
LAWS, FREDDY FREEMAN. *LAWS OF MAGIC.*
FOR *EXAMPLE,* IT'S UPON ME TO GRANT YOU A *POWER OF SHAZAM.*
MY *POWER.*
THE POWER TO *HEAL* YOURSELF.

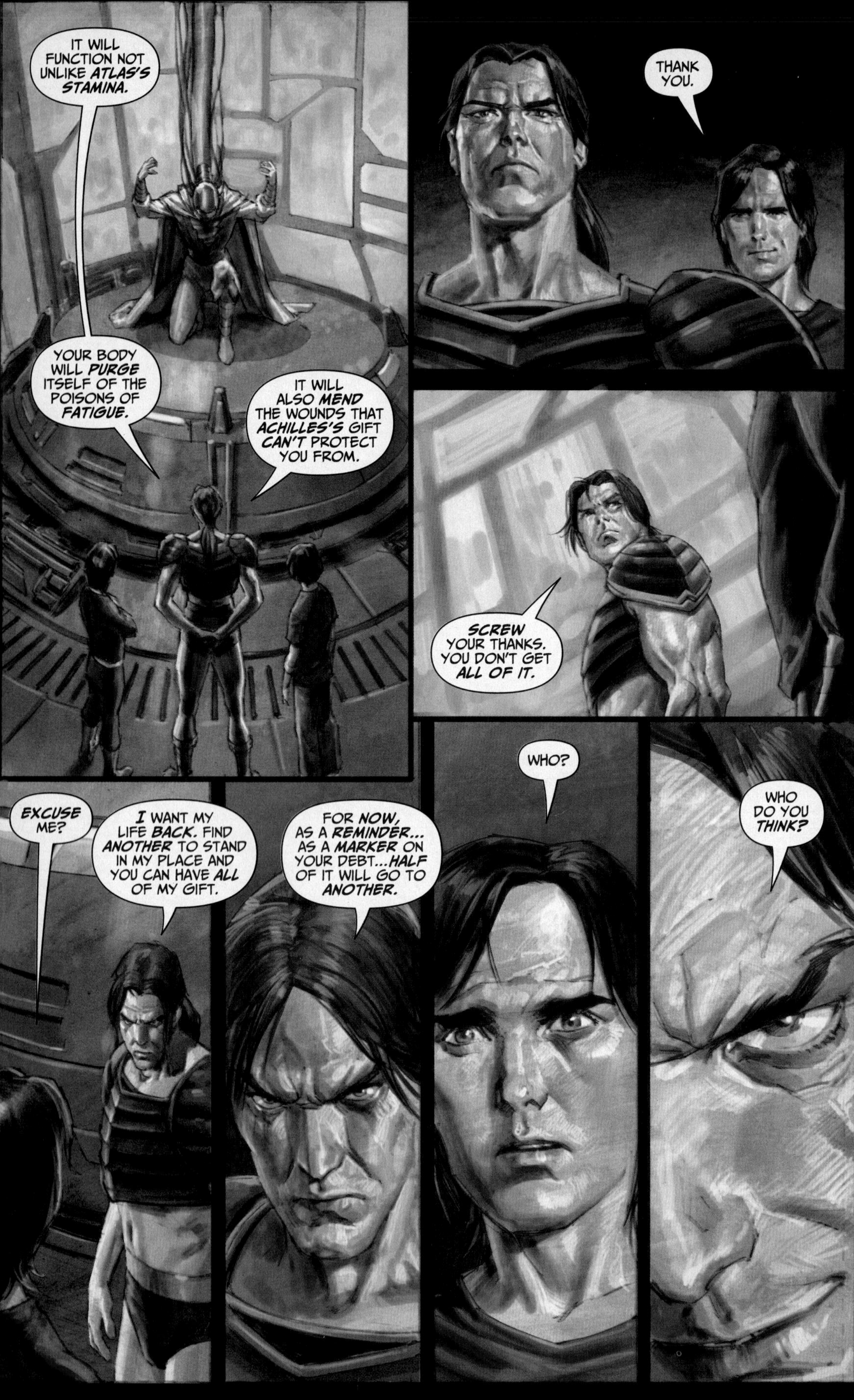
IT WILL FUNCTION NOT UNLIKE ATLAS'S STAMINA.
YOUR BODY WILL PURGE ITSELF OF THE POISONS OF FATIGUE.
IT WILL ALSO MEND THE WOUNDS THAT ACHILLES'S GIFT CAN'T PROTECT YOU FROM.
THANK YOU.
SCREW YOUR THANKS. YOU DON'T GET ALL OF IT.
EXCUSE ME?
I WANT MY LIFE BACK. FIND ANOTHER TO STAND IN MY PLACE AND YOU CAN HAVE ALL OF MY GIFT.
FOR NOW, AS A REMINDER... AS A MARKER ON YOUR DEBT...HALF OF IT WILL GO TO ANOTHER.
WHO?
WHO DO YOU THINK?

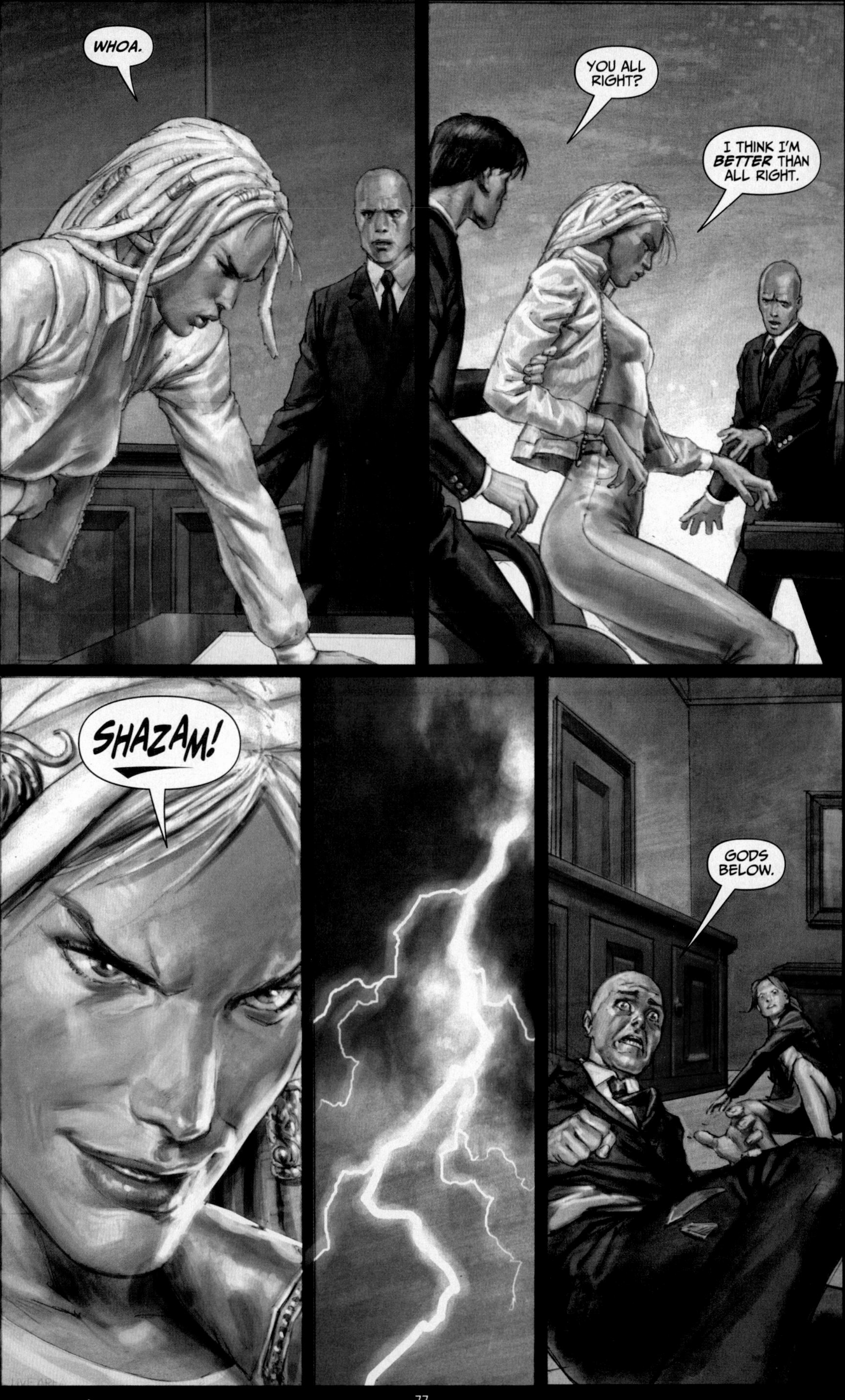
WHOA.
YOU ALL RIGHT?
I THINK I'M BETTER THAN ALL RIGHT.
SHAZAM!
GODS BELOW.

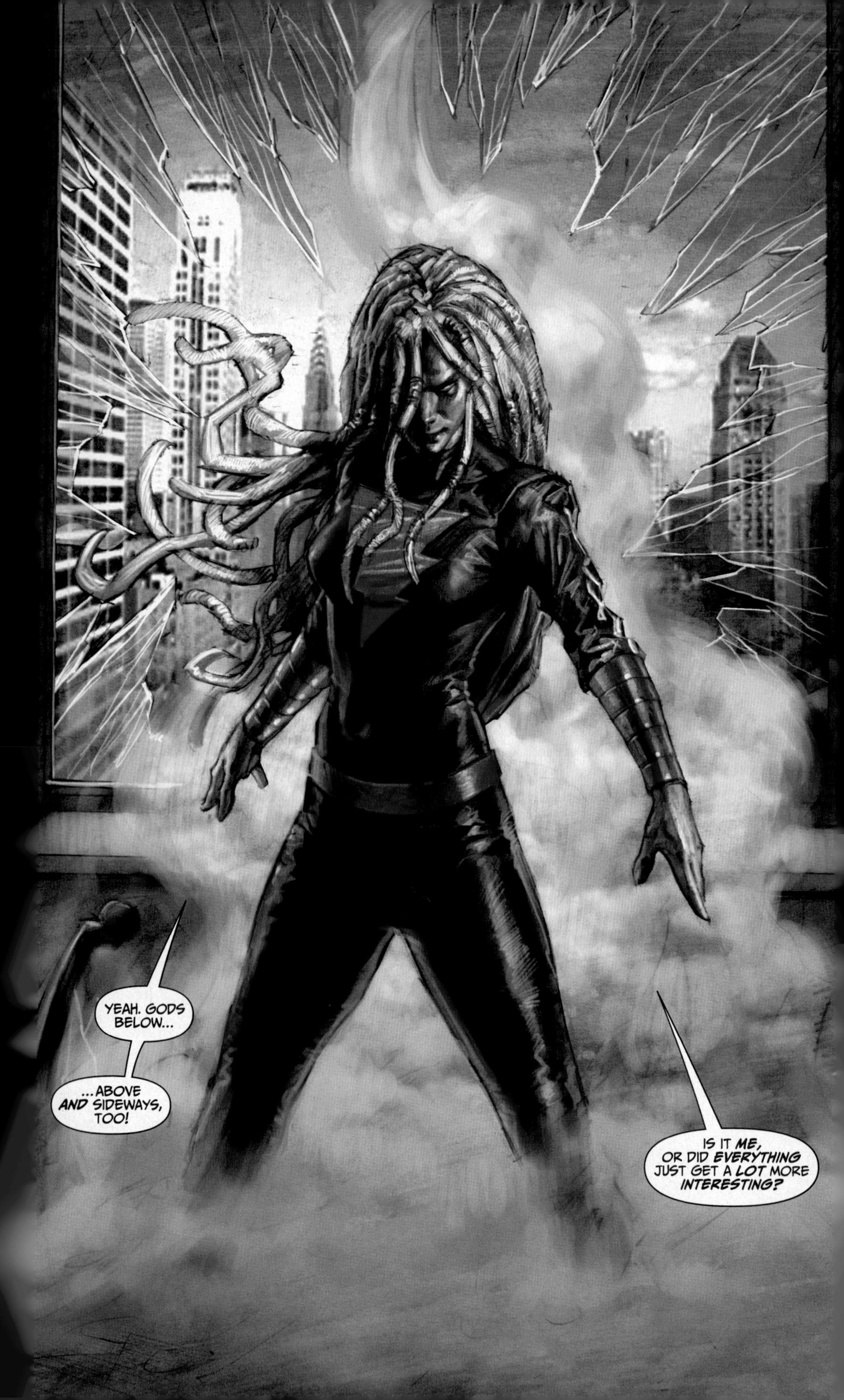
YEAH. GODS BELOW...
...ABOVE *AND* SIDEWAYS, TOO!
IS IT *ME*, OR DID *EVERYTHING* JUST GET A *LOT* MORE *INTERESTING?*

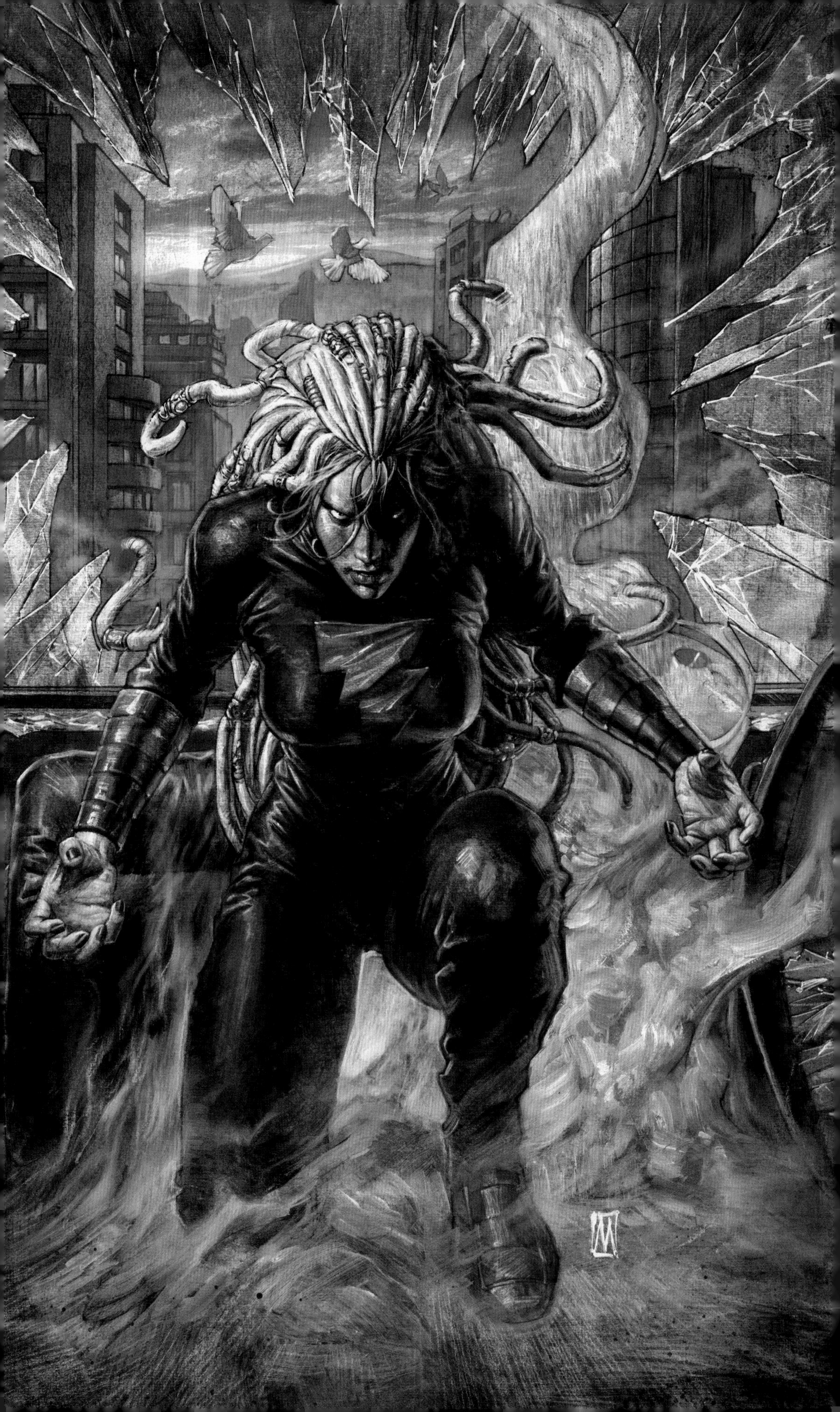

CHAPTER TEN:

MERCURY
RISING

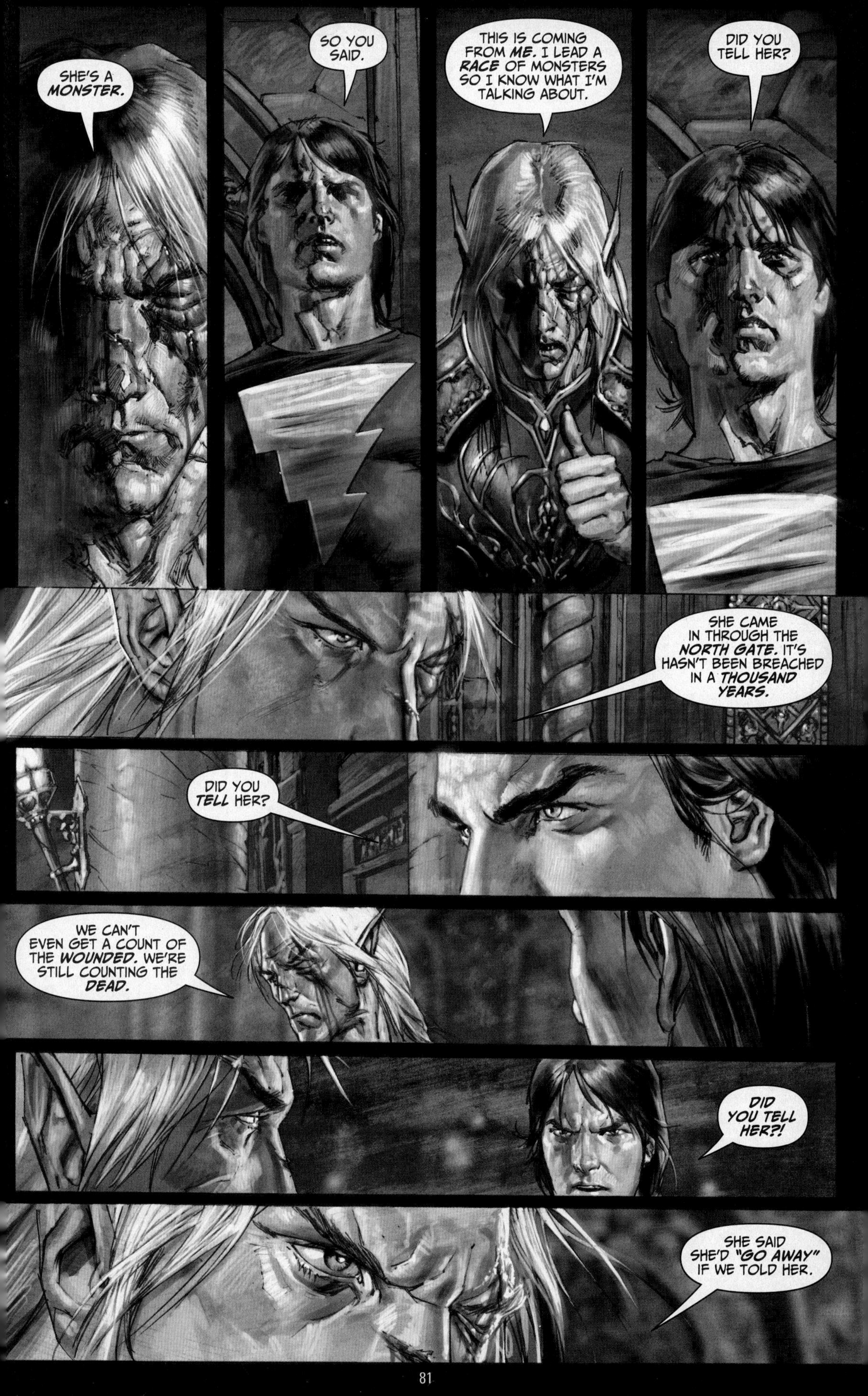
SHE'S A MONSTER.
SO YOU SAID.
THIS IS COMING FROM ME. I LEAD A RACE OF MONSTERS SO I KNOW WHAT I'M TALKING ABOUT.
DID YOU TELL HER?
SHE CAME IN THROUGH THE NORTH GATE. IT'S HASN'T BEEN BREACHED IN A THOUSAND YEARS.
DID YOU TELL HER?
WE CAN'T EVEN GET A COUNT OF THE WOUNDED. WE'RE STILL COUNTING THE DEAD.
DID YOU TELL HER?!
SHE SAID SHE'D "GO AWAY" IF WE TOLD HER.

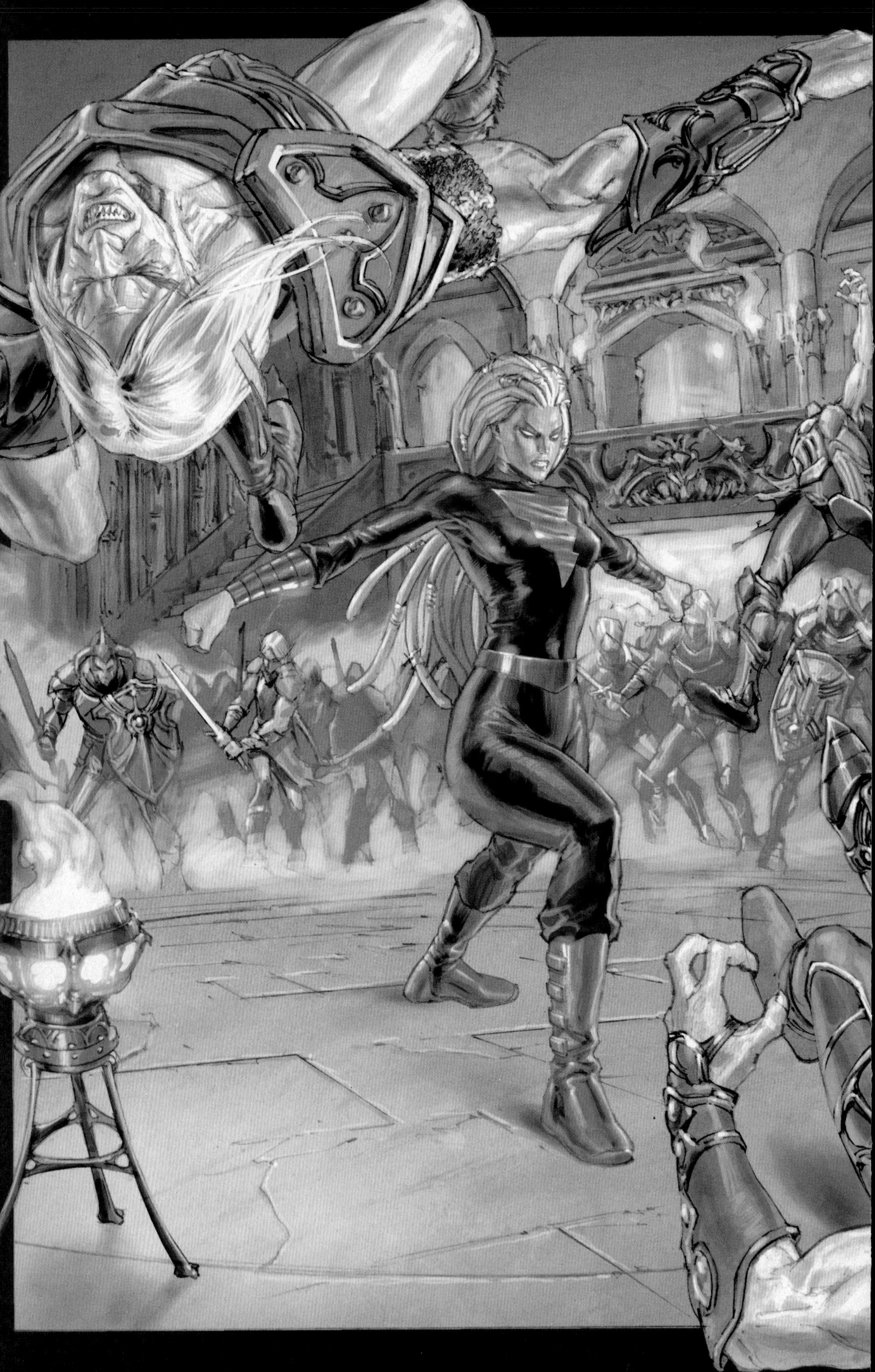

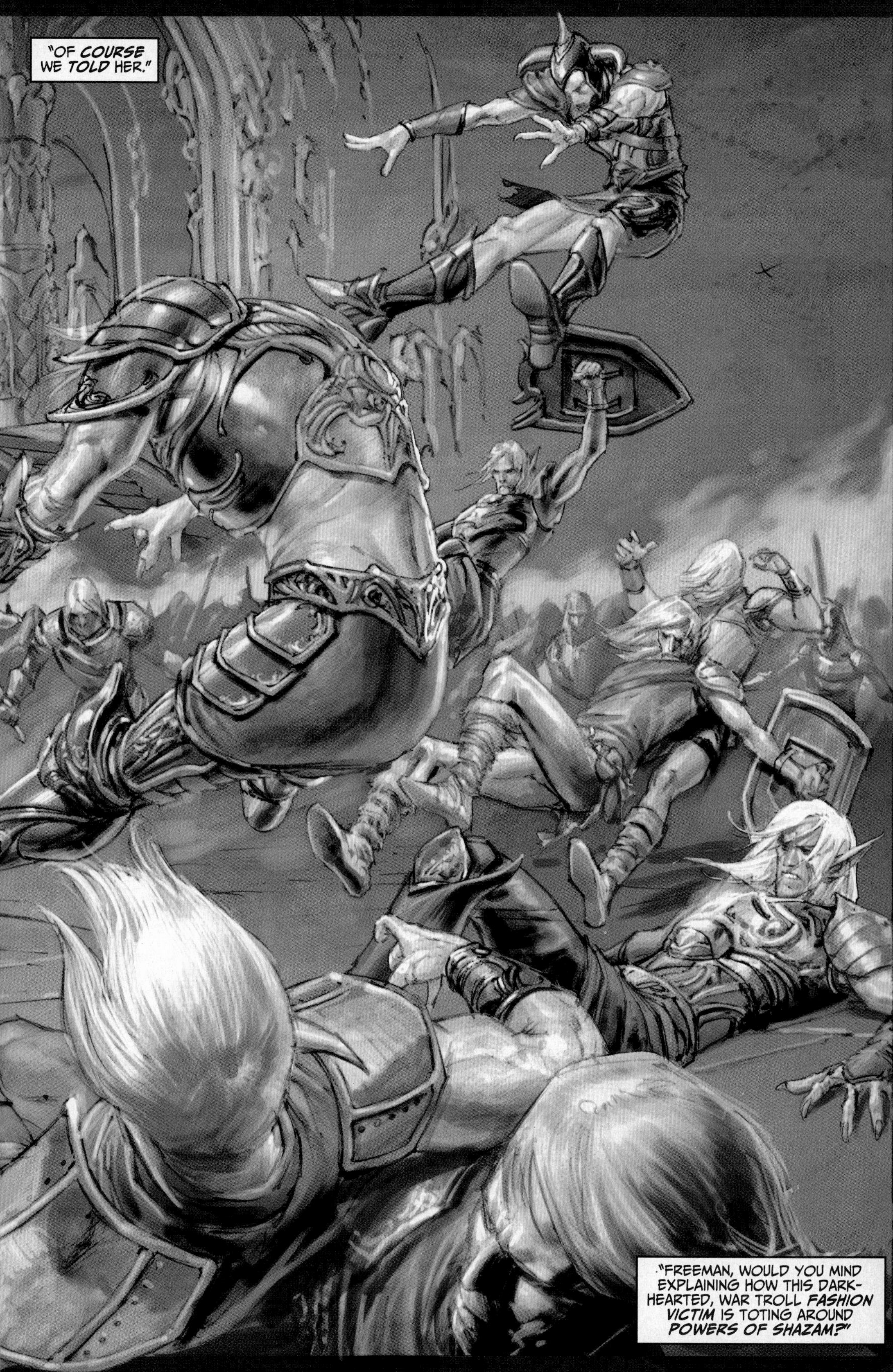
"OF COURSE WE TOLD HER."
"FREEMAN, WOULD YOU MIND EXPLAINING HOW THIS DARK-HEARTED, WAR TROLL FASHION VICTIM IS TOTING AROUND POWERS OF SHAZAM?"

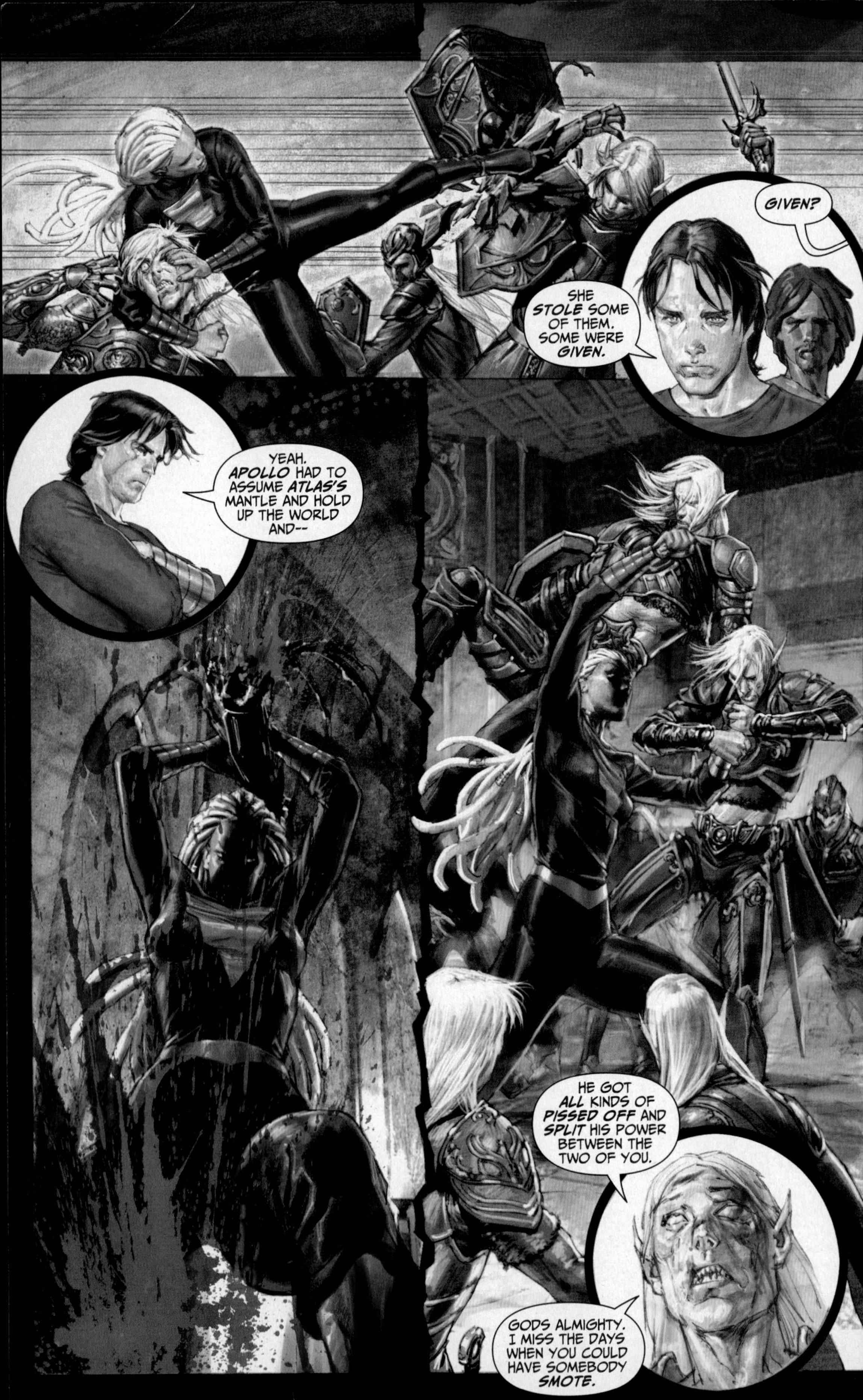
GIVEN?
SHE STOLE SOME OF THEM. SOME WERE GIVEN.
YEAH. APOLLO HAD TO ASSUME ATLAS'S MANTLE AND HOLD UP THE WORLD AND--
HE GOT ALL KINDS OF PISSED OFF AND SPLIT HIS POWER BETWEEN THE TWO OF YOU.
GODS ALMIGHTY. I MISS THE DAYS WHEN YOU COULD HAVE SOMEBODY SMOTE.

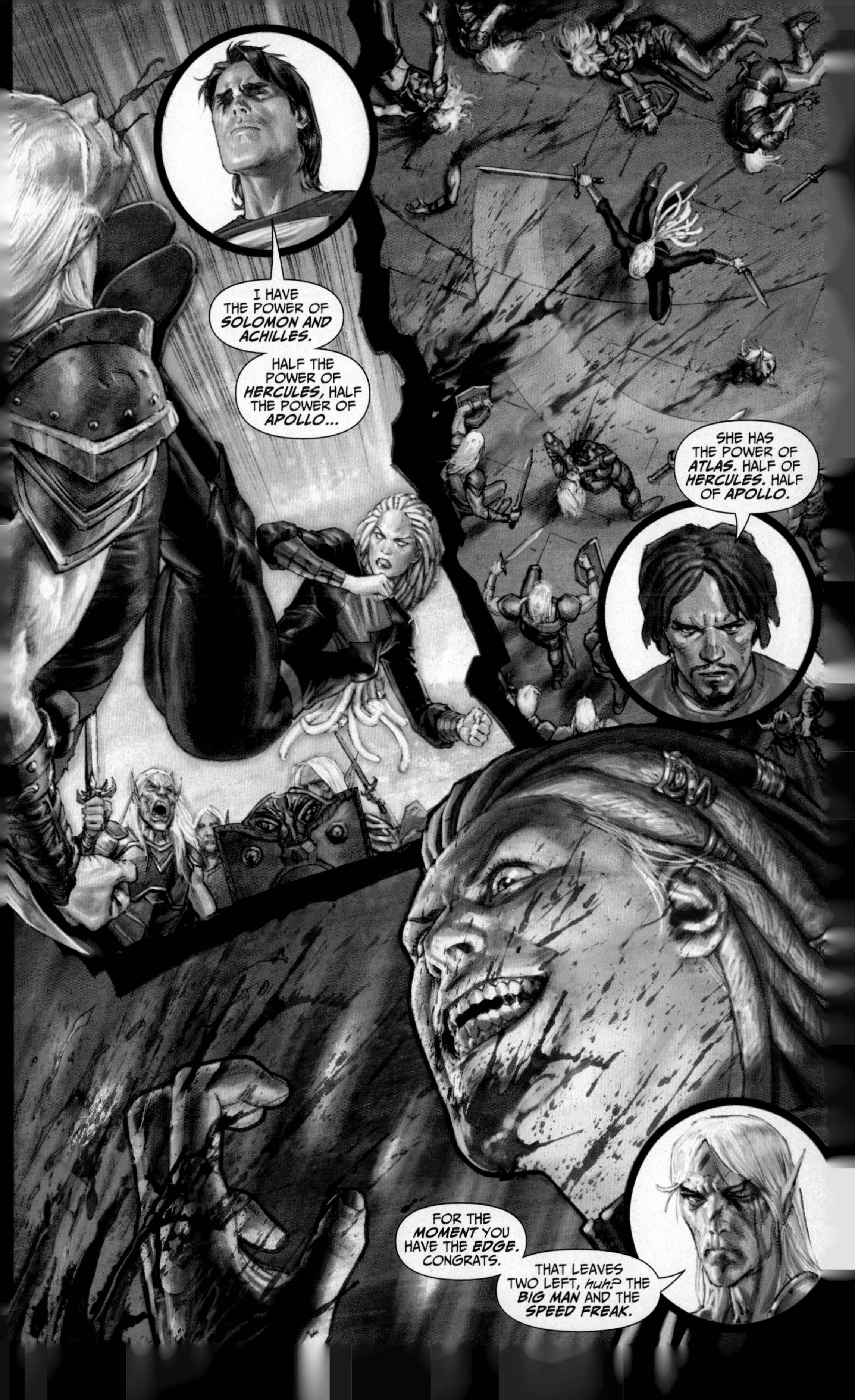
I HAVE THE POWER OF SOLOMON AND ACHILLES.
HALF THE POWER OF HERCULES, HALF THE POWER OF APOLLO...
SHE HAS THE POWER OF ATLAS. HALF OF HERCULES. HALF OF APOLLO.
FOR THE MOMENT YOU HAVE THE EDGE. CONGRATS.
THAT LEAVES TWO LEFT, huh? THE BIG MAN AND THE SPEED FREAK.

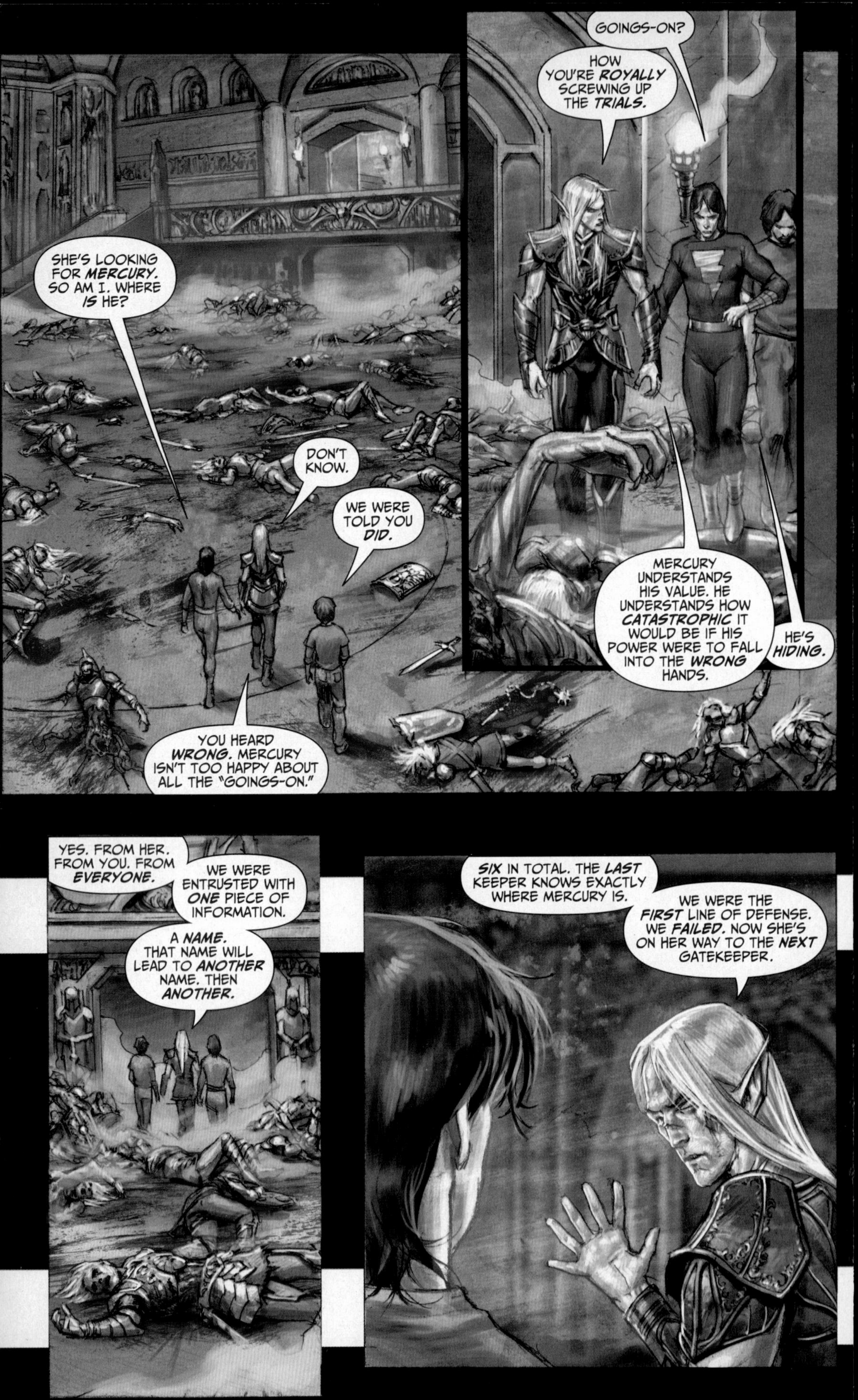
SHE'S LOOKING FOR MERCURY. SO AM I. WHERE IS HE?
DON'T KNOW.
WE WERE TOLD YOU DID.
YOU HEARD WRONG. MERCURY ISN'T TOO HAPPY ABOUT ALL THE "GOINGS-ON."
GOINGS-ON?
HOW YOU'RE ROYALLY SCREWING UP THE TRIALS.
MERCURY UNDERSTANDS HIS VALUE. HE UNDERSTANDS HOW CATASTROPHIC IT WOULD BE IF HIS POWER WERE TO FALL INTO THE WRONG HANDS.
HE'S HIDING.
YES. FROM HER. FROM YOU. FROM EVERYONE.
WE WERE ENTRUSTED WITH ONE PIECE OF INFORMATION.
A NAME. THAT NAME WILL LEAD TO ANOTHER NAME. THEN ANOTHER.
SIX IN TOTAL. THE LAST KEEPER KNOWS EXACTLY WHERE MERCURY IS.
WE WERE THE FIRST LINE OF DEFENSE. WE FAILED. NOW SHE'S ON HER WAY TO THE NEXT GATEKEEPER.

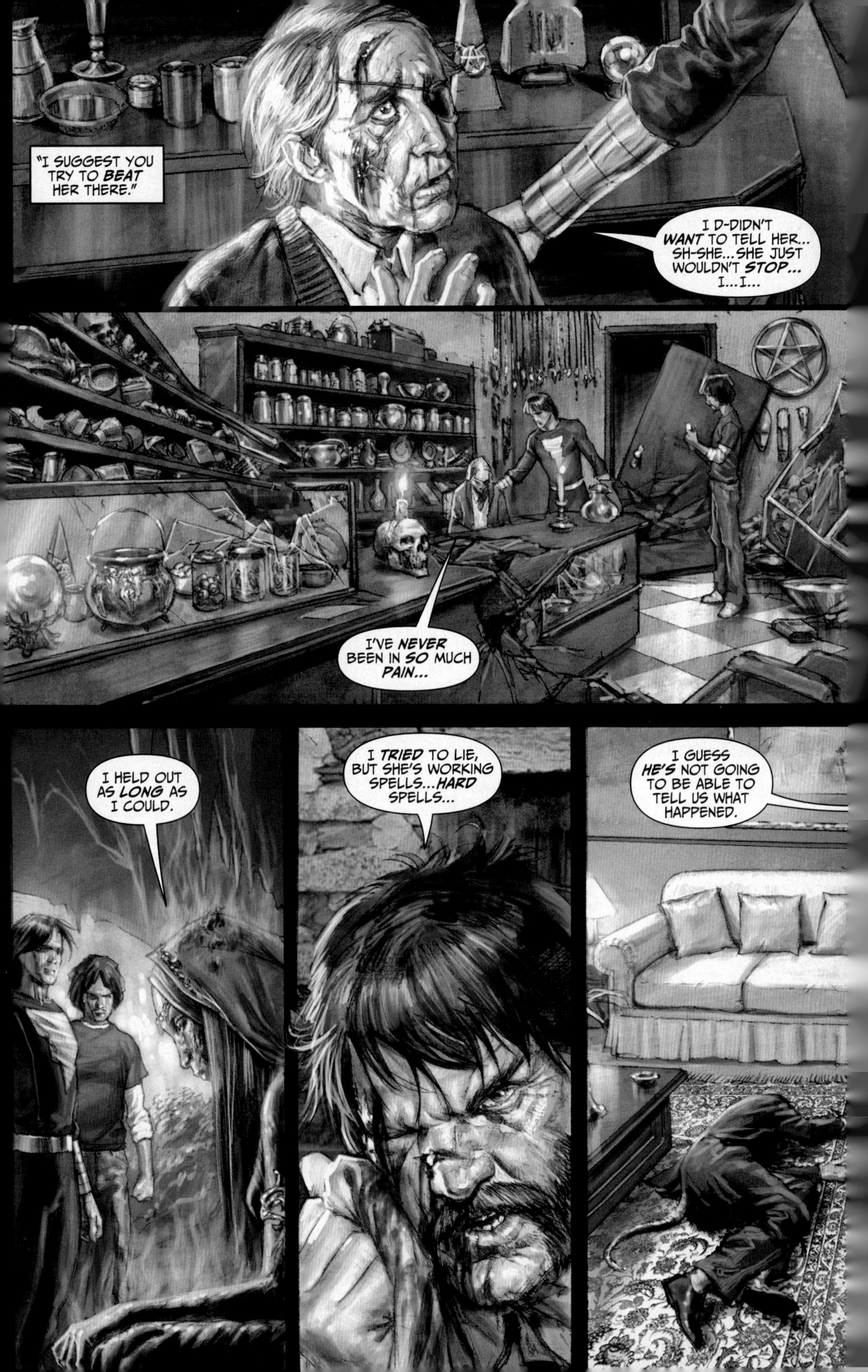
"I SUGGEST YOU TRY TO BEAT HER THERE."
I D-DIDN'T WANT TO TELL HER... SH-SHE...SHE JUST WOULDN'T STOP... I...I...
I'VE NEVER BEEN IN SO MUCH PAIN...
I HELD OUT AS LONG AS I COULD.
I TRIED TO LIE, BUT SHE'S WORKING SPELLS...HARD SPELLS...
I GUESS HE'S NOT GOING TO BE ABLE TO TELL US WHAT HAPPENED.

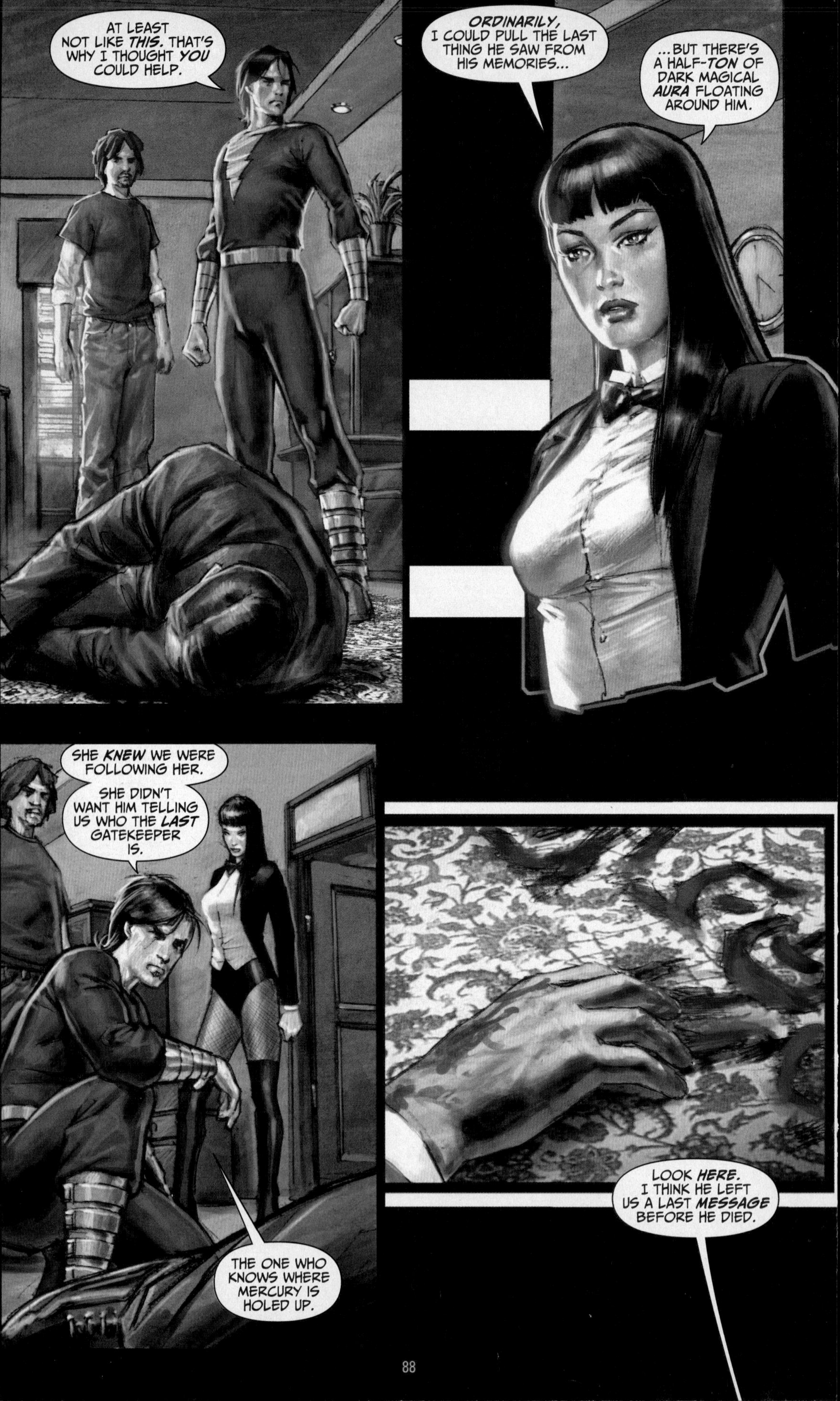
AT LEAST NOT LIKE THIS. THAT'S WHY I THOUGHT YOU COULD HELP.
ORDINARILY, I COULD PULL THE LAST THING HE SAW FROM HIS MEMORIES...
...BUT THERE'S A HALF-TON OF DARK MAGICAL AURA FLOATING AROUND HIM.
SHE KNEW WE WERE FOLLOWING HER.
SHE DIDN'T WANT HIM TELLING US WHO THE LAST GATEKEEPER IS.
THE ONE WHO KNOWS WHERE MERCURY IS HOLED UP.
LOOK HERE. I THINK HE LEFT US A LAST MESSAGE BEFORE HE DIED.

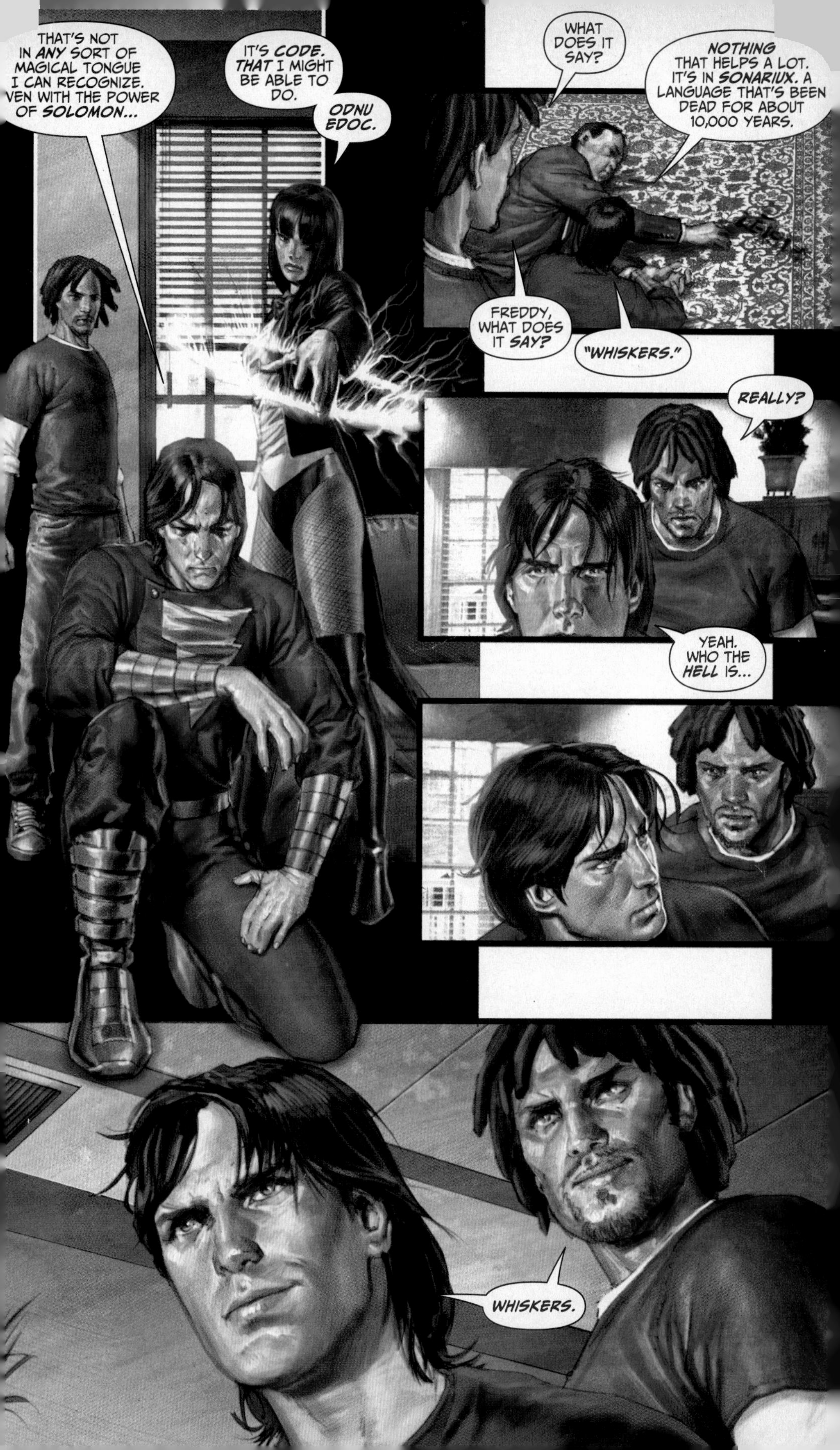
THAT'S NOT IN ANY SORT OF MAGICAL TONGUE I CAN RECOGNIZE. VEN WITH THE POWER OF SOLOMON...
IT'S CODE. THAT I MIGHT BE ABLE TO DO.
ODNU EDOC.
WHAT DOES IT SAY?
NOTHING THAT HELPS A LOT. IT'S IN SONARIUX. A LANGUAGE THAT'S BEEN DEAD FOR ABOUT 10,000 YEARS.
FREDDY, WHAT DOES IT SAY?
"WHISKERS."
REALLY?
YEAH. WHO THE HELL IS...
WHISKERS.

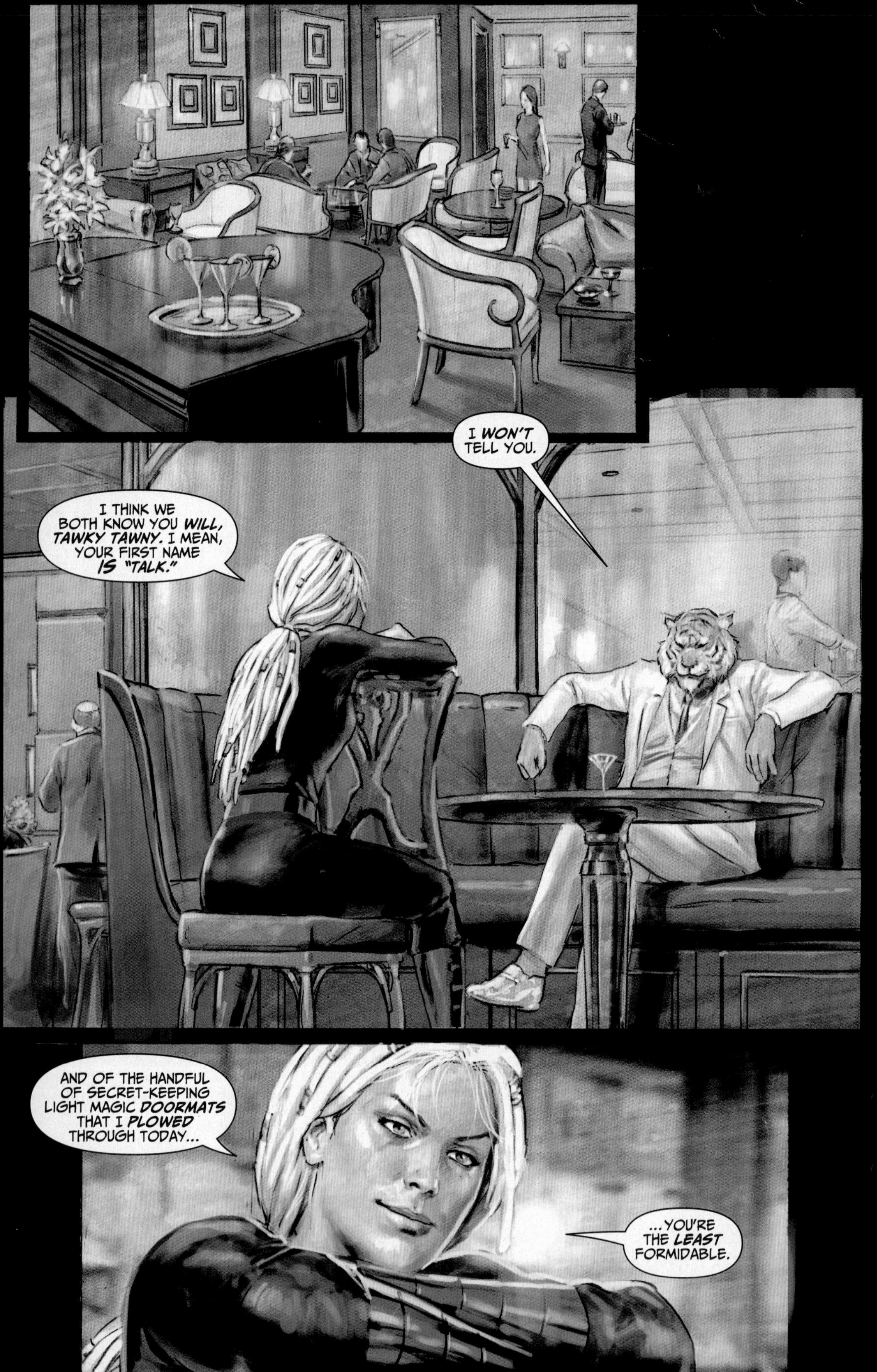

I WON'T TELL YOU.
I THINK WE BOTH KNOW YOU WILL, TAWKY TAWNY. I MEAN, YOUR FIRST NAME IS "TALK."
AND OF THE HANDFUL OF SECRET-KEEPING LIGHT MAGIC DOORMATS THAT I PLOWED THROUGH TODAY...
...YOU'RE THE LEAST FORMIDABLE.

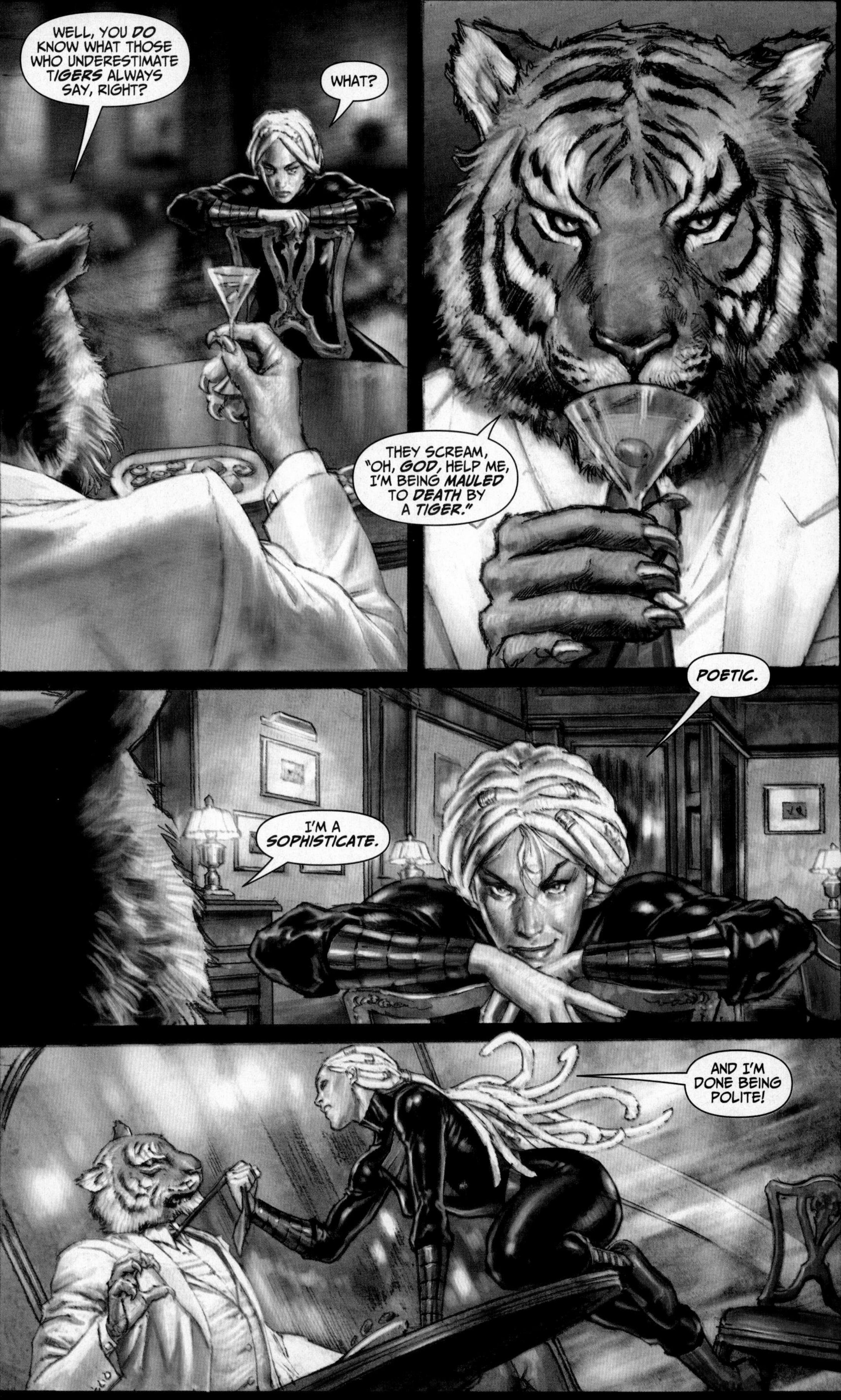
WELL, YOU DO KNOW WHAT THOSE WHO UNDERESTIMATE TIGERS ALWAYS SAY, RIGHT?
WHAT?
THEY SCREAM, "OH, GOD, HELP ME, I'M BEING MAULED TO DEATH BY A TIGER."
POETIC.
I'M A SOPHISTICATE.
AND I'M DONE BEING POLITE!

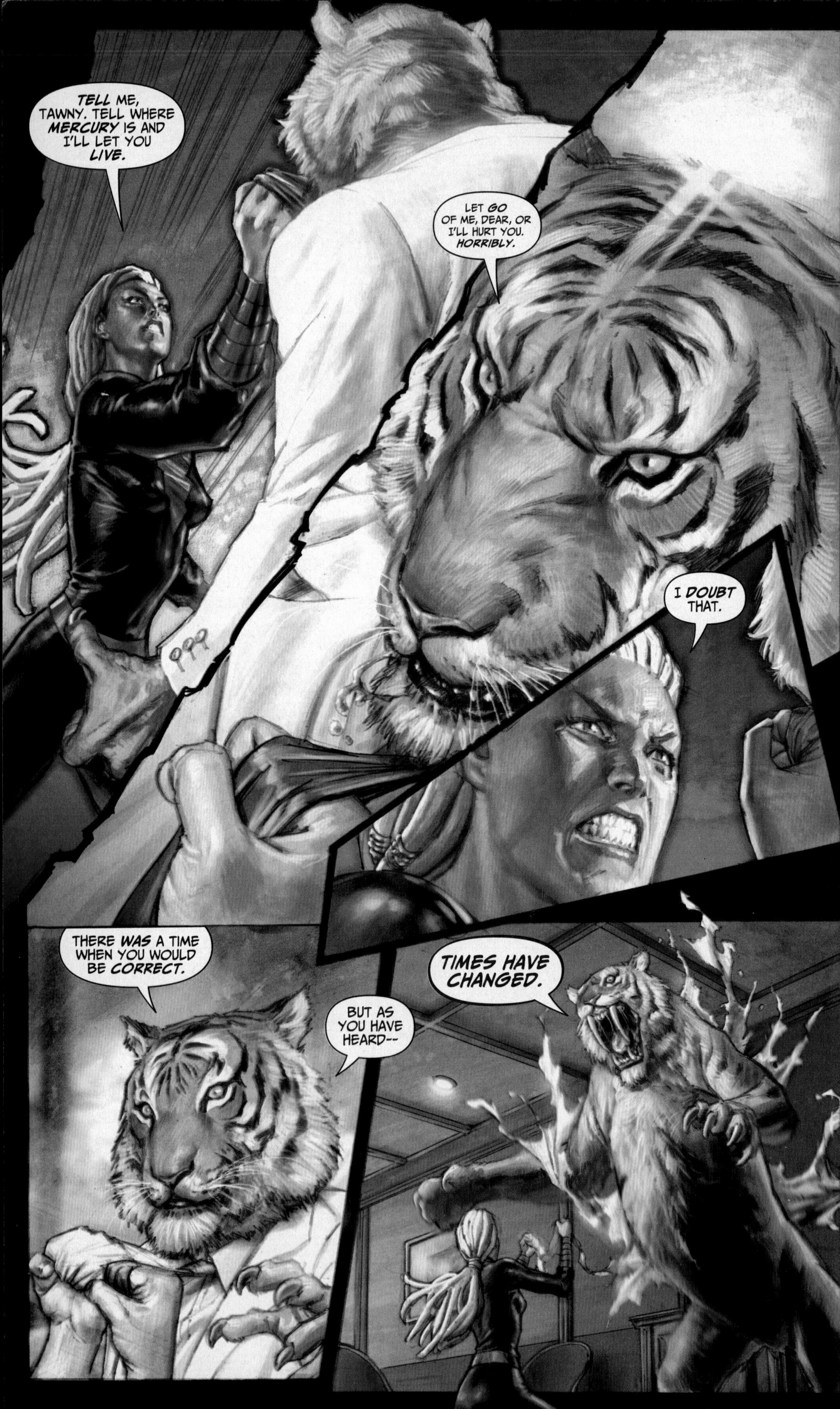
TELL ME, TAWNY. TELL WHERE MERCURY IS AND I'LL LET YOU LIVE.
LET GO OF ME, DEAR, OR I'LL HURT YOU. HORRIBLY.
I DOUBT THAT.
THERE WAS A TIME WHEN YOU WOULD BE CORRECT.
BUT AS YOU HAVE HEARD--
TIMES HAVE CHANGED.

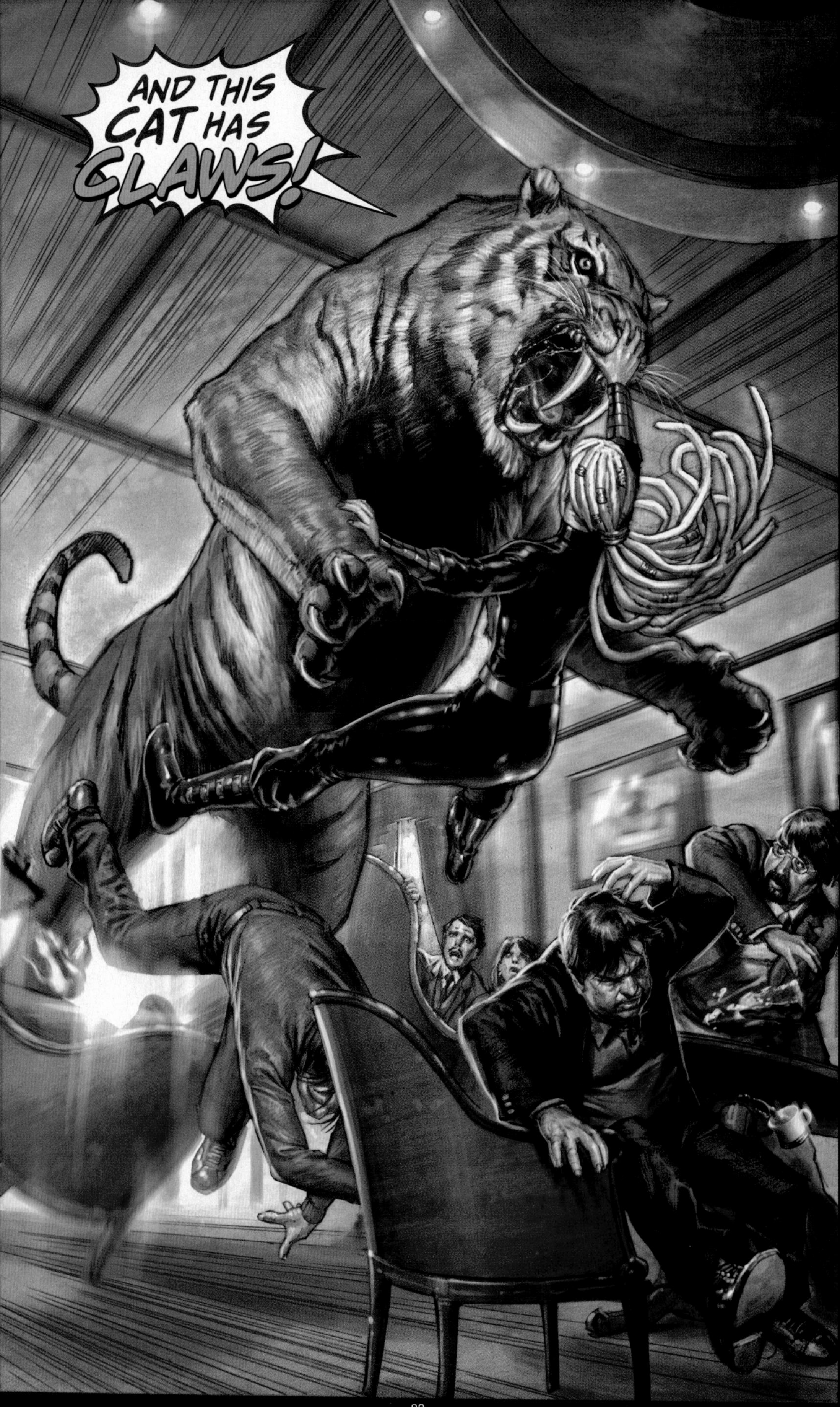
AND THIS CAT HAS CLAWS!

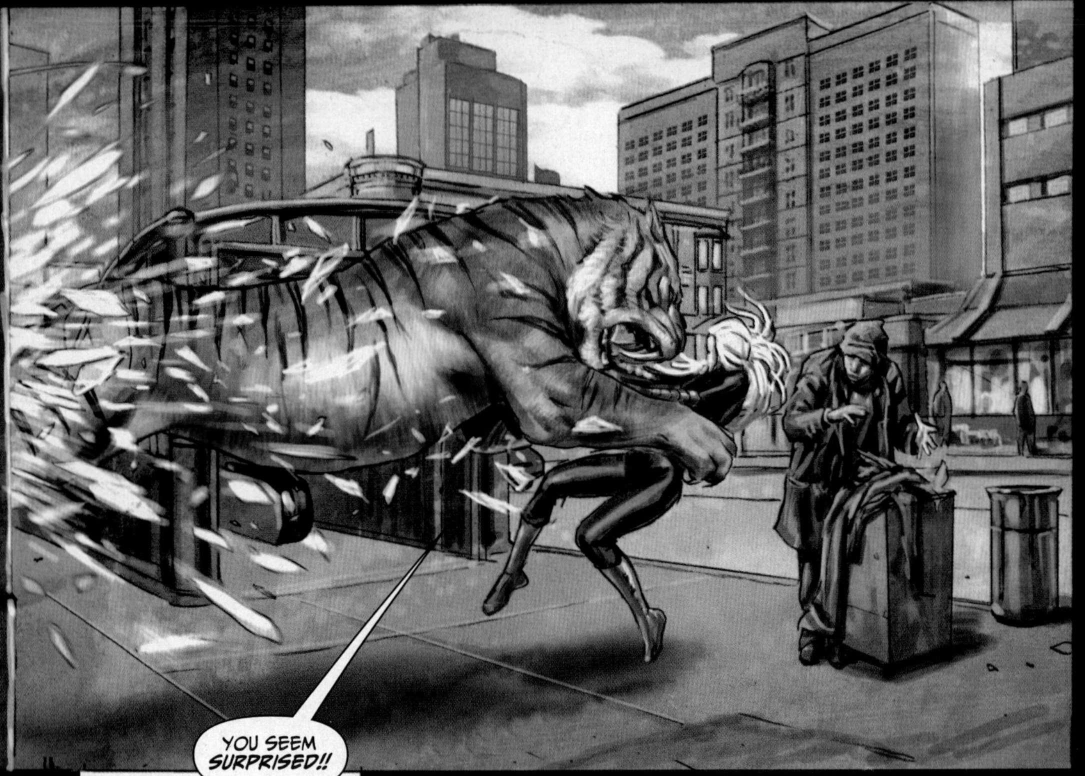
YOU SEEM SURPRISED!!

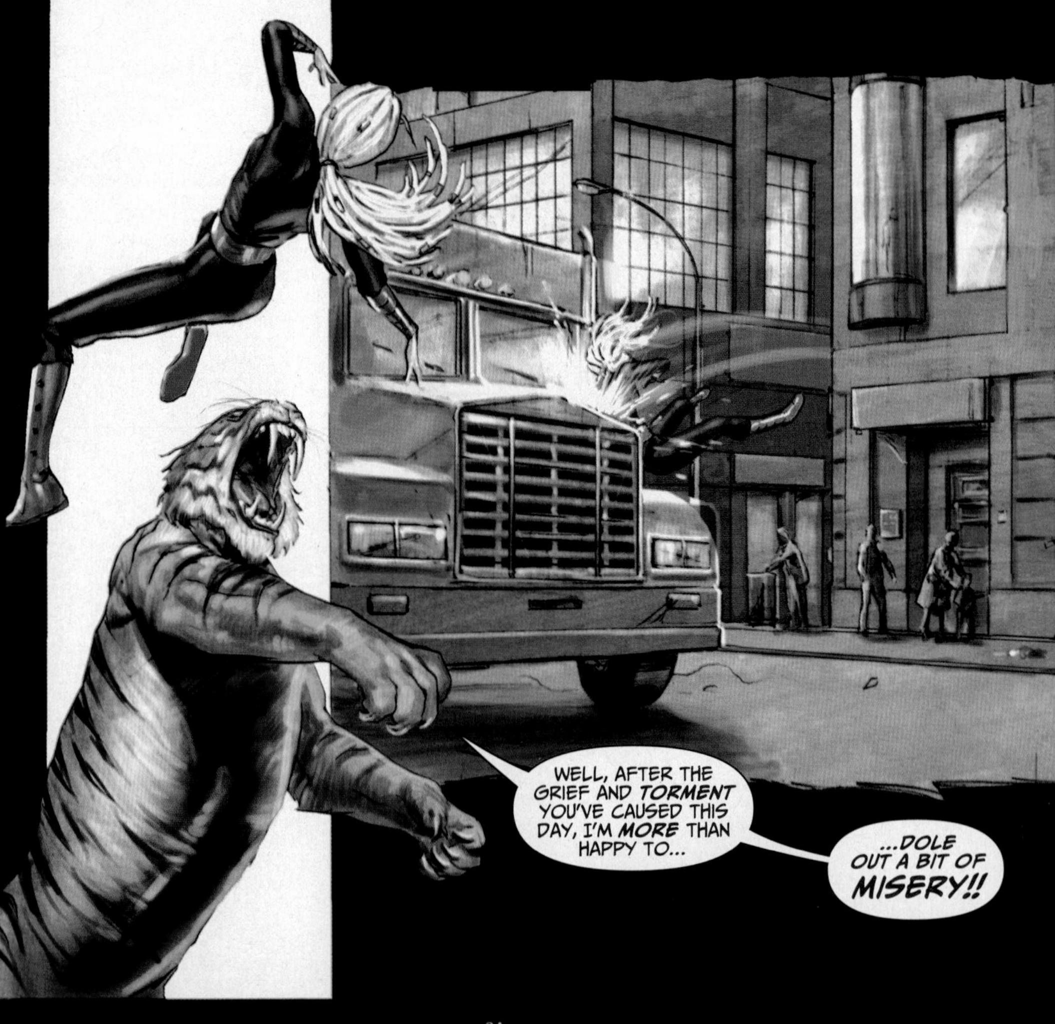
WELL, AFTER THE GRIEF AND TORMENT YOU'VE CAUSED THIS DAY, I'M MORE THAN HAPPY TO...
...DOLE OUT A BIT OF MISERY!!

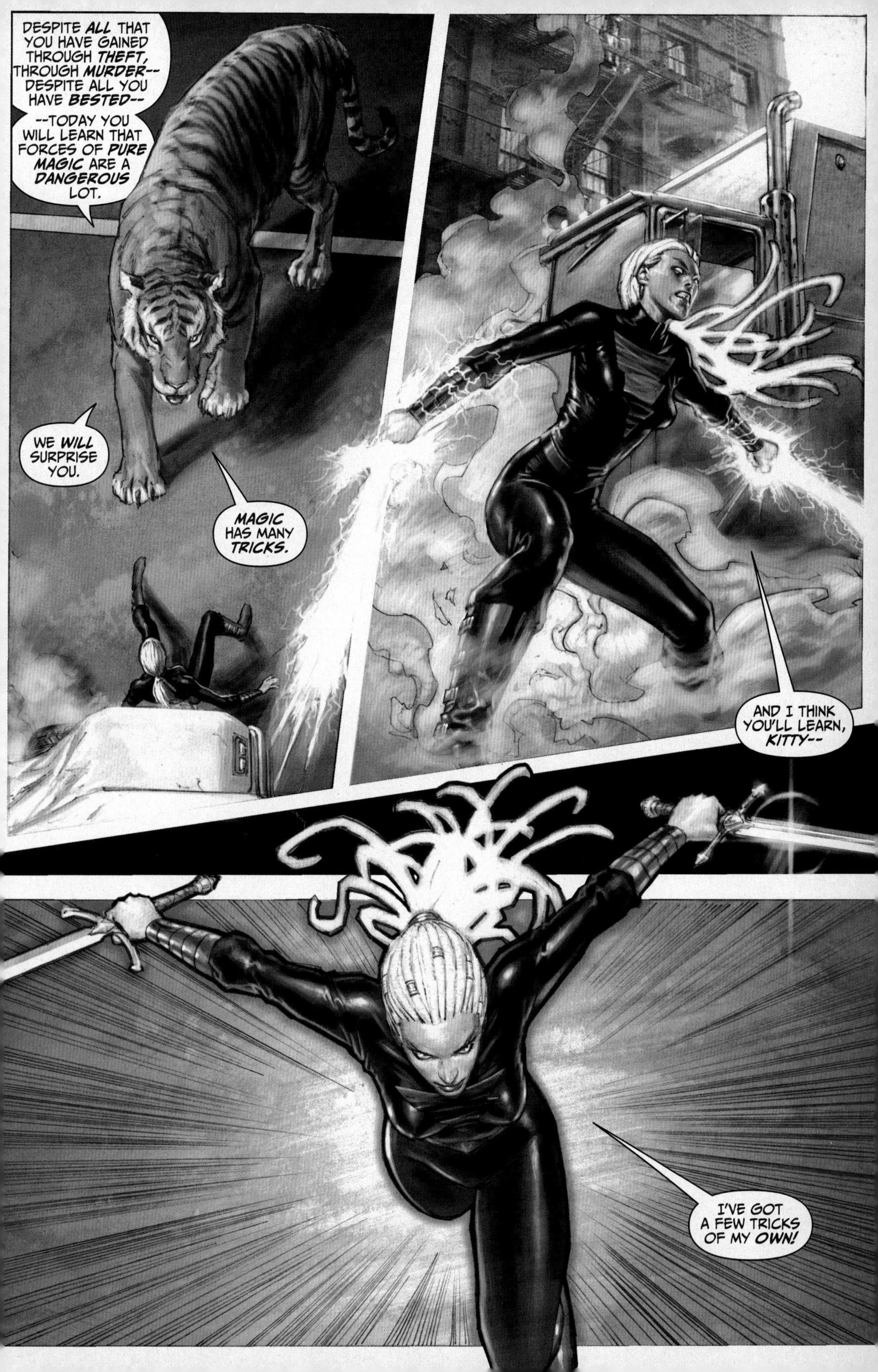
DESPITE ALL THAT YOU HAVE GAINED THROUGH THEFT, THROUGH MURDER-- DESPITE ALL YOU HAVE BESTED--
--TODAY YOU WILL LEARN THAT FORCES OF PURE MAGIC ARE A DANGEROUS LOT.
WE WILL SURPRISE YOU.
MAGIC HAS MANY TRICKS.
AND I THINK YOU'LL LEARN, KITTY--
I'VE GOT A FEW TRICKS OF MY OWN!

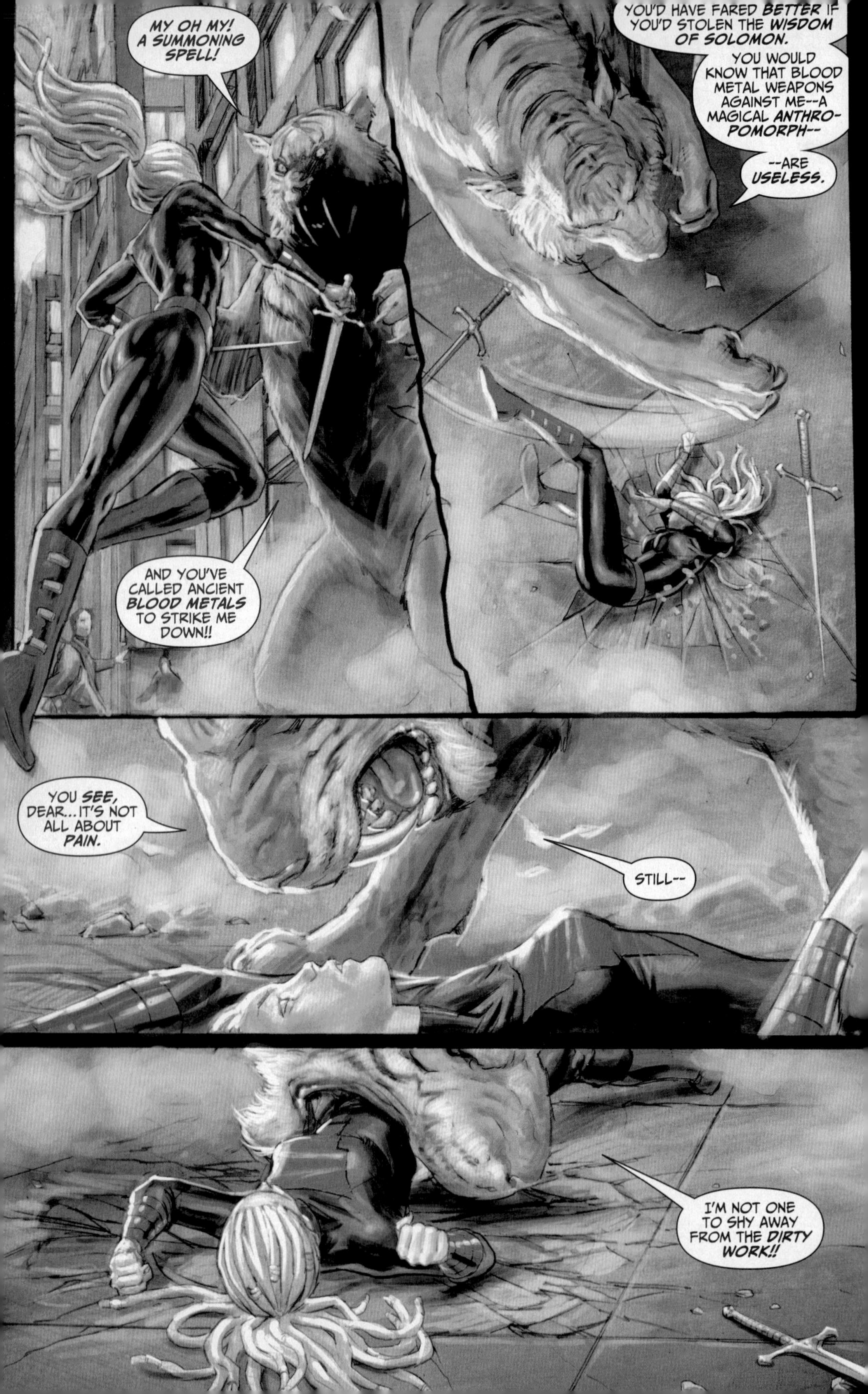
MY OH MY! A SUMMONING SPELL!
AND YOU'VE CALLED ANCIENT BLOOD METALS TO STRIKE ME DOWN!!
YOU'D HAVE FARED BETTER IF YOU'D STOLEN THE WISDOM OF SOLOMON.
YOU WOULD KNOW THAT BLOOD METAL WEAPONS AGAINST ME--A MAGICAL ANTHRO-POMORPH--
--ARE USELESS.
YOU SEE, DEAR...IT'S NOT ALL ABOUT PAIN.
STILL--
I'M NOT ONE TO SHY AWAY FROM THE DIRTY WORK!!

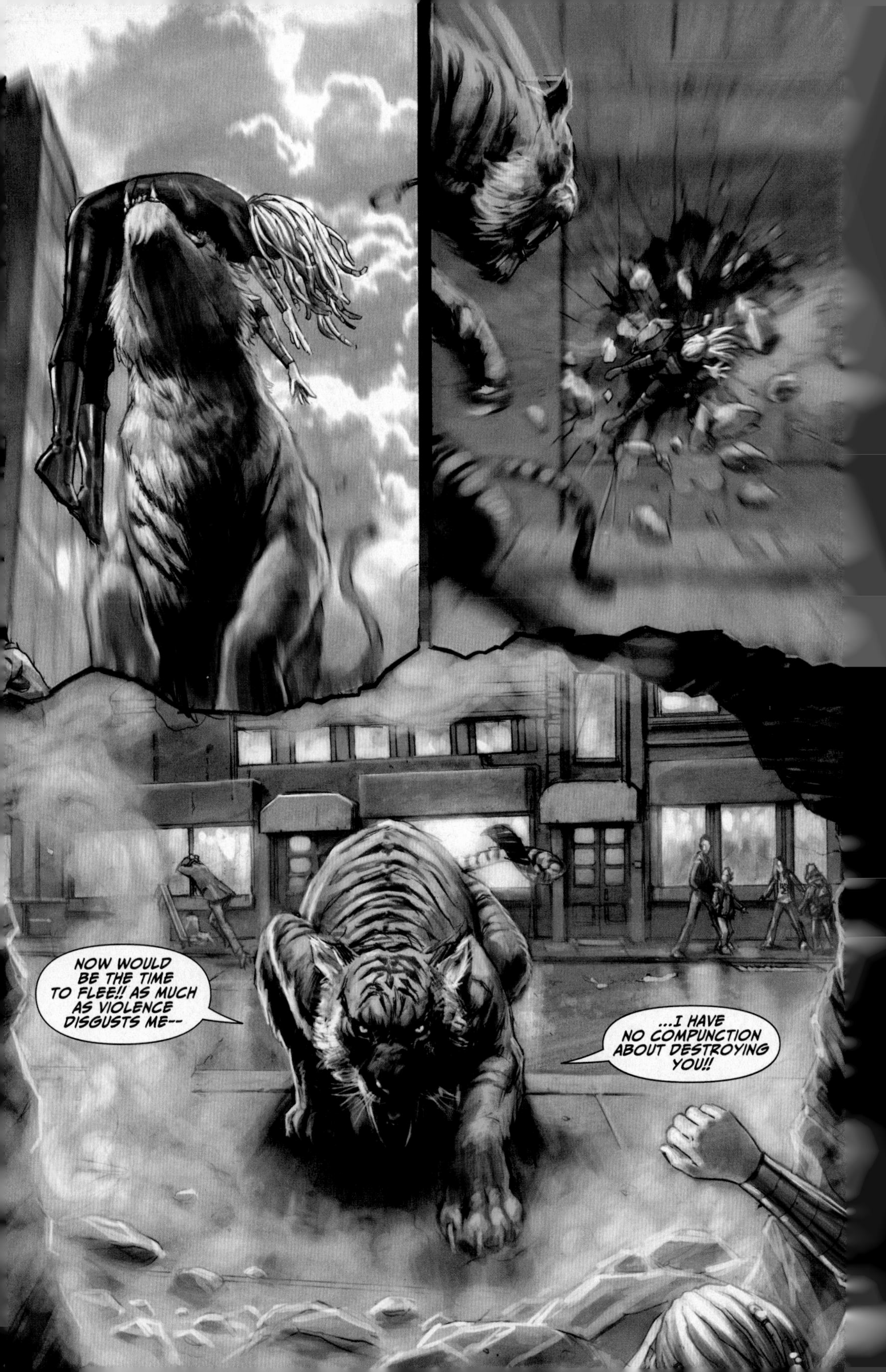
NOW WOULD BE THE TIME TO FLEE!! AS MUCH AS VIOLENCE DISGUSTS ME--
...I HAVE NO COMPUNCTION ABOUT DESTROYING YOU!!

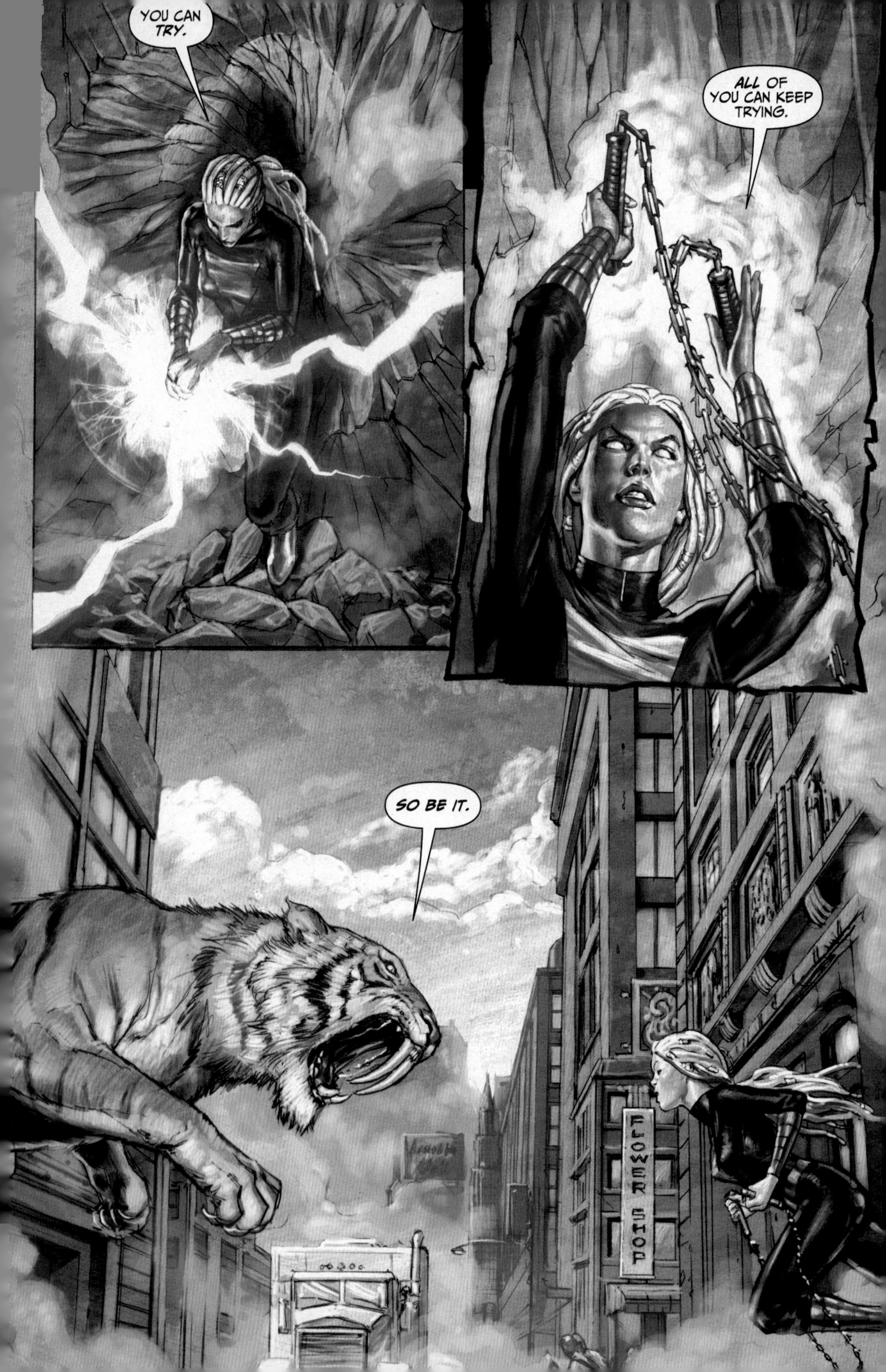
YOU CAN TRY.
ALL OF YOU CAN KEEP TRYING.
SO BE IT.
FLOWER SHOP

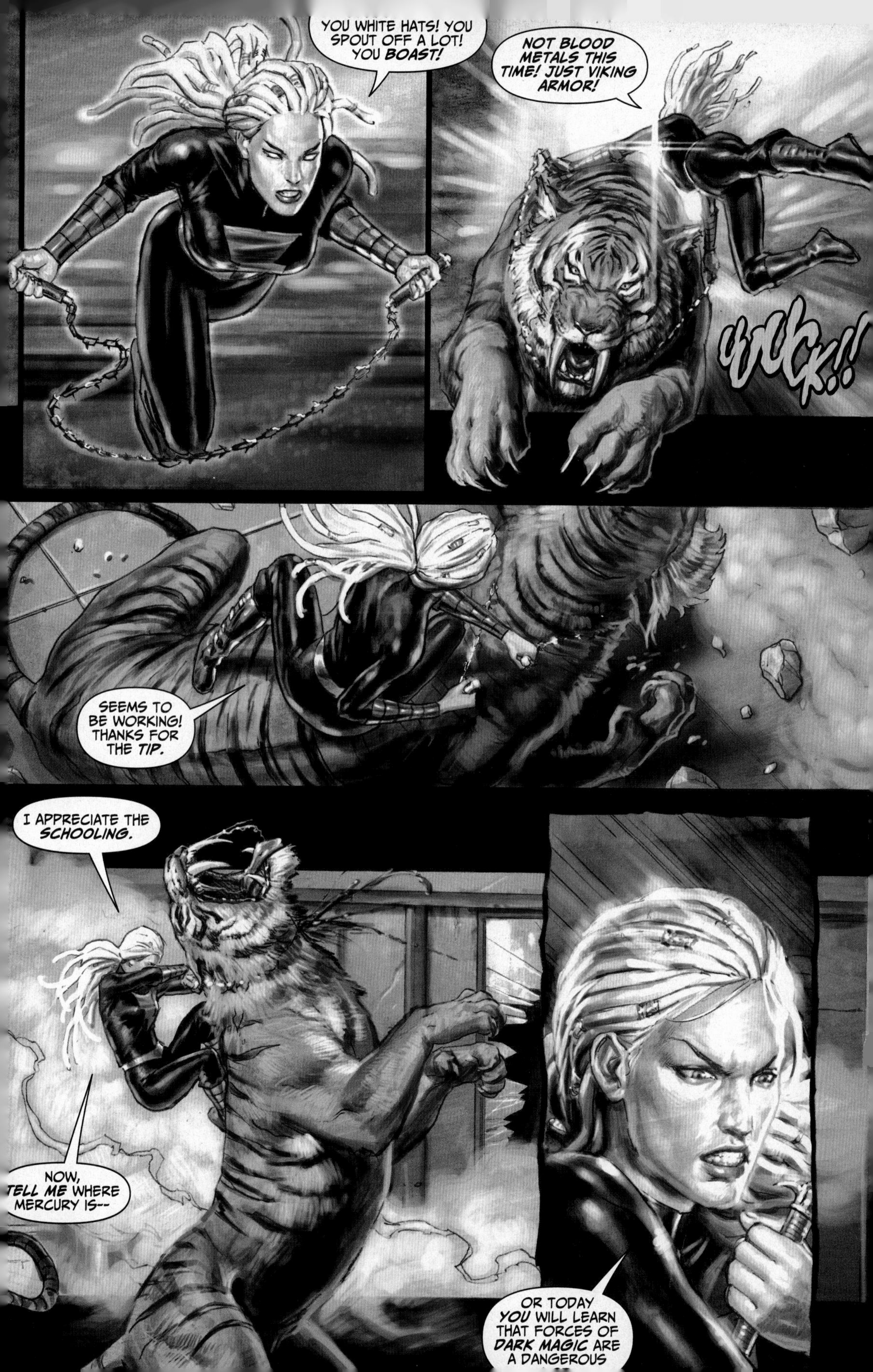
YOU WHITE HATS! YOU SPOUT OFF A LOT! YOU BOAST!
NOT BLOOD METALS THIS TIME! JUST VIKING ARMOR!
SEEMS TO BE WORKING! THANKS FOR THE TIP.
I APPRECIATE THE SCHOOLING.
NOW, TELL ME WHERE MERCURY IS--
OR TODAY YOU WILL LEARN THAT FORCES OF DARK MAGIC ARE A DANGEROUS

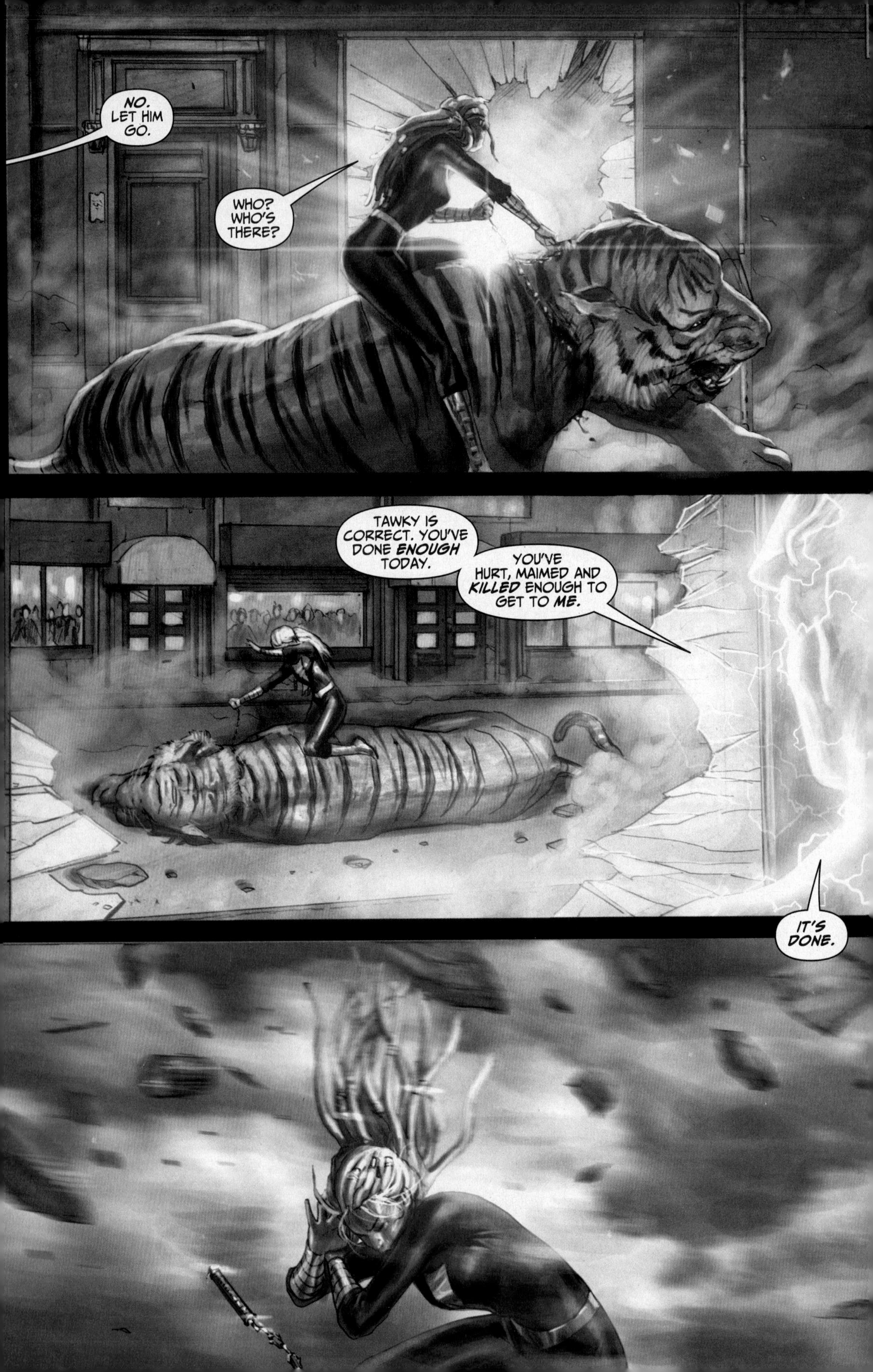
NO. LET HIM GO.
WHO? WHO'S THERE?
TAWKY IS CORRECT. YOU'VE DONE ENOUGH TODAY.
YOU'VE HURT, MAIMED AND KILLED ENOUGH TO GET TO ME.
IT'S DONE.

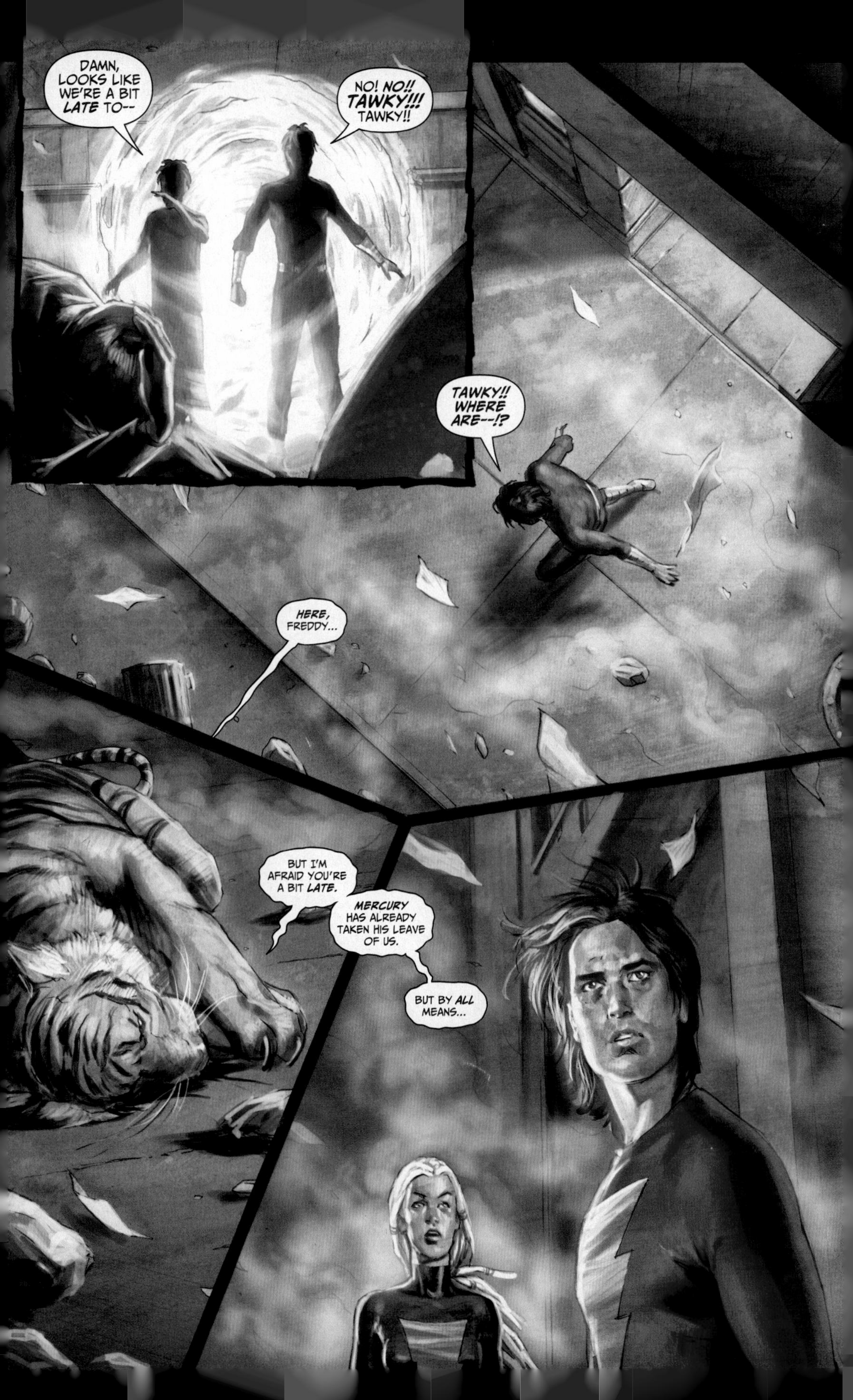
DAMN, LOOKS LIKE WE'RE A BIT LATE TO--
NO! NO!! TAWKY!!! TAWKY!!
TAWKY!! WHERE ARE--!?
HERE, FREDDY...
BUT I'M AFRAID YOU'RE A BIT LATE.
MERCURY HAS ALREADY TAKEN HIS LEAVE OF US.
BUT BY ALL MEANS...

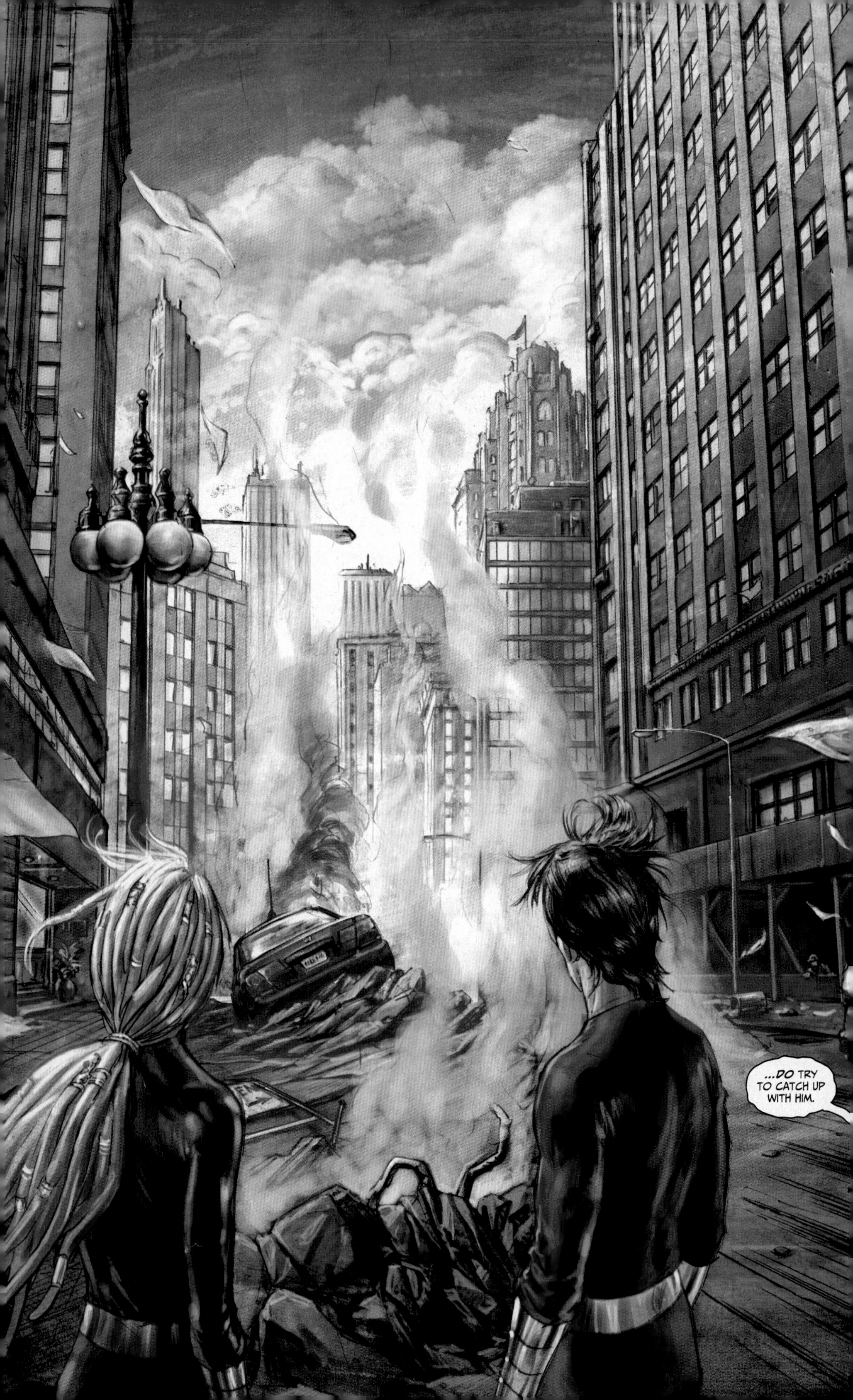
...DO TRY TO CATCH UP WITH HIM.

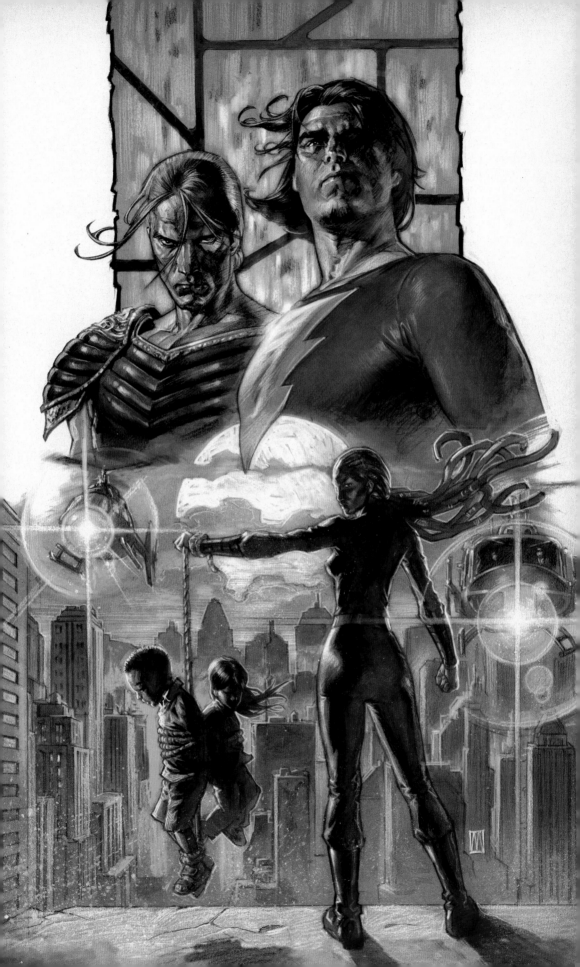

CHAPTER ELEVEN:

THERE'S MAGIC IN THE AIR

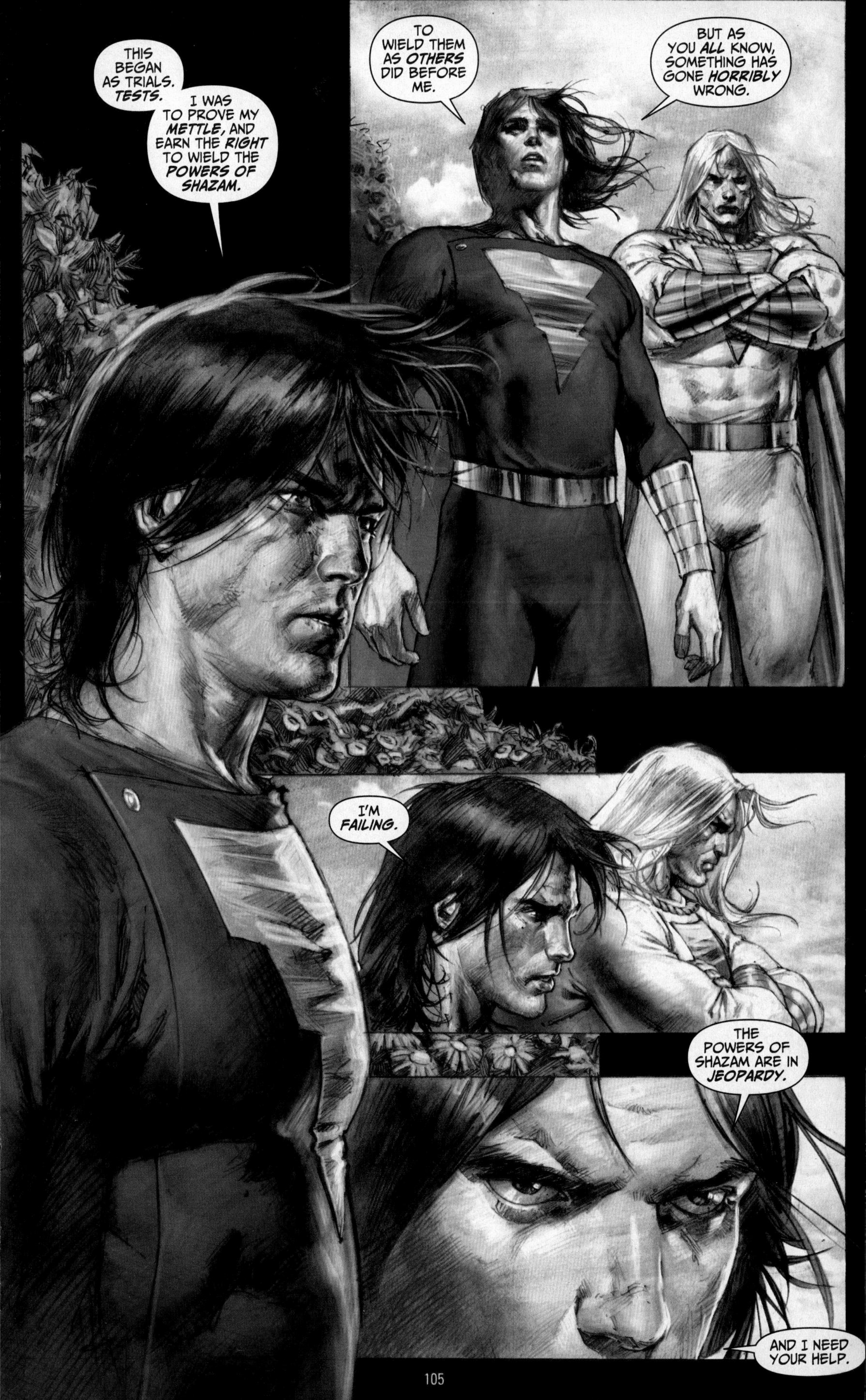

THIS BEGAN AS TRIALS. TESTS.
I WAS TO PROVE MY METTLE, AND EARN THE RIGHT TO WIELD THE POWERS OF SHAZAM.
TO WIELD THEM AS OTHERS DID BEFORE ME.
BUT AS YOU ALL KNOW, SOMETHING HAS GONE HORRIBLY WRONG.
I'M FAILING.
THE POWERS OF SHAZAM ARE IN JEOPARDY.
AND I NEED YOUR HELP.

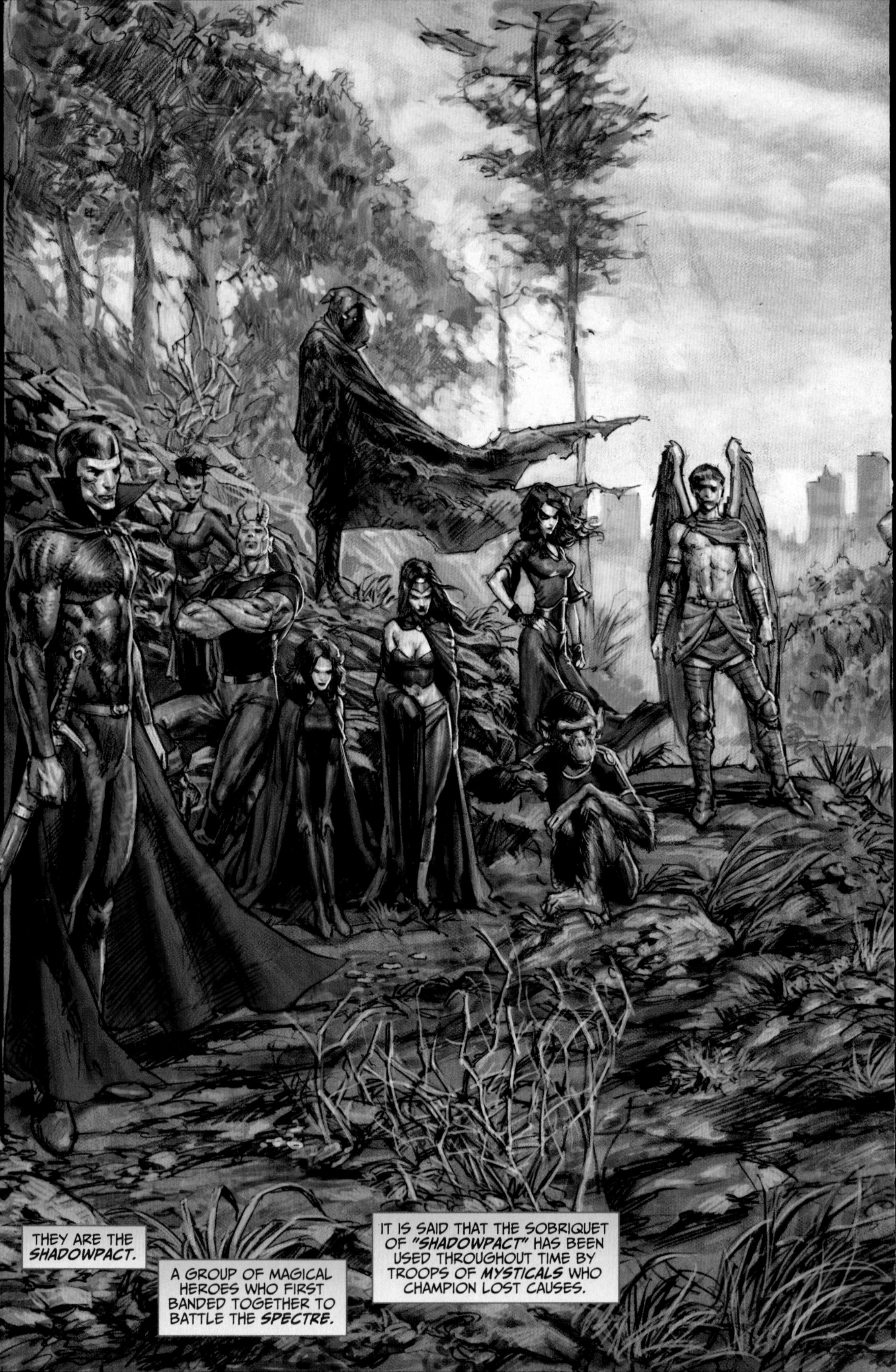
THEY ARE THE SHADOWPACT.
A GROUP OF MAGICAL HEROES WHO FIRST BANDED TOGETHER TO BATTLE THE SPECTRE.
IT IS SAID THAT THE SOBRIQUET OF "SHADOWPACT" HAS BEEN USED THROUGHOUT TIME BY TROOPS OF MYSTICALS WHO CHAMPION LOST CAUSES.

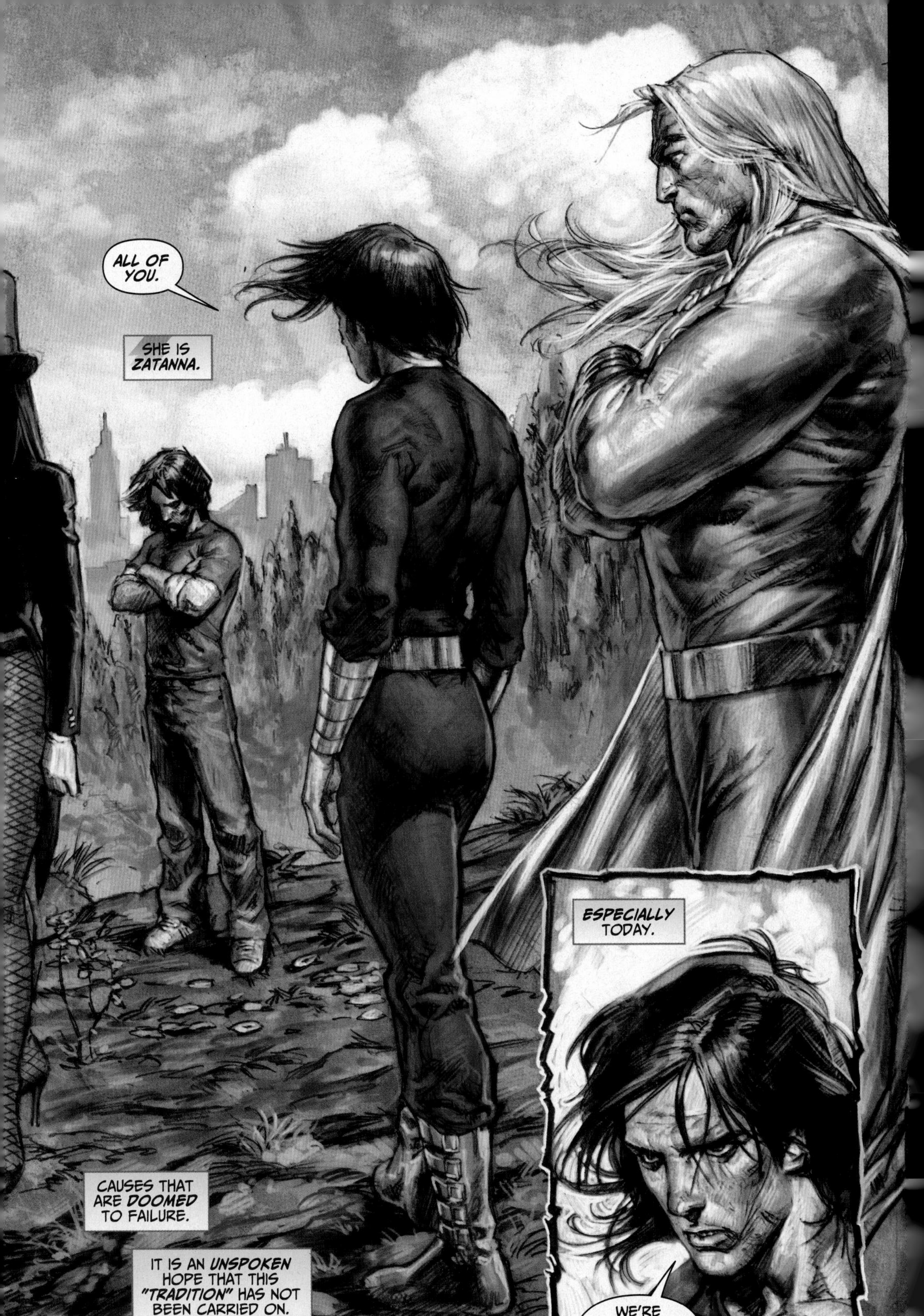
ALL OF YOU.
SHE IS ZATANNA.
CAUSES THAT ARE DOOMED TO FAILURE.
IT IS AN UNSPOKEN HOPE THAT THIS "TRADITION" HAS NOT BEEN CARRIED ON.
ESPECIALLY TODAY.
WE'RE LOOKING FOR MERCURY. THE MAGICAL GOD OF SPEED.

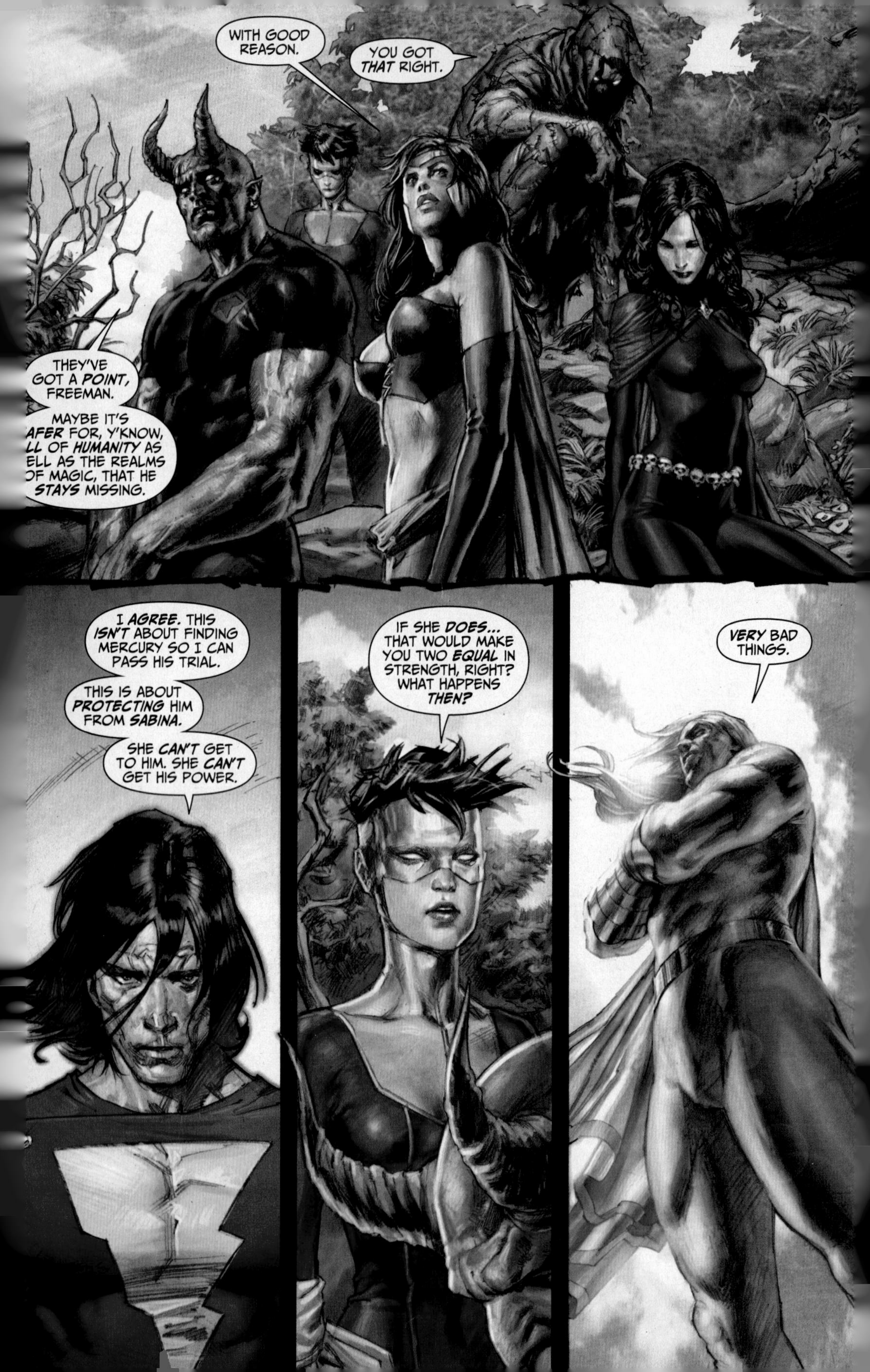
WITH GOOD REASON.
YOU GOT *THAT* RIGHT.
THEY'VE GOT A *POINT,* FREEMAN.
MAYBE IT'S SAFER FOR, Y'KNOW, ALL OF *HUMANITY* AS WELL AS THE REALMS OF MAGIC, THAT HE *STAYS* MISSING.
I *AGREE.* THIS *ISN'T* ABOUT FINDING MERCURY SO I CAN PASS HIS TRIAL.
THIS IS ABOUT *PROTECTING* HIM FROM *SABINA.*
SHE *CAN'T* GET TO HIM. SHE *CAN'T* GET HIS POWER.
IF SHE *DOES*... THAT WOULD MAKE YOU TWO *EQUAL* IN STRENGTH, RIGHT? WHAT HAPPENS *THEN?*
VERY BAD THINGS.

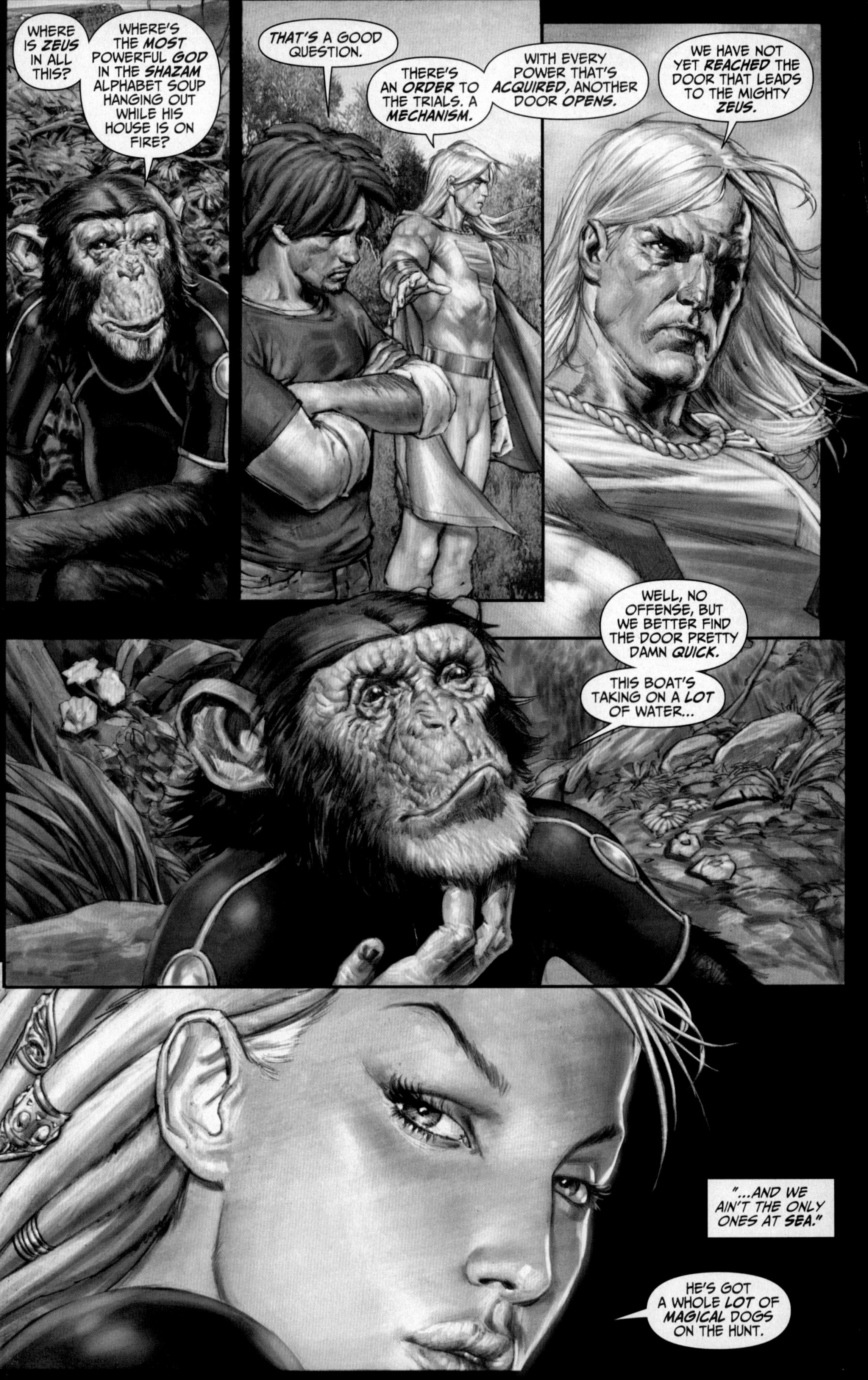
WHERE IS ZEUS IN ALL THIS?
WHERE'S THE MOST POWERFUL GOD IN THE SHAZAM ALPHABET SOUP HANGING OUT WHILE HIS HOUSE IS ON FIRE?
THAT'S A GOOD QUESTION.
THERE'S AN ORDER TO THE TRIALS. A MECHANISM.
WITH EVERY POWER THAT'S ACQUIRED, ANOTHER DOOR OPENS.
WE HAVE NOT YET REACHED THE DOOR THAT LEADS TO THE MIGHTY ZEUS.
WELL, NO OFFENSE, BUT WE BETTER FIND THE DOOR PRETTY DAMN QUICK.
THIS BOAT'S TAKING ON A LOT OF WATER...
"...AND WE AIN'T THE ONLY ONES AT SEA."
HE'S GOT A WHOLE LOT OF MAGICAL DOGS ON THE HUNT.

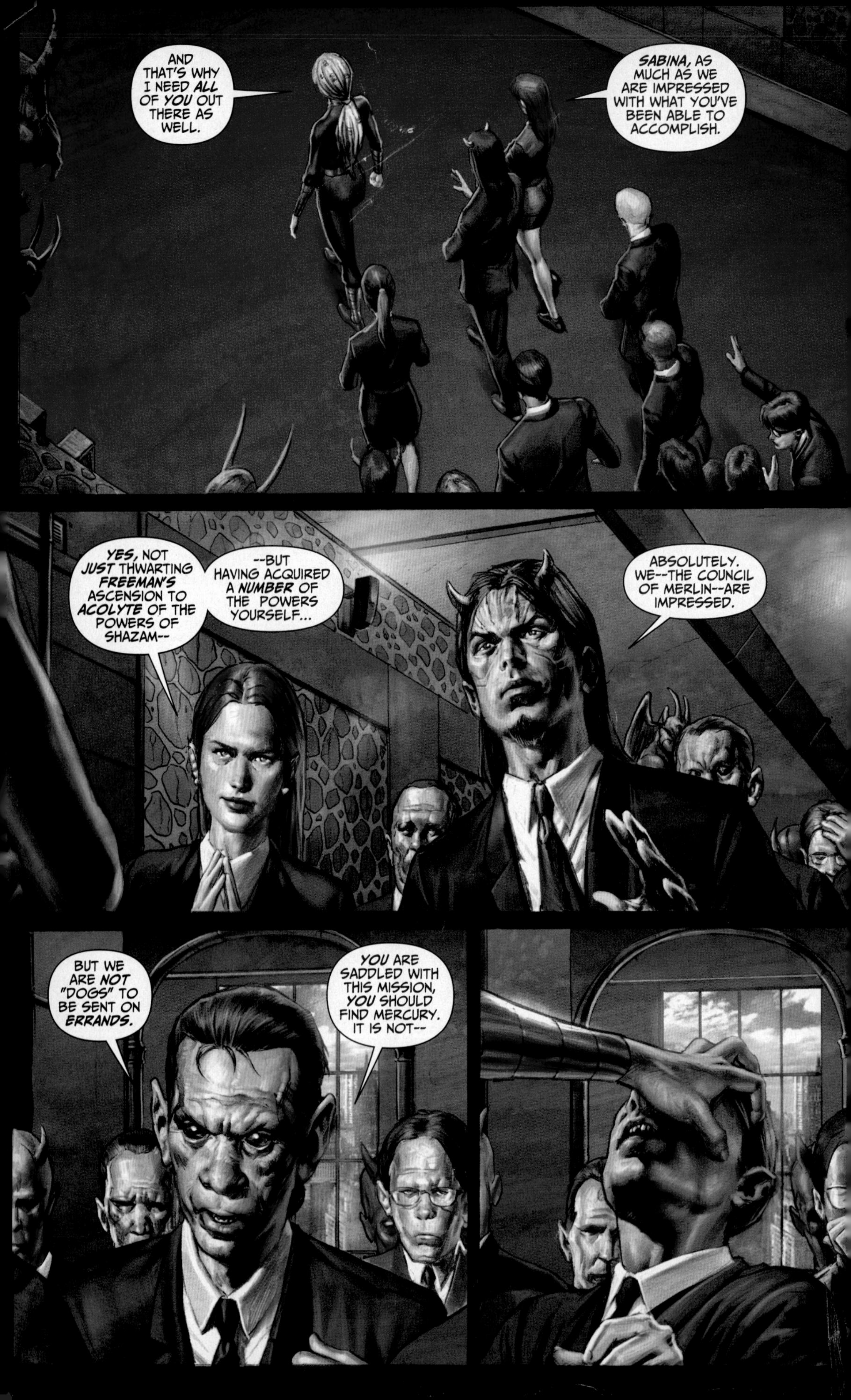
AND THAT'S WHY I NEED ALL OF YOU OUT THERE AS WELL.
SABINA, AS MUCH AS WE ARE IMPRESSED WITH WHAT YOU'VE BEEN ABLE TO ACCOMPLISH.
YES, NOT JUST THWARTING FREEMAN'S ASCENSION TO ACOLYTE OF THE POWERS OF SHAZAM--
--BUT HAVING ACQUIRED A NUMBER OF THE POWERS YOURSELF...
ABSOLUTELY. WE--THE COUNCIL OF MERLIN--ARE IMPRESSED.
BUT WE ARE NOT "DOGS" TO BE SENT ON ERRANDS.
YOU ARE SADDLED WITH THIS MISSION, YOU SHOULD FIND MERCURY. IT IS NOT--

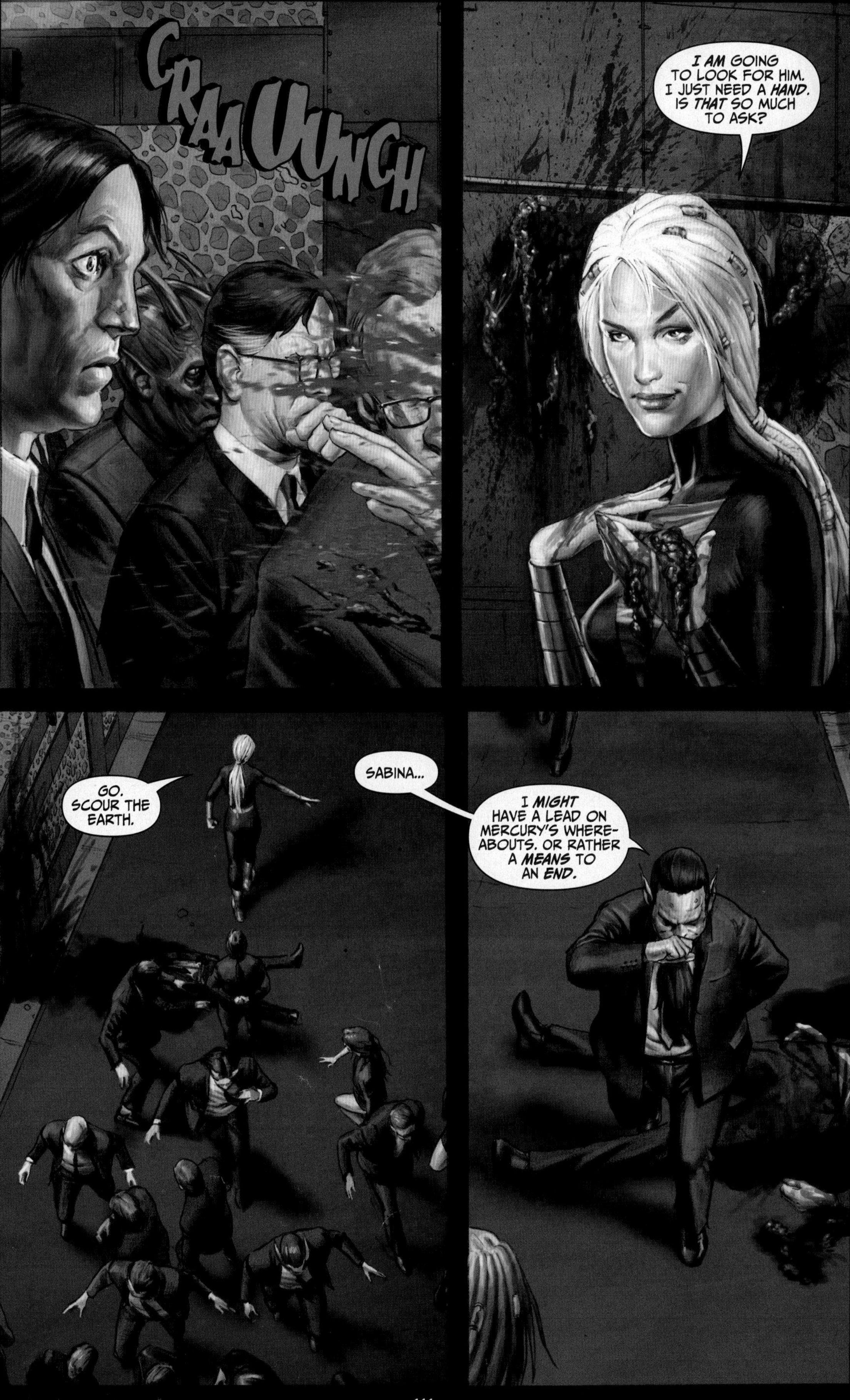
CRAAUUNCH
I AM GOING TO LOOK FOR HIM. I JUST NEED A HAND. IS THAT SO MUCH TO ASK?
GO. SCOUR THE EARTH.
SABINA...
I MIGHT HAVE A LEAD ON MERCURY'S WHERE-ABOUTS. OR RATHER A MEANS TO AN END.

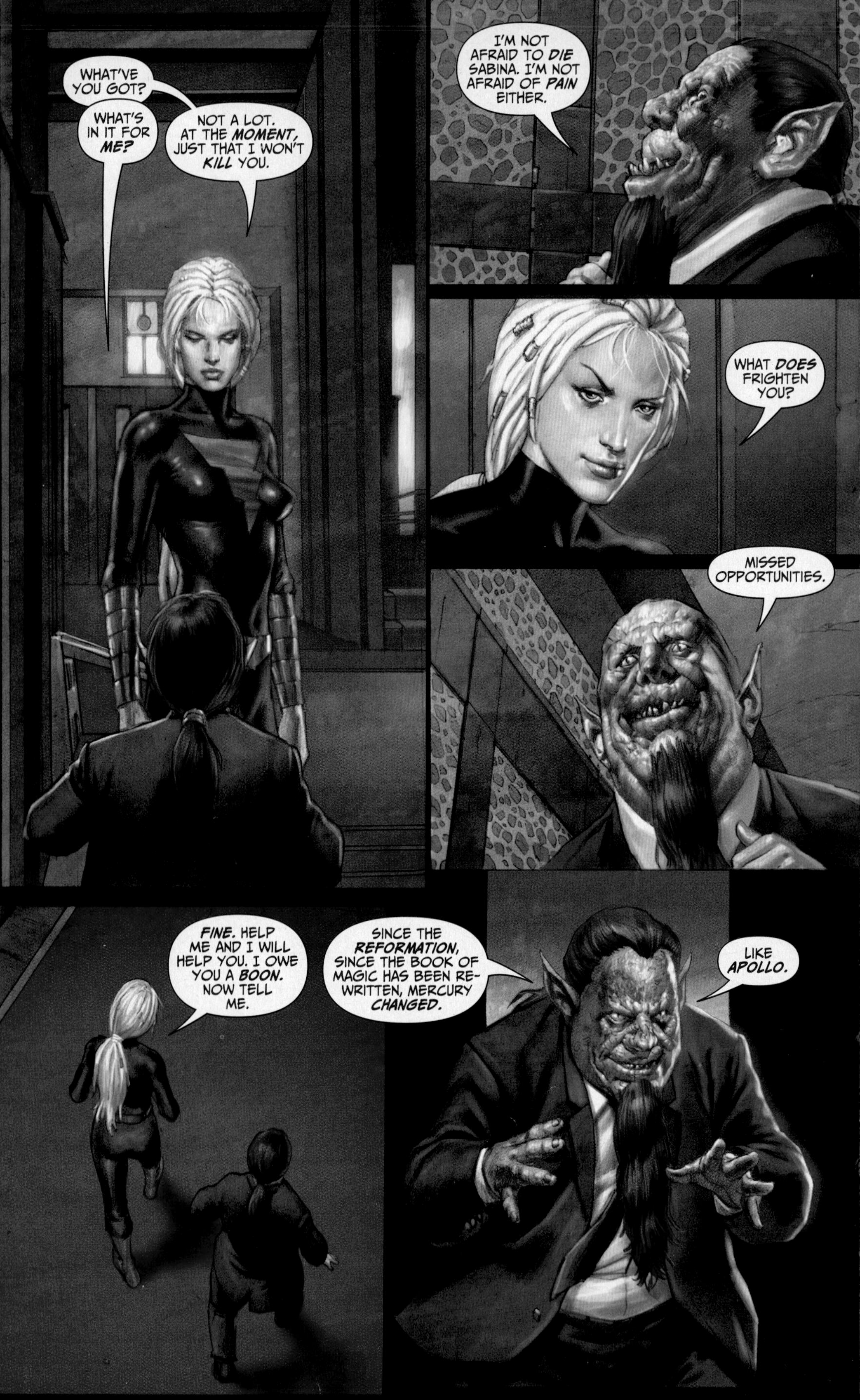
WHAT'VE YOU GOT?
WHAT'S IN IT FOR ME?
NOT A LOT. AT THE MOMENT, JUST THAT I WON'T KILL YOU.
I'M NOT AFRAID TO DIE SABINA. I'M NOT AFRAID OF PAIN EITHER.
WHAT DOES FRIGHTEN YOU?
MISSED OPPORTUNITIES.
FINE. HELP ME AND I WILL HELP YOU. I OWE YOU A BOON. NOW TELL ME.
SINCE THE REFORMATION, SINCE THE BOOK OF MAGIC HAS BEEN RE-WRITTEN, MERCURY CHANGED.
LIKE APOLLO.

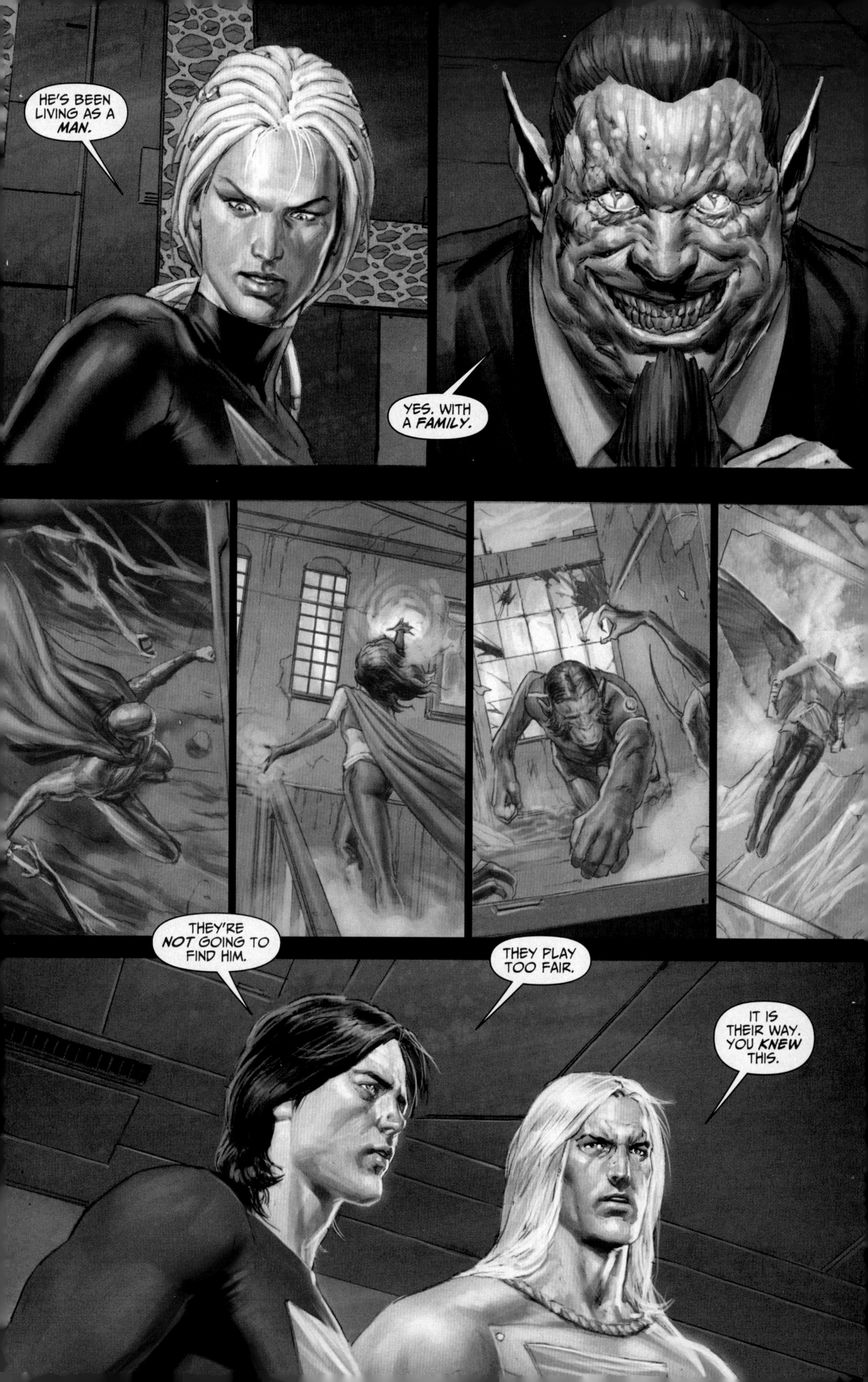
HE'S BEEN LIVING AS A MAN.
YES. WITH A FAMILY.
THEY'RE NOT GOING TO FIND HIM.
THEY PLAY TOO FAIR.
IT IS THEIR WAY. YOU KNEW THIS.

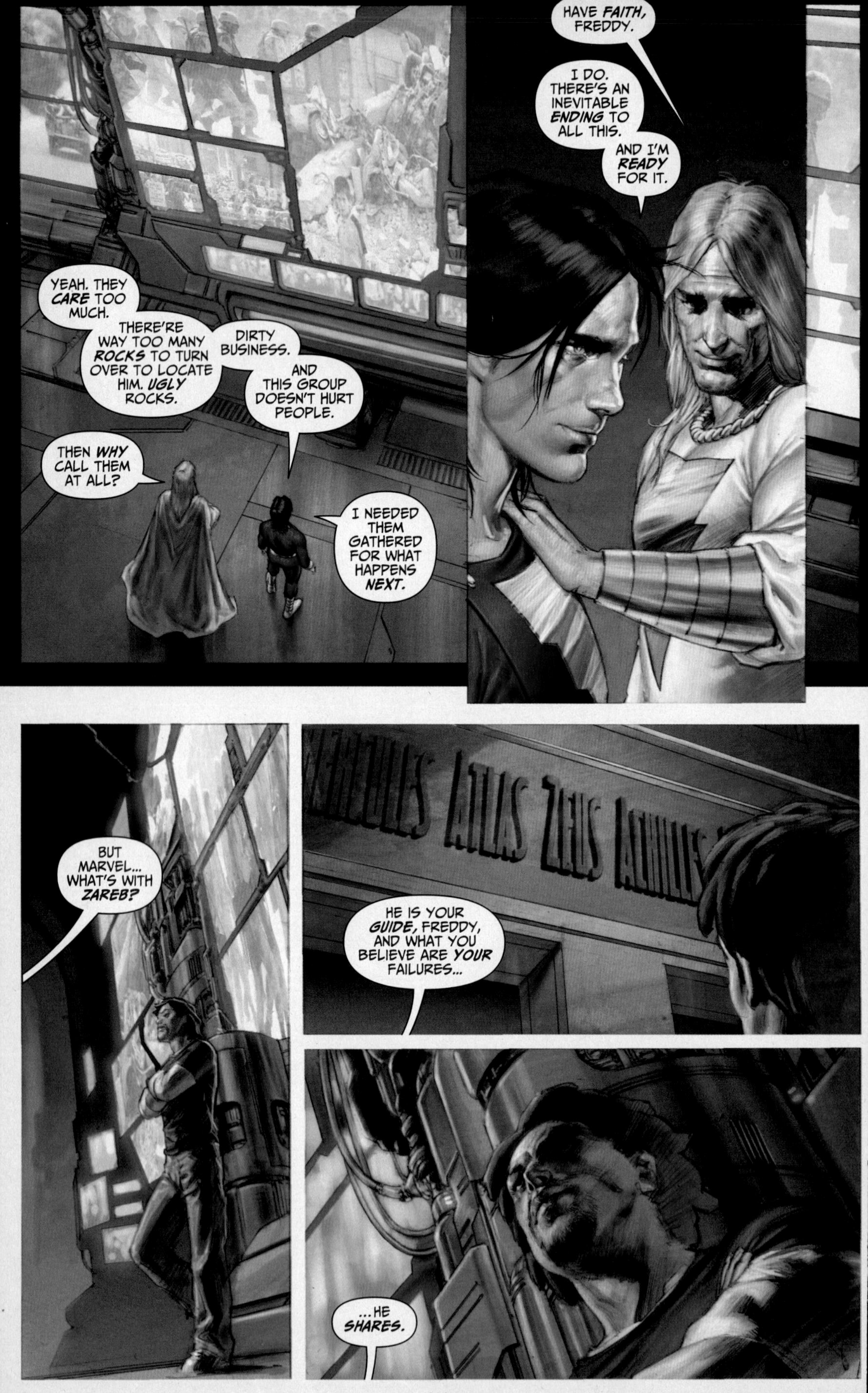
YEAH. THEY CARE TOO MUCH.
THERE'RE WAY TOO MANY ROCKS TO TURN OVER TO LOCATE HIM. UGLY ROCKS.
DIRTY BUSINESS.
AND THIS GROUP DOESN'T HURT PEOPLE.
THEN WHY CALL THEM AT ALL?
I NEEDED THEM GATHERED FOR WHAT HAPPENS NEXT.
HAVE FAITH, FREDDY.
I DO. THERE'S AN INEVITABLE ENDING TO ALL THIS.
AND I'M READY FOR IT.
BUT MARVEL... WHAT'S WITH ZAREB?
ATLAS ZEUS
HE IS YOUR GUIDE, FREDDY, AND WHAT YOU BELIEVE ARE YOUR FAILURES...
...HE SHARES.

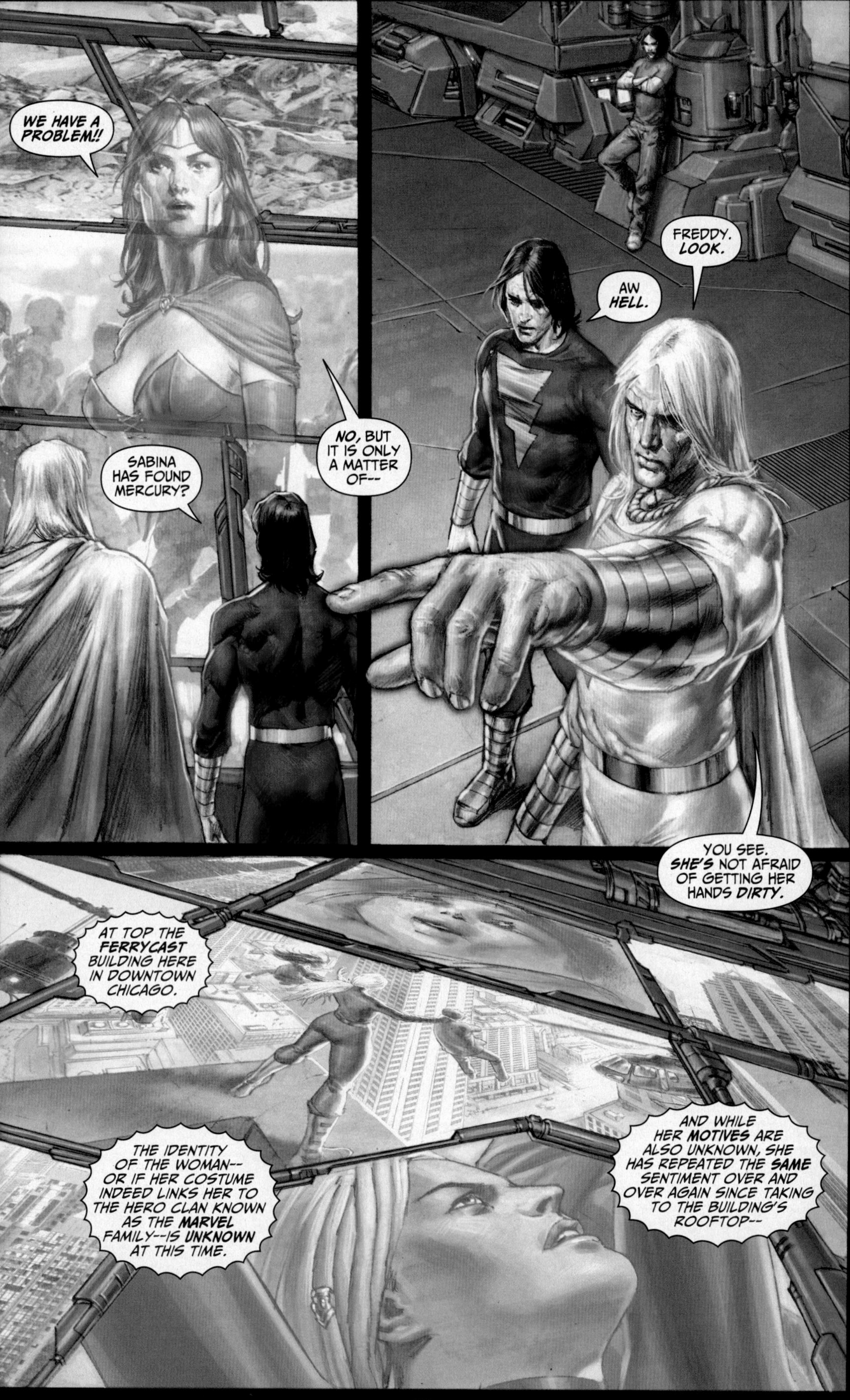
WE HAVE A PROBLEM!!
SABINA HAS FOUND MERCURY?
NO, BUT IT IS ONLY A MATTER OF--
FREDDY. LOOK.
AW HELL.
YOU SEE. SHE'S NOT AFRAID OF GETTING HER HANDS DIRTY.
AT TOP THE FERRYCAST BUILDING HERE IN DOWNTOWN CHICAGO.
THE IDENTITY OF THE WOMAN-- OR IF HER COSTUME INDEED LINKS HER TO THE HERO CLAN KNOWN AS THE MARVEL FAMILY--IS UNKNOWN AT THIS TIME.
AND WHILE HER MOTIVES ARE ALSO UNKNOWN, SHE HAS REPEATED THE SAME SENTIMENT OVER AND OVER AGAIN SINCE TAKING TO THE BUILDING'S ROOFTOP--

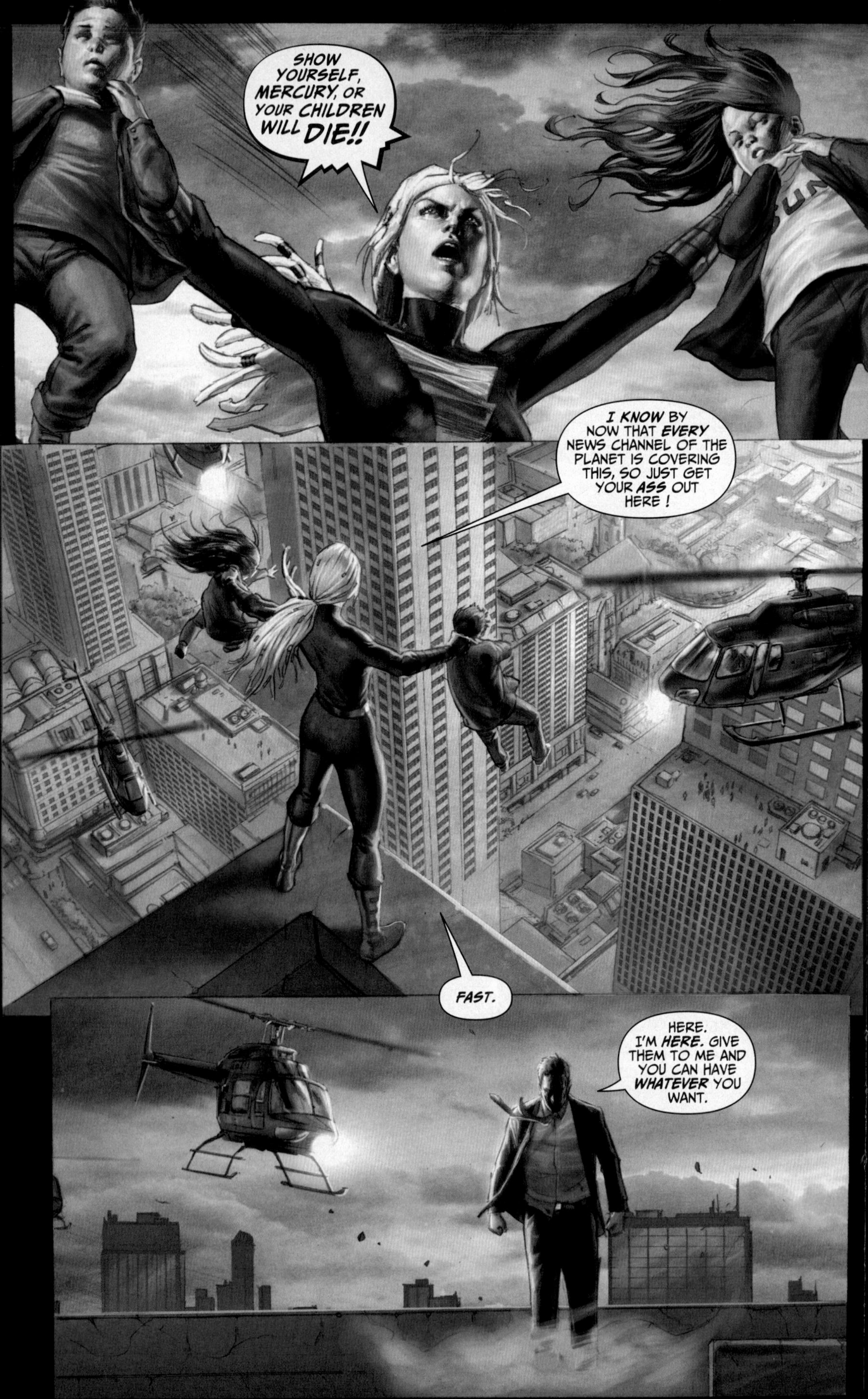
SHOW YOURSELF, MERCURY, OR YOUR CHILDREN WILL DIE!!
I KNOW BY NOW THAT EVERY NEWS CHANNEL OF THE PLANET IS COVERING THIS, SO JUST GET YOUR ASS OUT HERE !
FAST.
HERE. I'M HERE. GIVE THEM TO ME AND YOU CAN HAVE WHATEVER YOU WANT.

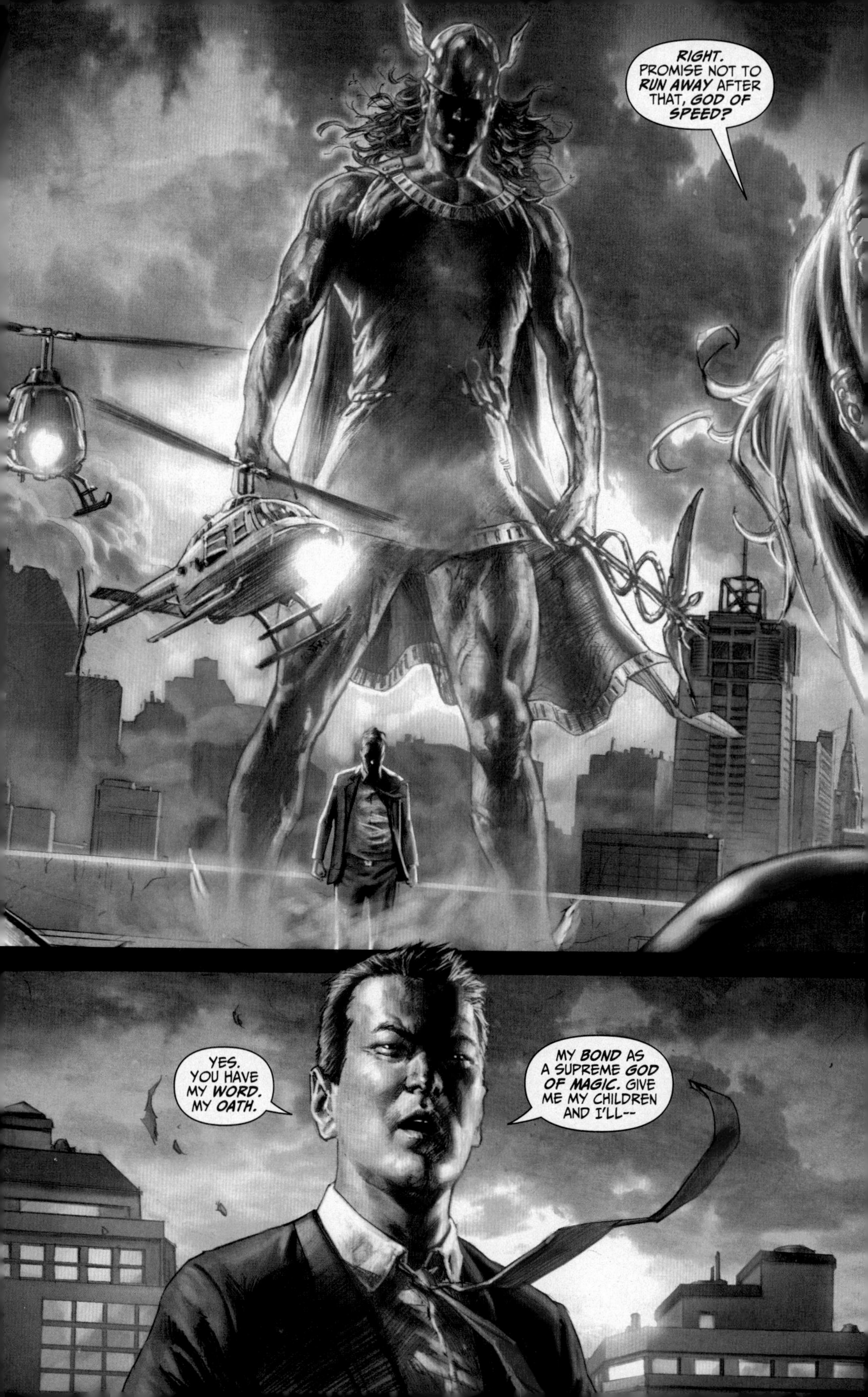
RIGHT. PROMISE NOT TO RUN AWAY AFTER THAT, GOD OF SPEED?
YES. YOU HAVE MY WORD. MY OATH.
MY BOND AS A SUPREME GOD OF MAGIC. GIVE ME MY CHILDREN AND I'LL--

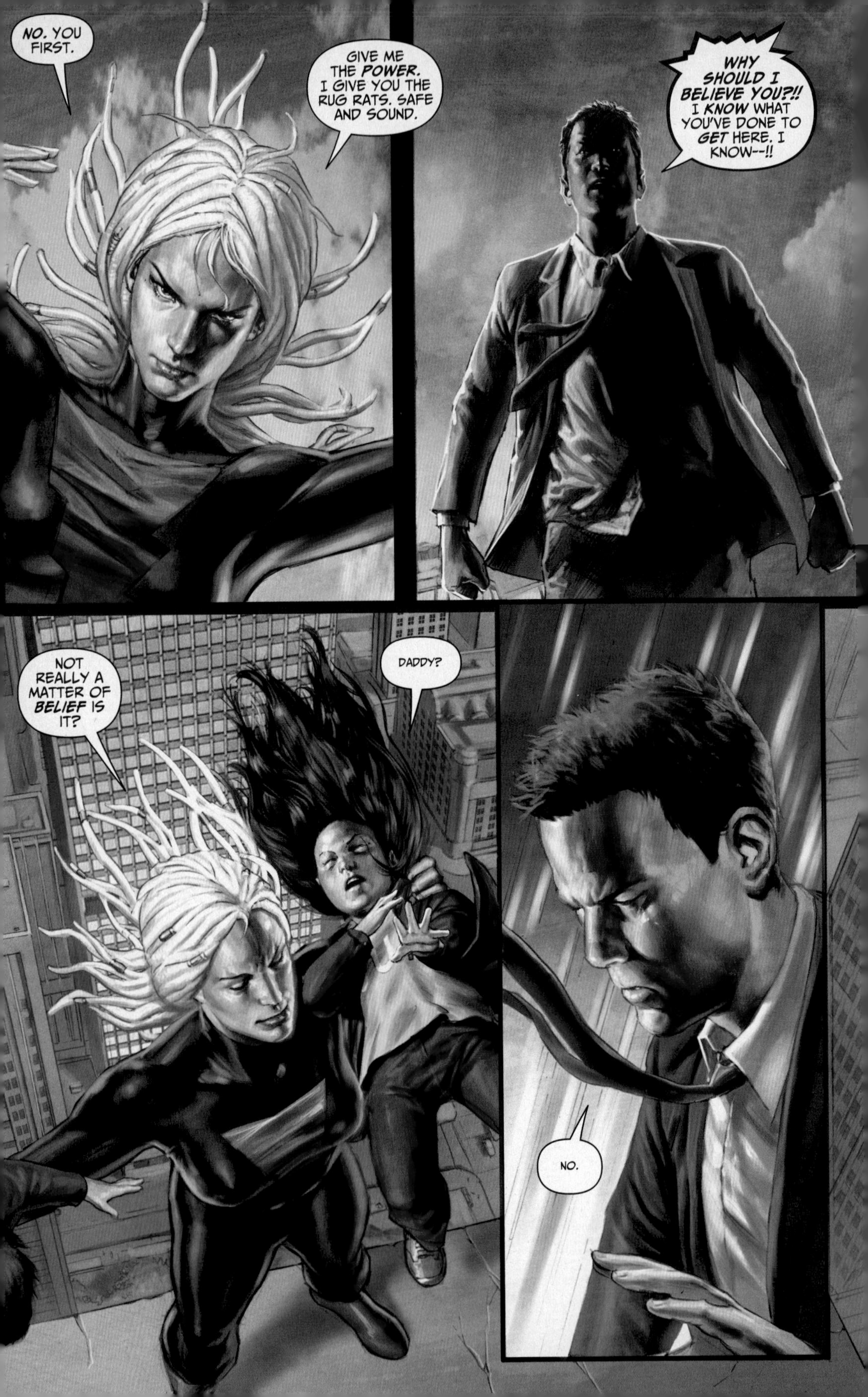
NO. YOU FIRST.
GIVE ME THE POWER. I GIVE YOU THE RUG RATS. SAFE AND SOUND.
WHY SHOULD I BELIEVE YOU?!! I KNOW WHAT YOU'VE DONE TO GET HERE. I KNOW--!!
NOT REALLY A MATTER OF BELIEF IS IT?
DADDY?
NO.

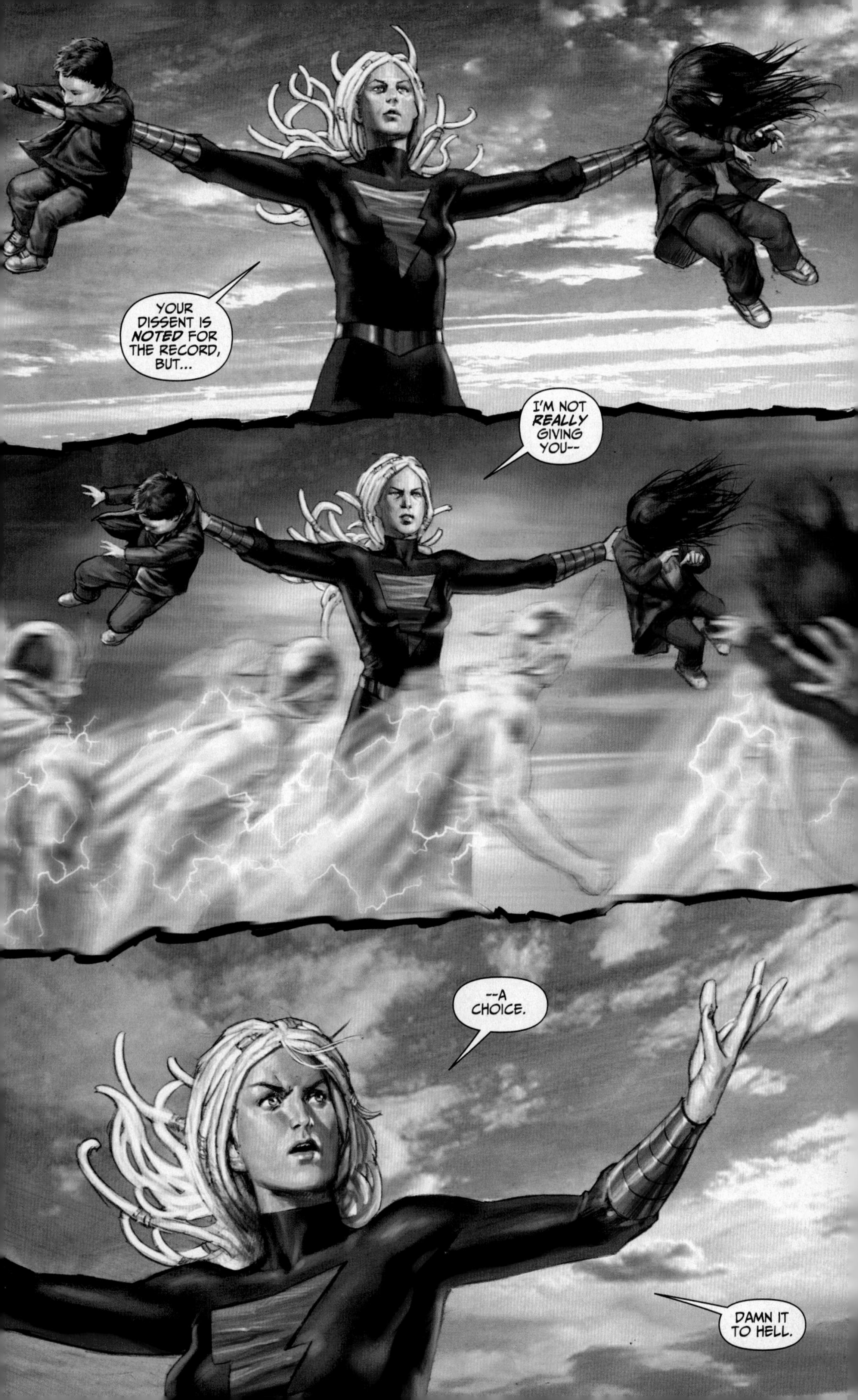
YOUR DISSENT IS NOTED FOR THE RECORD, BUT...
I'M NOT REALLY GIVING YOU--
--A CHOICE.
DAMN IT TO HELL.

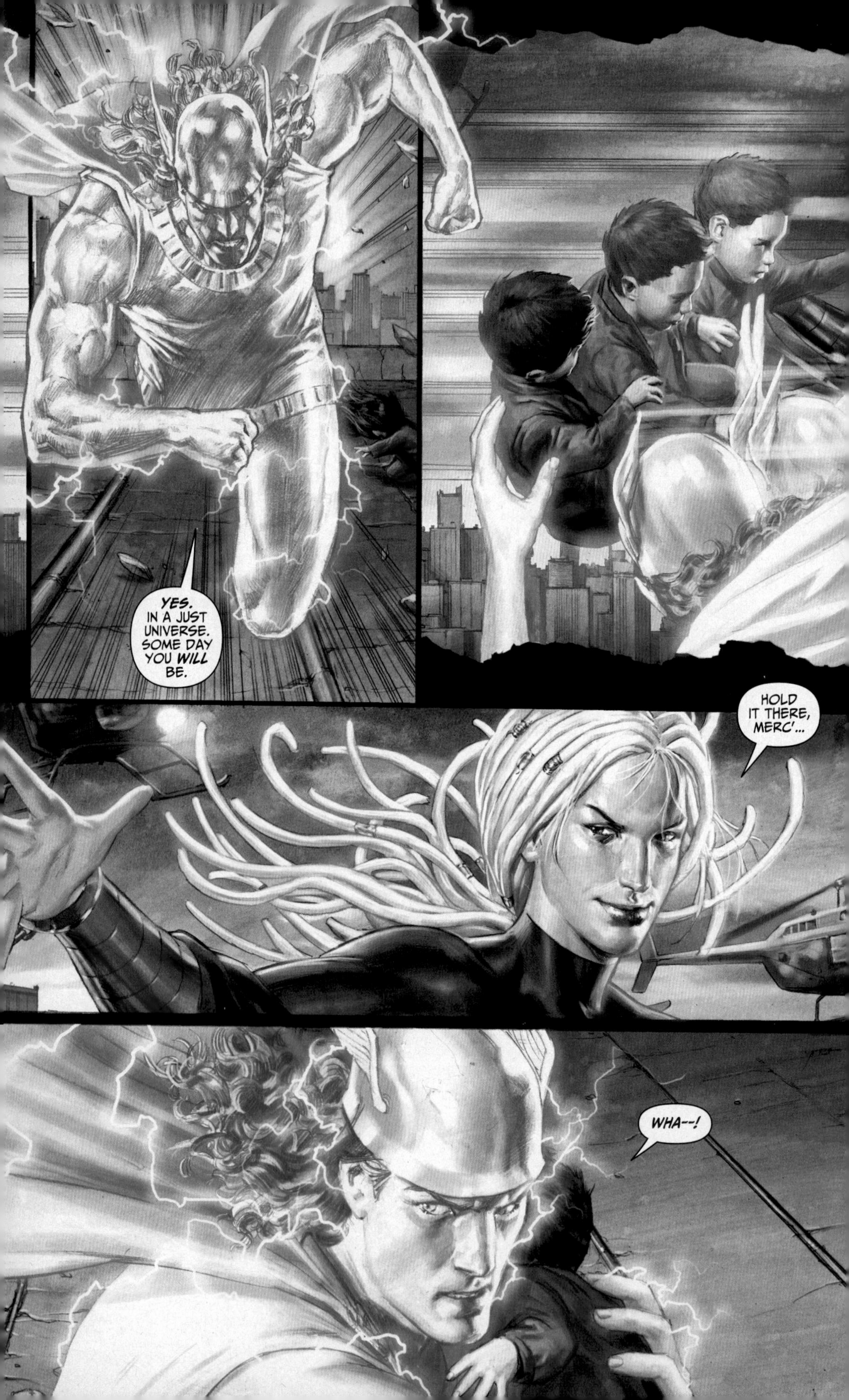
YES. IN A JUST UNIVERSE. SOME DAY YOU WILL BE.
HOLD IT THERE, MERC'...
WHA--!

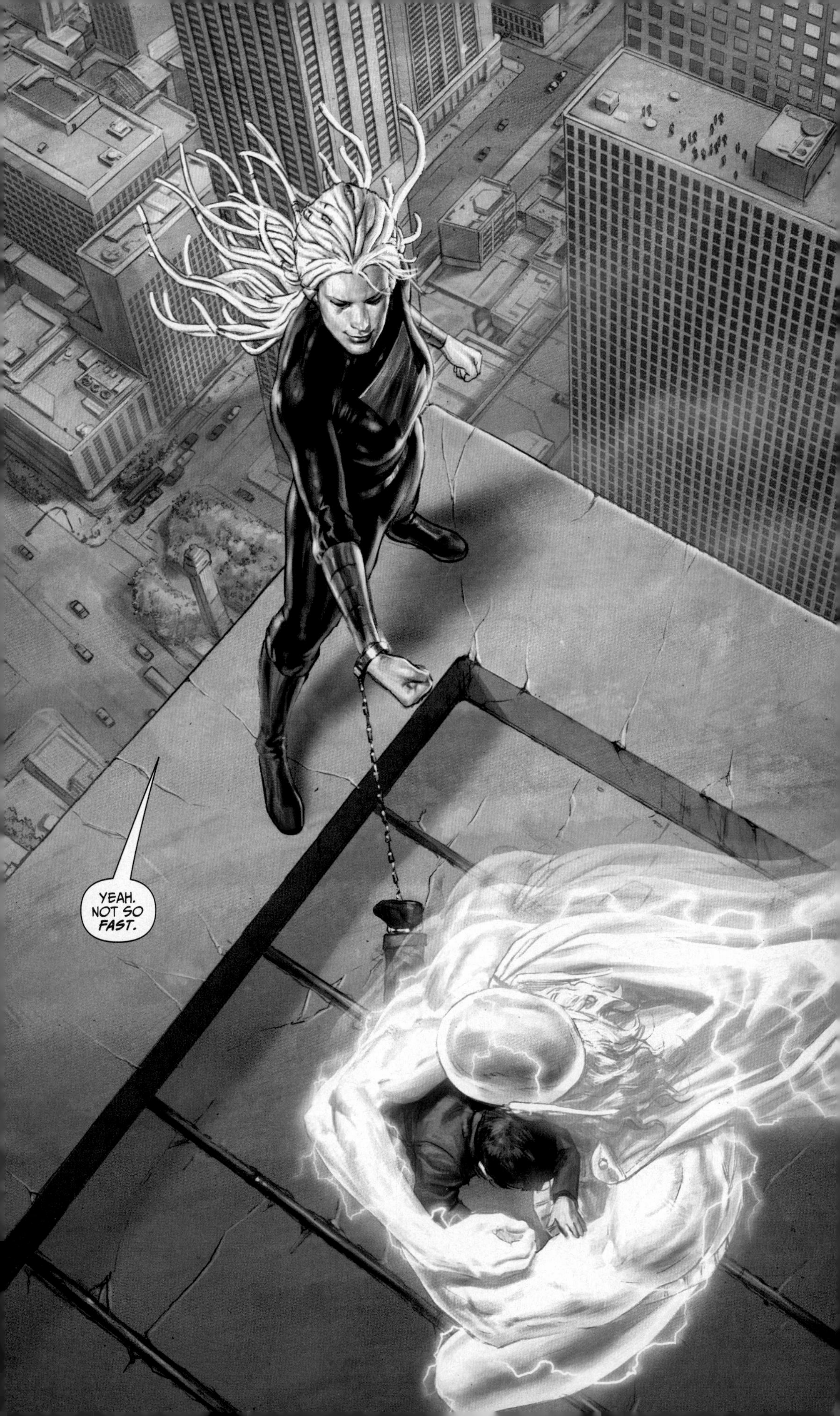
YEAH. NOT SO FAST.

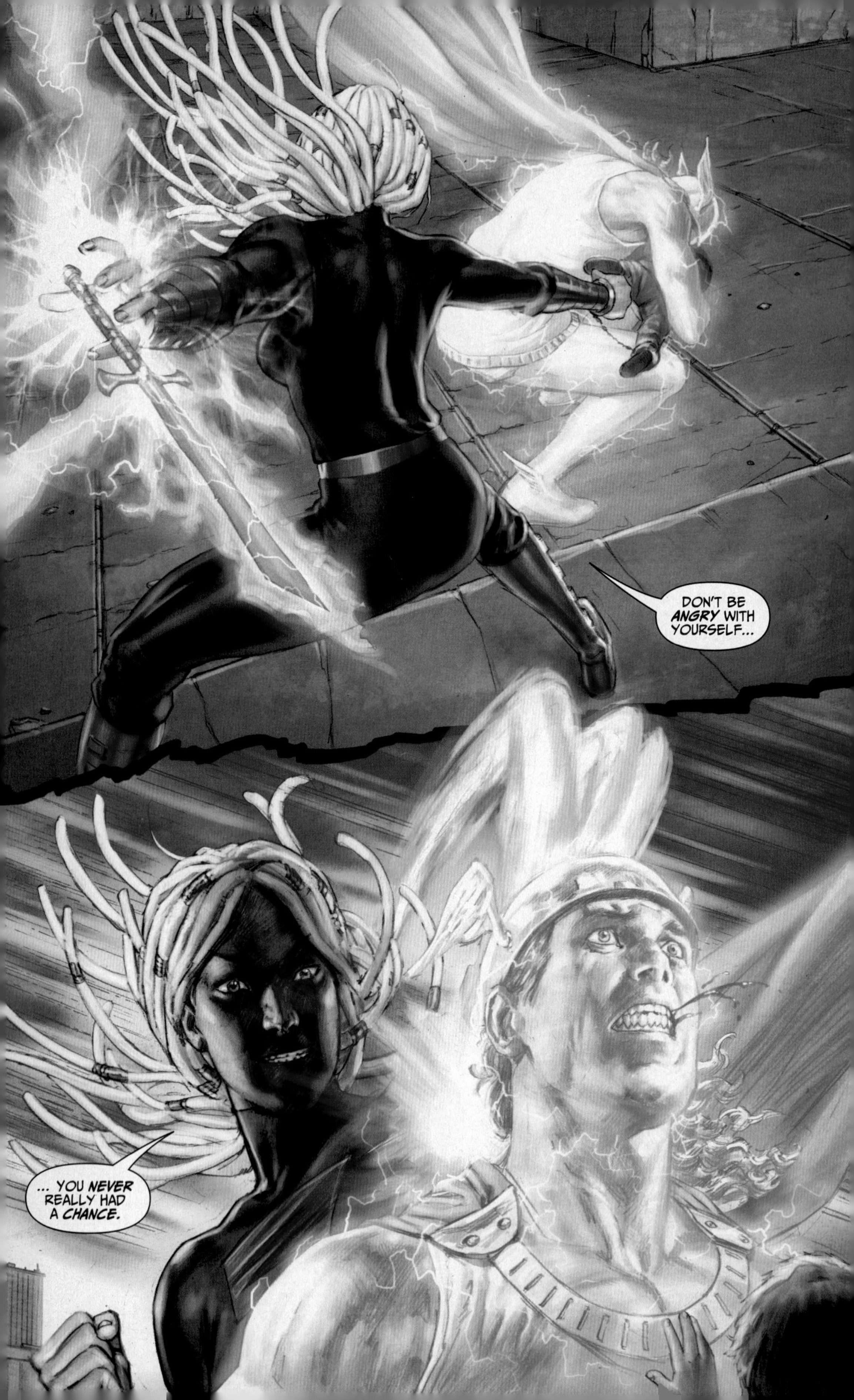
DON'T BE ANGRY WITH YOURSELF...
... YOU NEVER REALLY HAD A CHANCE.

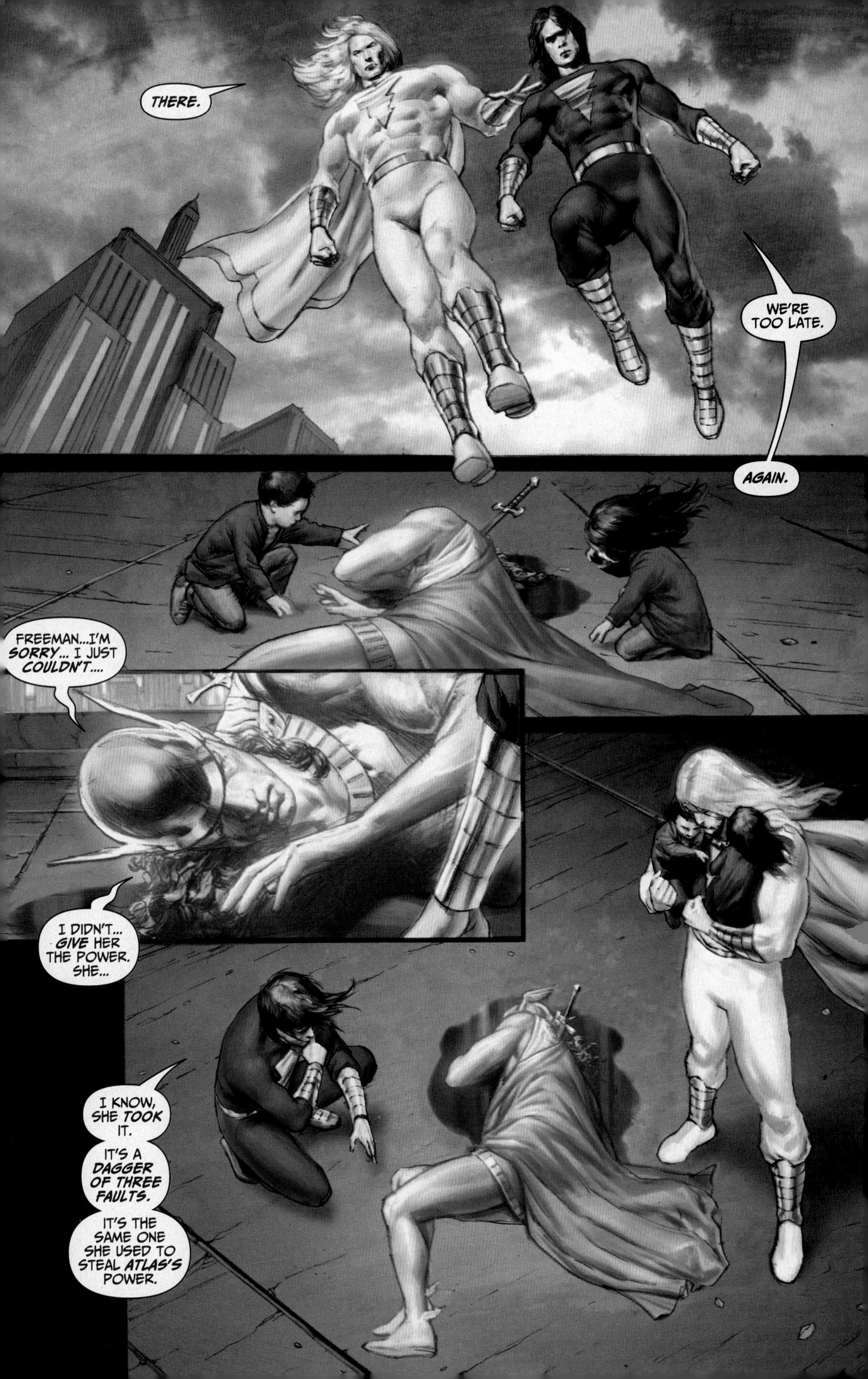
THERE.
WE'RE TOO LATE.
AGAIN.
FREEMAN...I'M SORRY... I JUST COULDN'T....
I DIDN'T... GIVE HER THE POWER. SHE...
I KNOW, SHE TOOK IT.
IT'S A DAGGER OF THREE FAULTS.
IT'S THE SAME ONE SHE USED TO STEAL ATLAS'S POWER.

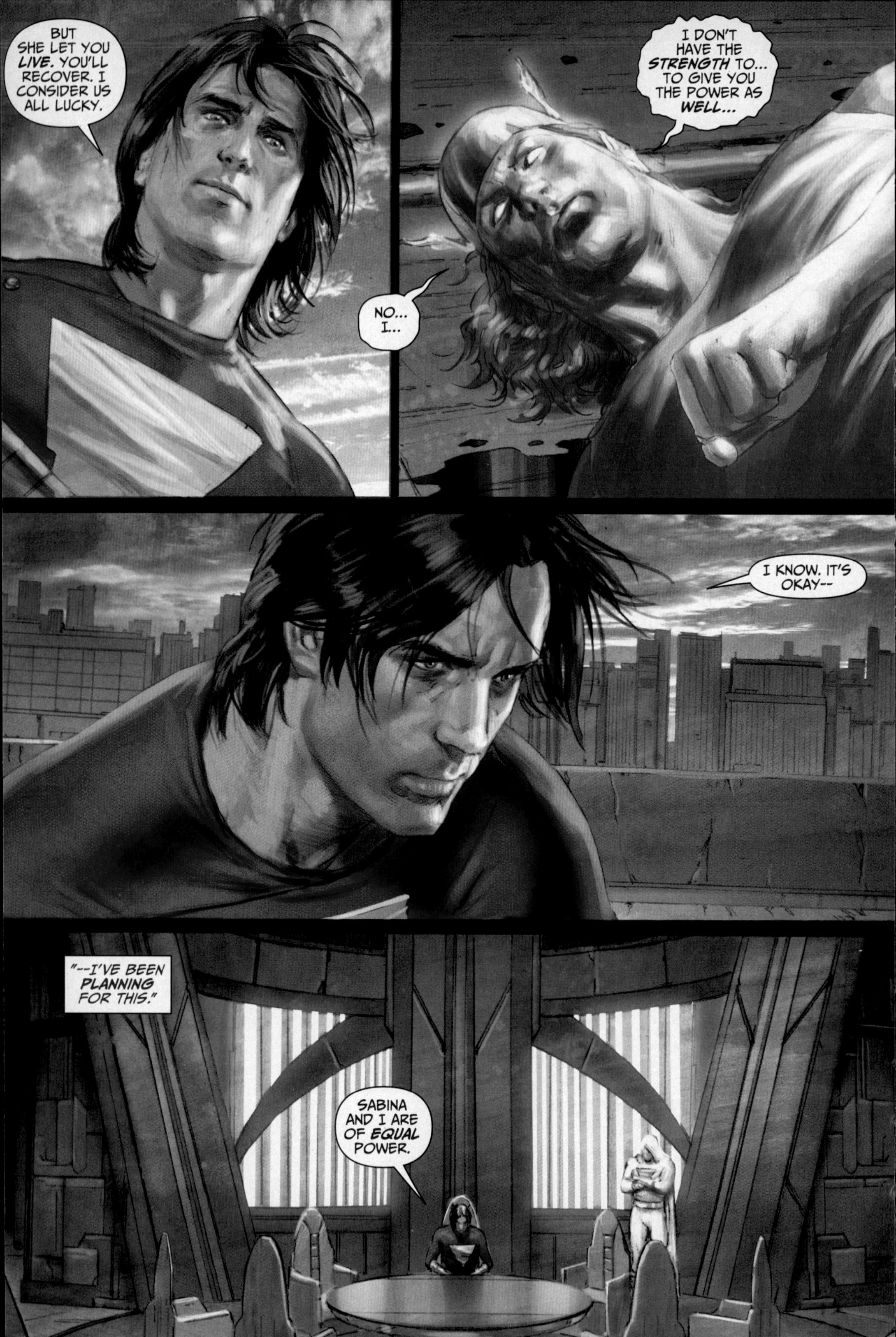
BUT SHE LET YOU LIVE. YOU'LL RECOVER. I CONSIDER US ALL LUCKY.
I DON'T HAVE THE STRENGTH TO... TO GIVE YOU THE POWER AS WELL...
NO... I...
I KNOW. IT'S OKAY--
"--I'VE BEEN PLANNING FOR THIS."
SABINA AND I ARE OF EQUAL POWER.

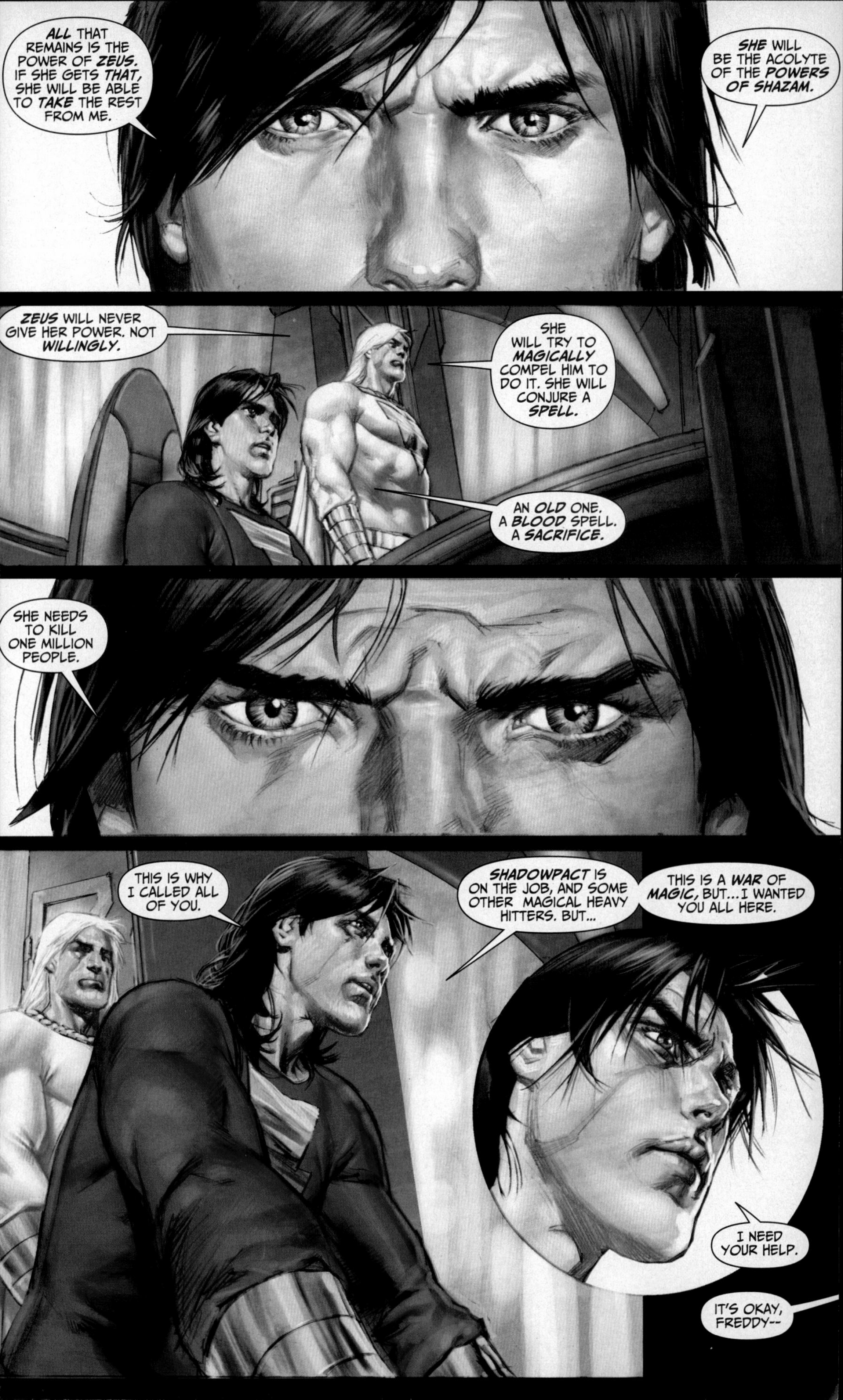
ALL THAT REMAINS IS THE POWER OF ZEUS. IF SHE GETS THAT, SHE WILL BE ABLE TO TAKE THE REST FROM ME.
SHE WILL BE THE ACOLYTE OF THE POWERS OF SHAZAM.
ZEUS WILL NEVER GIVE HER POWER. NOT WILLINGLY.
SHE WILL TRY TO MAGICALLY COMPEL HIM TO DO IT. SHE WILL CONJURE A SPELL.
AN OLD ONE. A BLOOD SPELL. A SACRIFICE.
SHE NEEDS TO KILL ONE MILLION PEOPLE.
THIS IS WHY I CALLED ALL OF YOU.
SHADOWPACT IS ON THE JOB, AND SOME OTHER MAGICAL HEAVY HITTERS. BUT...
THIS IS A WAR OF MAGIC, BUT...I WANTED YOU ALL HERE.
I NEED YOUR HELP.
IT'S OKAY, FREDDY--

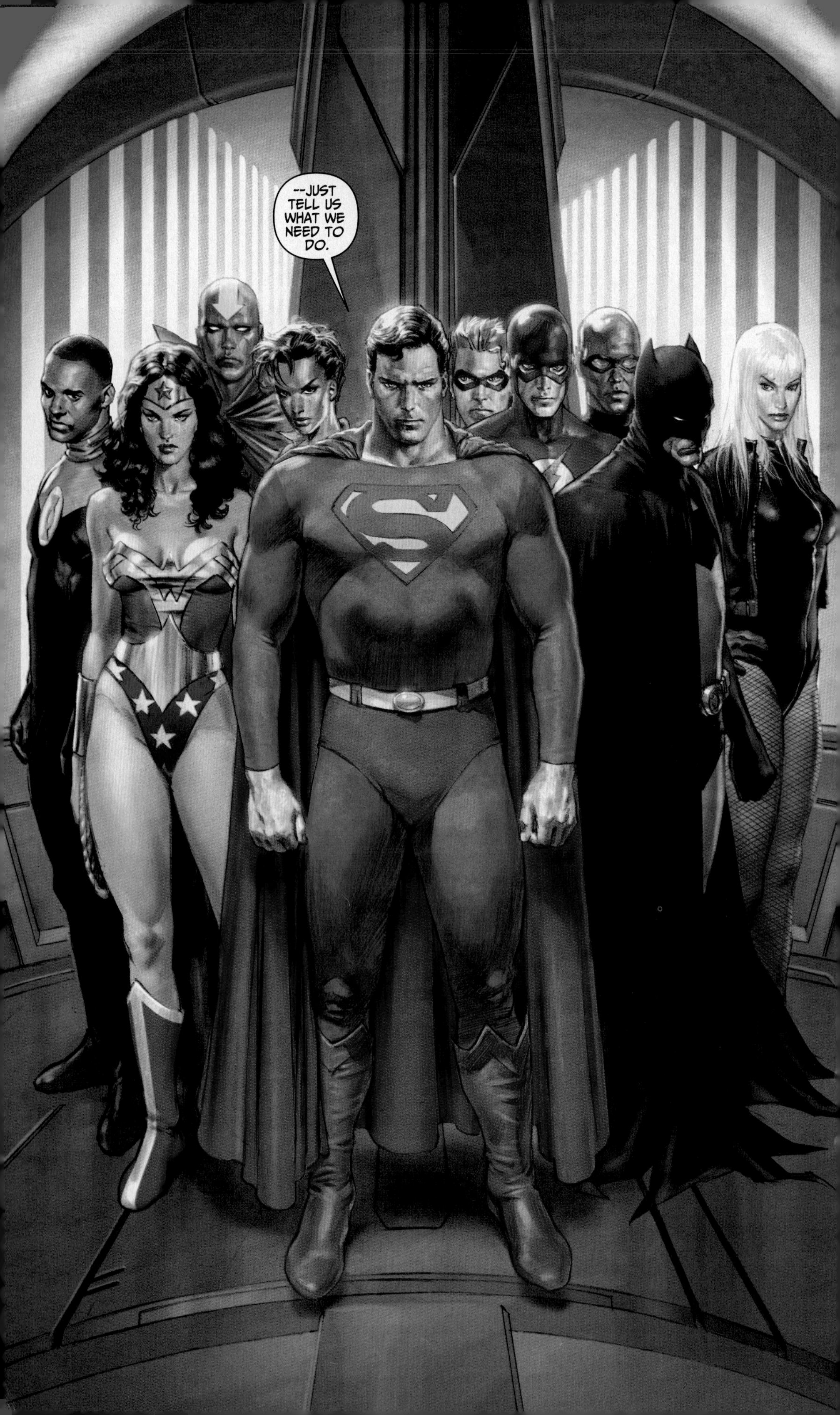
--JUST TELL US WHAT WE NEED TO DO.

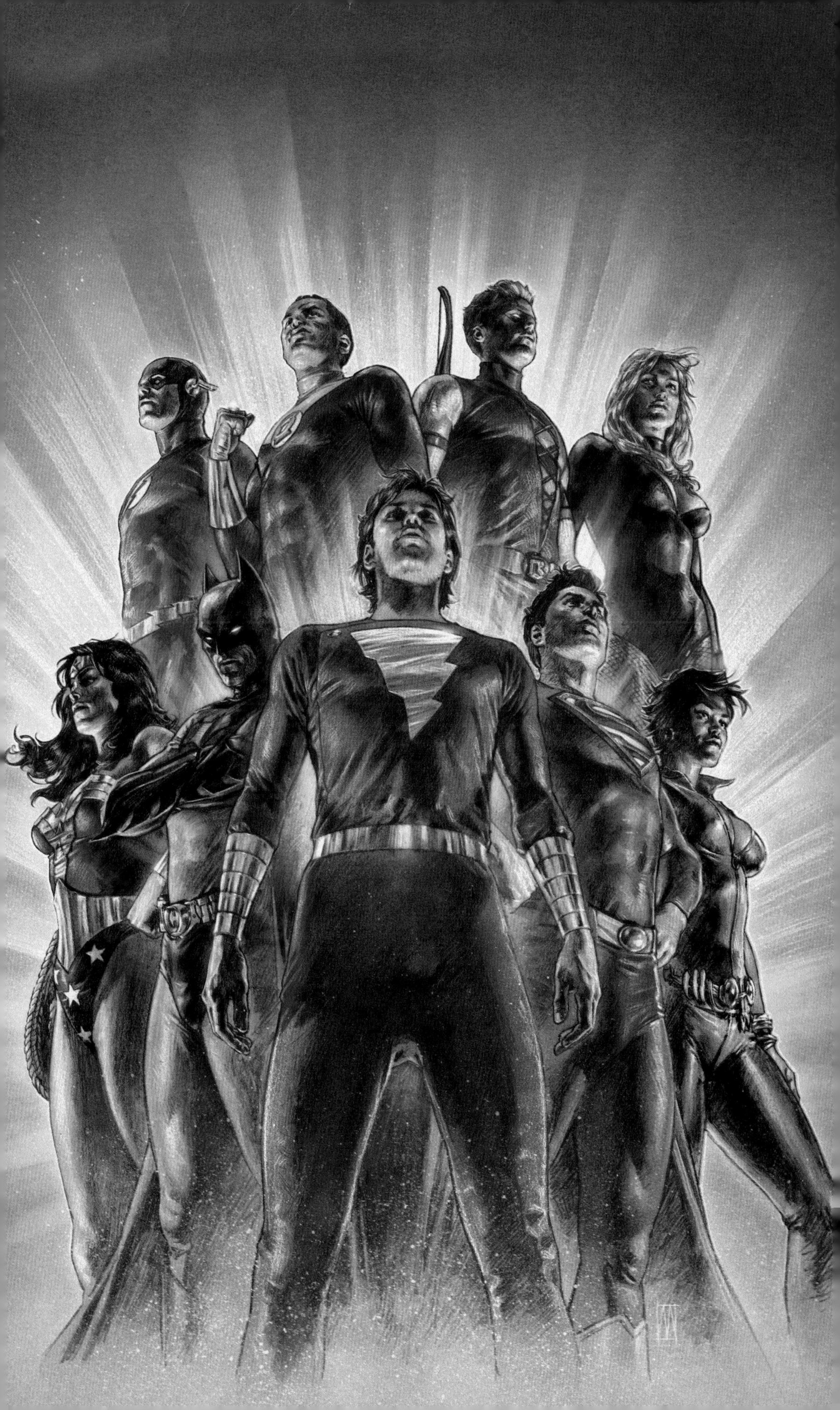

CHAPTER TWELVE:

VERDICT

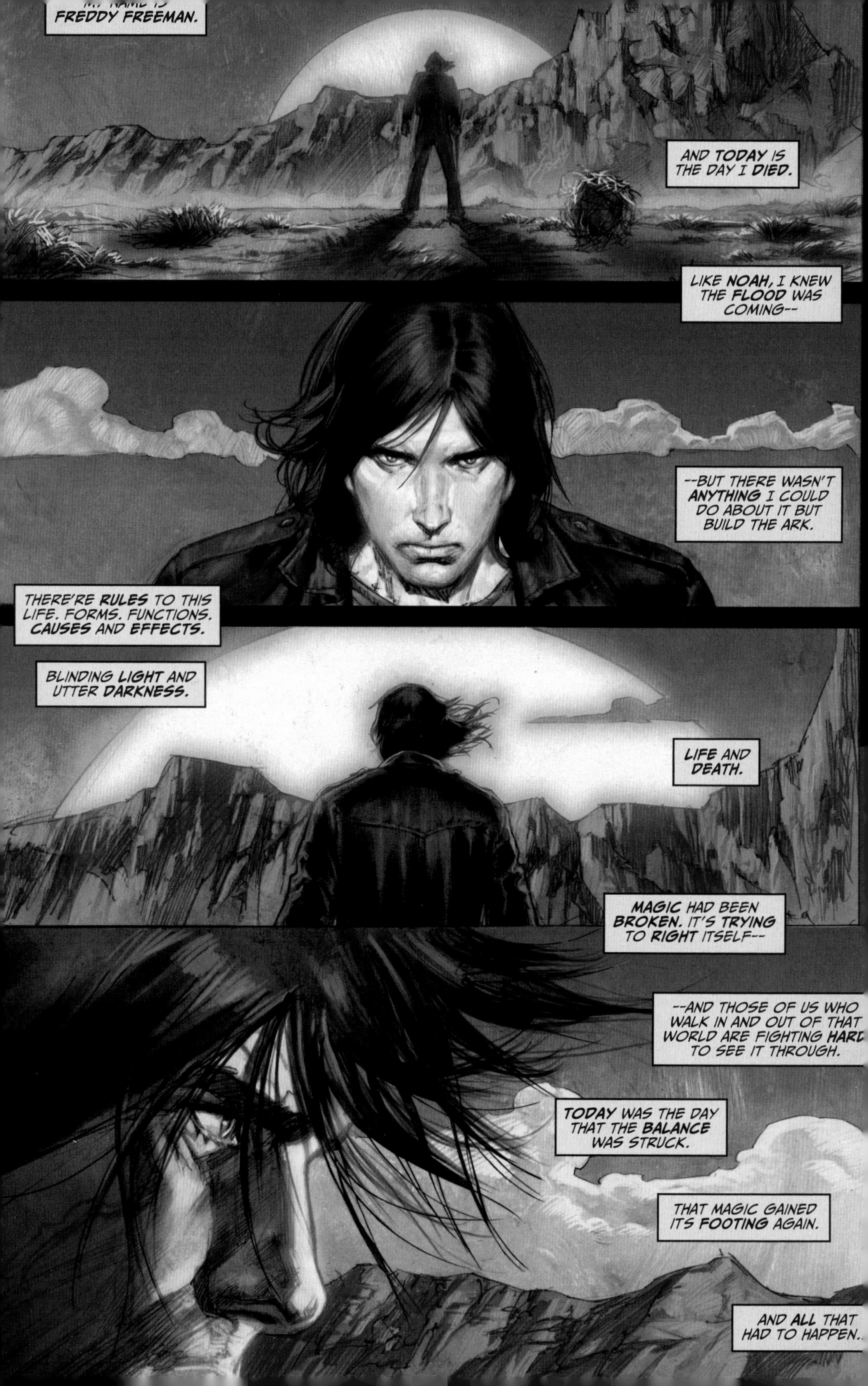
FREDDY FREEMAN.
AND TODAY IS THE DAY I DIED.
LIKE NOAH, I KNEW THE FLOOD WAS COMING--
--BUT THERE WASN'T ANYTHING I COULD DO ABOUT IT BUT BUILD THE ARK.
THERE'RE RULES TO THIS LIFE. FORMS. FUNCTIONS. CAUSES AND EFFECTS.
BLINDING LIGHT AND UTTER DARKNESS.
LIFE AND DEATH.
MAGIC HAD BEEN BROKEN. IT'S TRYING TO RIGHT ITSELF--
--AND THOSE OF US WHO WALK IN AND OUT OF THAT WORLD ARE FIGHTING HARD TO SEE IT THROUGH.
TODAY WAS THE DAY THAT THE BALANCE WAS STRUCK.
THAT MAGIC GAINED ITS FOOTING AGAIN.
AND ALL THAT HAD TO HAPPEN.

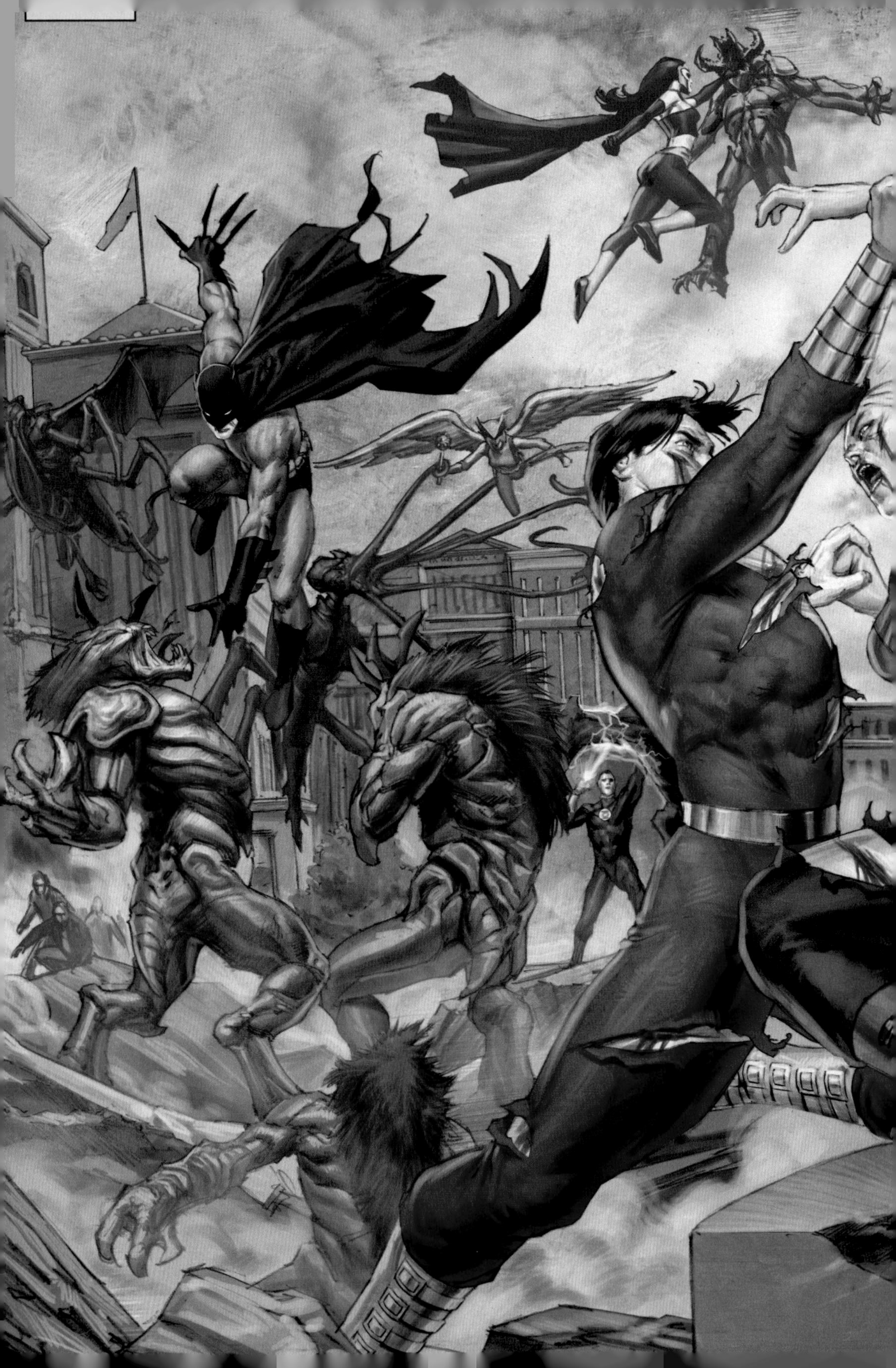

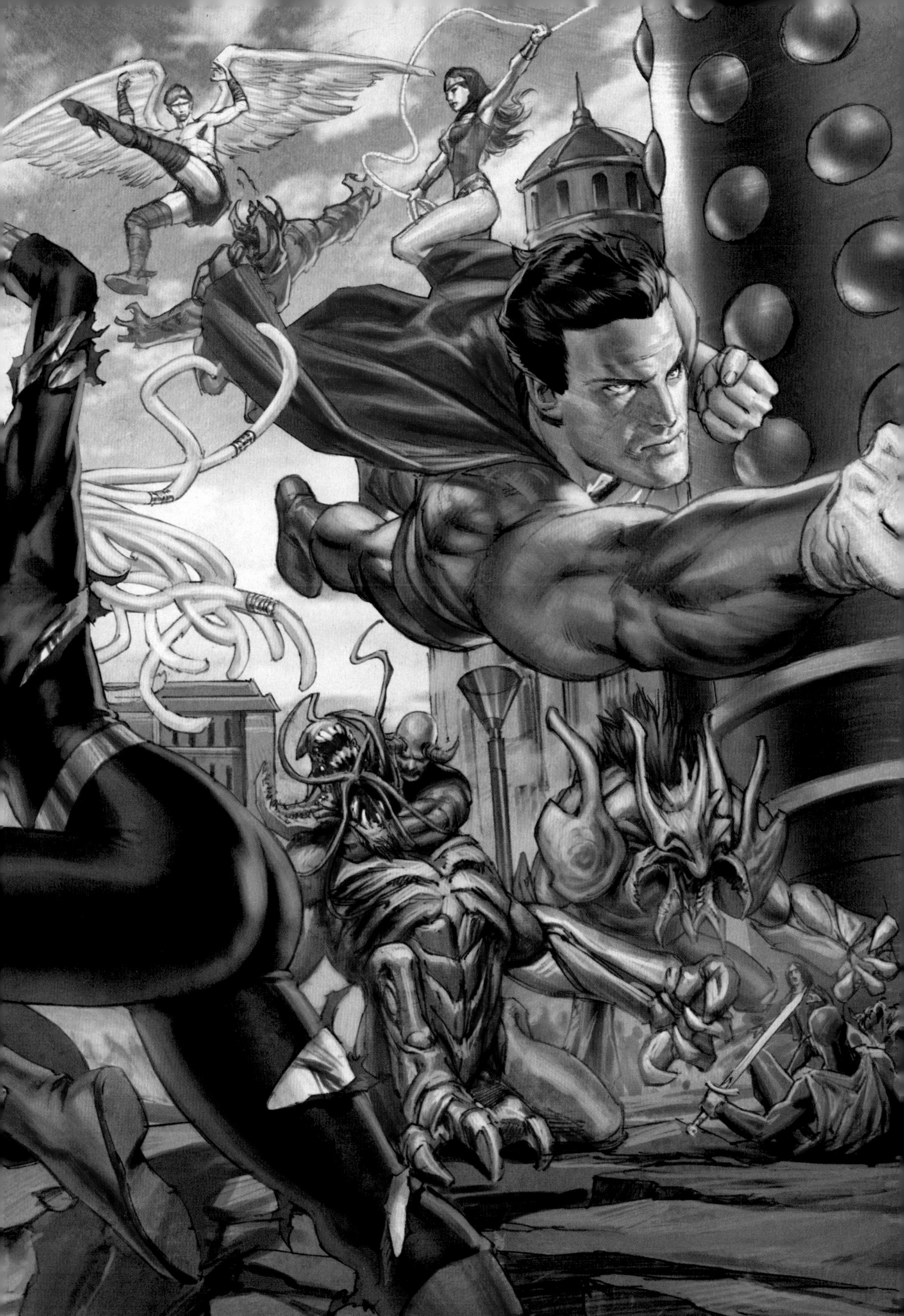

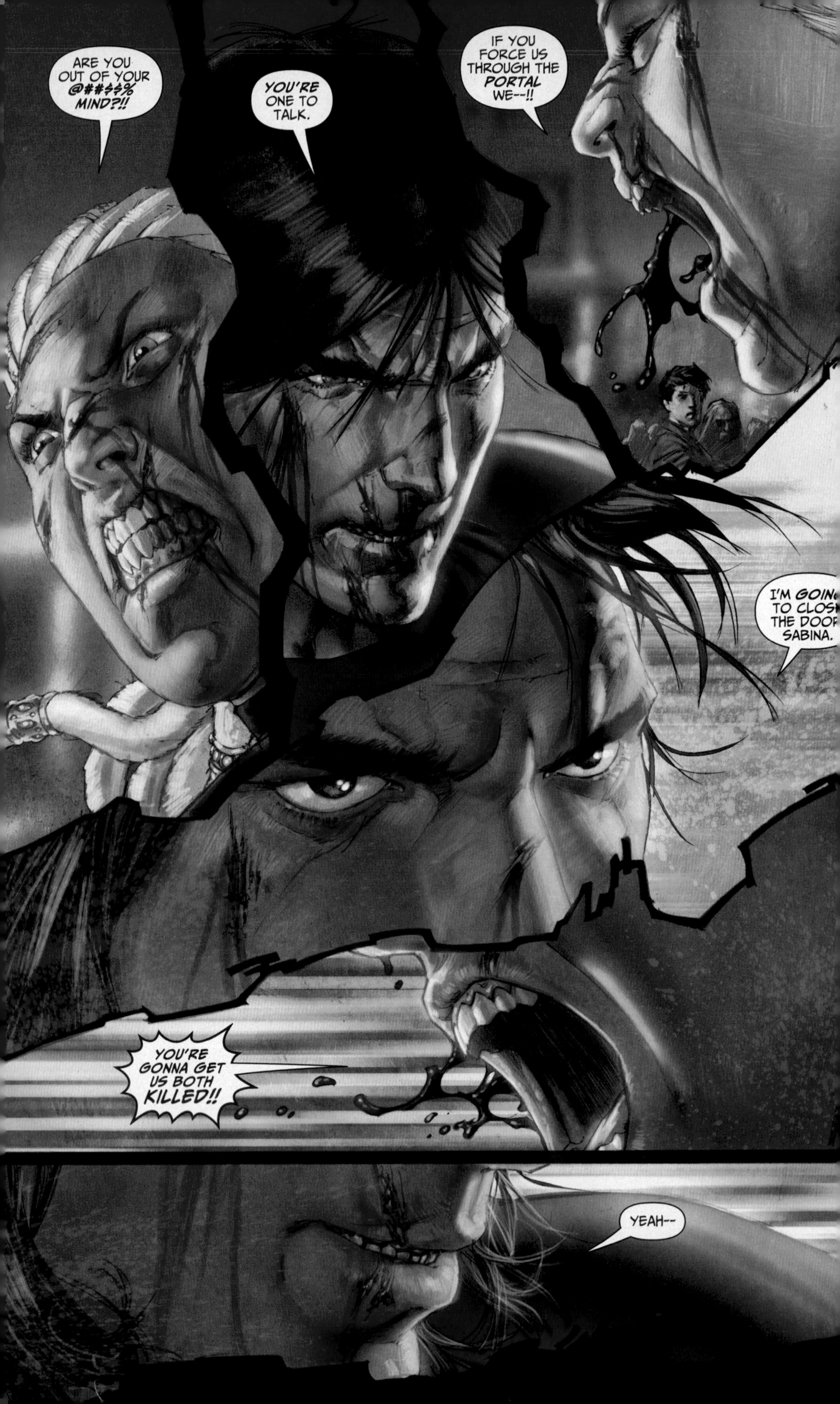
ARE YOU OUT OF YOUR @#$$$% MIND?!!
YOU'RE ONE TO TALK.
IF YOU FORCE US THROUGH THE PORTAL WE--!!
I'M GOIN TO CLOS THE DOOR SABINA.
YOU'RE GONNA GET US BOTH KILLED!!
YEAH--

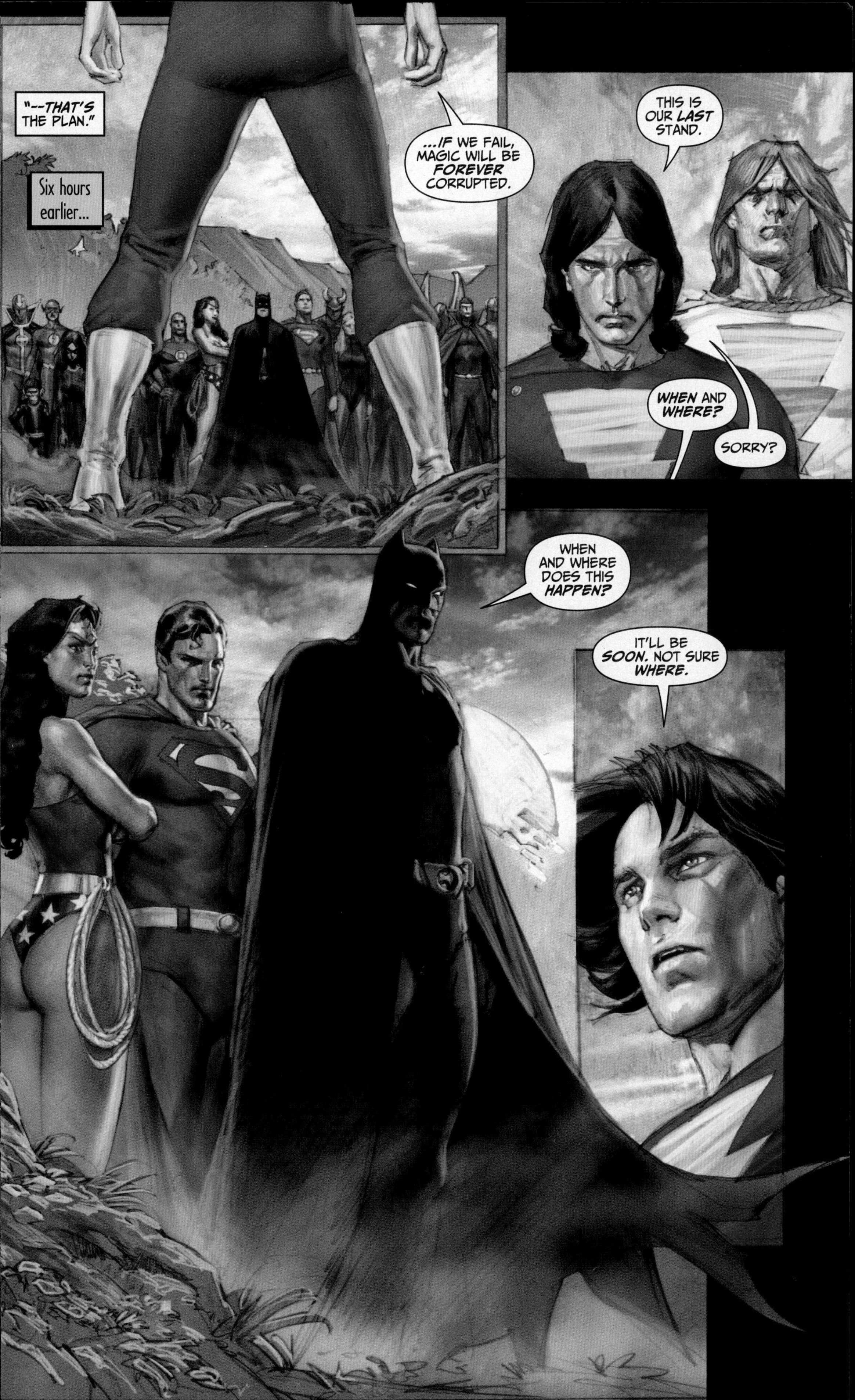
"--THAT'S THE PLAN."
Six hours earlier...
...IF WE FAIL, MAGIC WILL BE FOREVER CORRUPTED.
THIS IS OUR LAST STAND.
WHEN AND WHERE?
SORRY?
WHEN AND WHERE DOES THIS HAPPEN?
IT'LL BE SOON. NOT SURE WHERE.

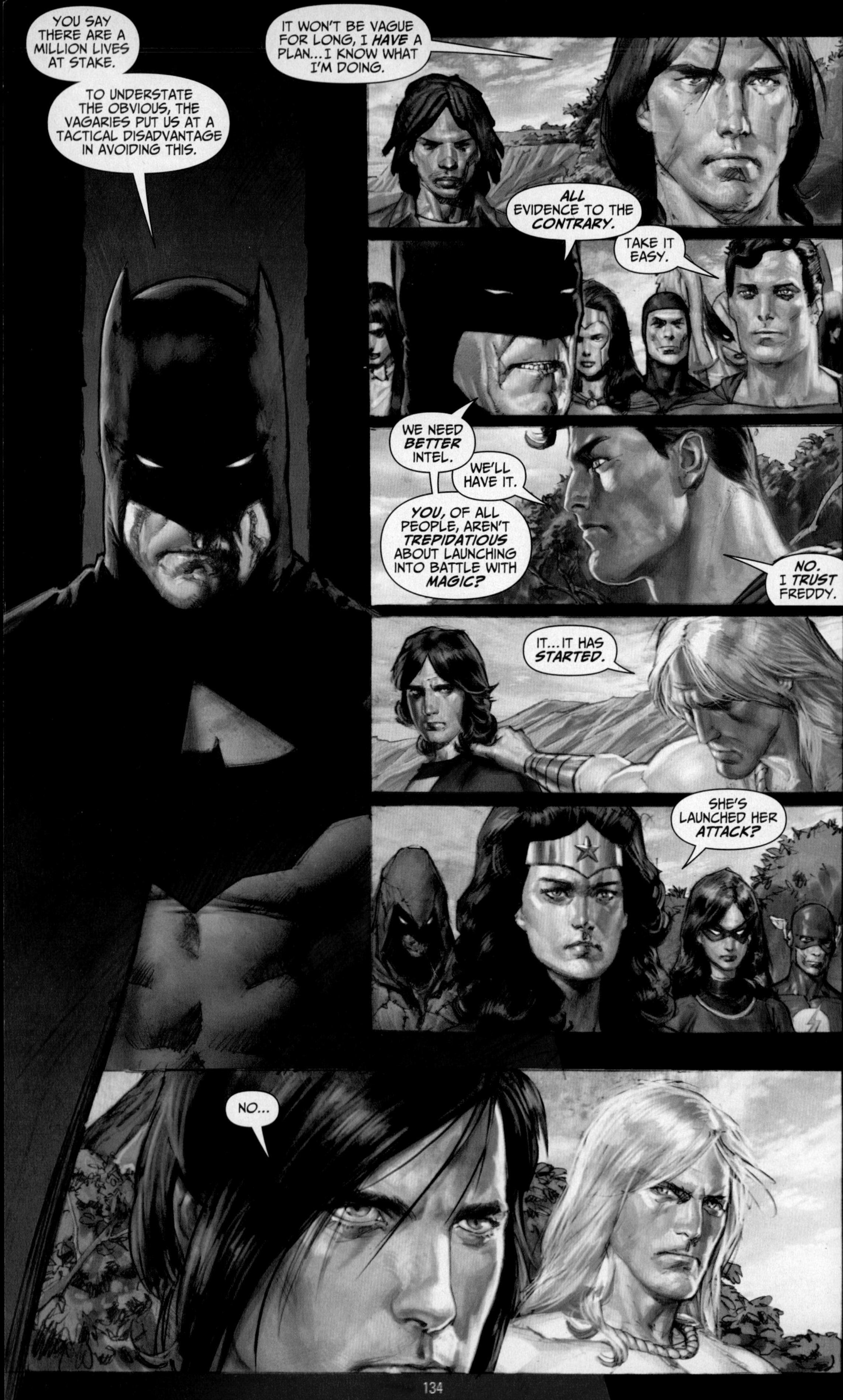
YOU SAY THERE ARE A MILLION LIVES AT STAKE.
TO UNDERSTATE THE OBVIOUS, THE VAGARIES PUT US AT A TACTICAL DISADVANTAGE IN AVOIDING THIS.
IT WON'T BE VAGUE FOR LONG, I *HAVE* A PLAN... I KNOW WHAT I'M DOING.
ALL EVIDENCE TO THE *CONTRARY.*
TAKE IT EASY.
WE NEED *BETTER* INTEL.
WE'LL HAVE IT.
YOU, OF ALL PEOPLE, AREN'T *TREPIDATIOUS* ABOUT LAUNCHING INTO BATTLE WITH *MAGIC?*
NO. I *TRUST* FREDDY.
IT... IT HAS *STARTED.*
SHE'S LAUNCHED HER *ATTACK?*
NO...

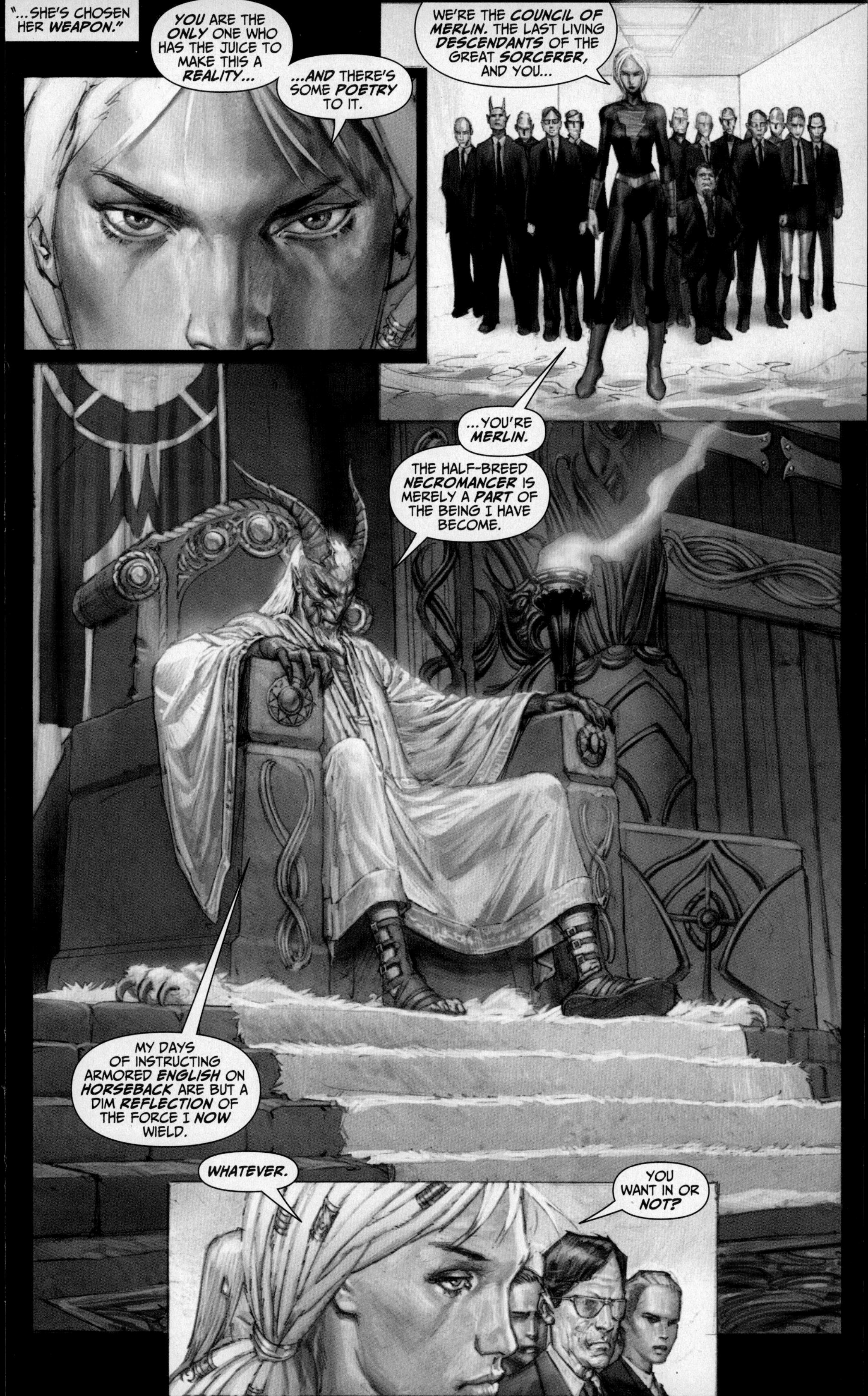
"...SHE'S CHOSEN HER WEAPON."
YOU ARE THE ONLY ONE WHO HAS THE JUICE TO MAKE THIS A REALITY...
...AND THERE'S SOME POETRY TO IT.
WE'RE THE COUNCIL OF MERLIN. THE LAST LIVING DESCENDANTS OF THE GREAT SORCERER, AND YOU...
...YOU'RE MERLIN.
THE HALF-BREED NECROMANCER IS MERELY A PART OF THE BEING I HAVE BECOME.
MY DAYS OF INSTRUCTING ARMORED ENGLISH ON HORSEBACK ARE BUT A DIM REFLECTION OF THE FORCE I NOW WIELD.
WHATEVER.
YOU WANT IN OR NOT?

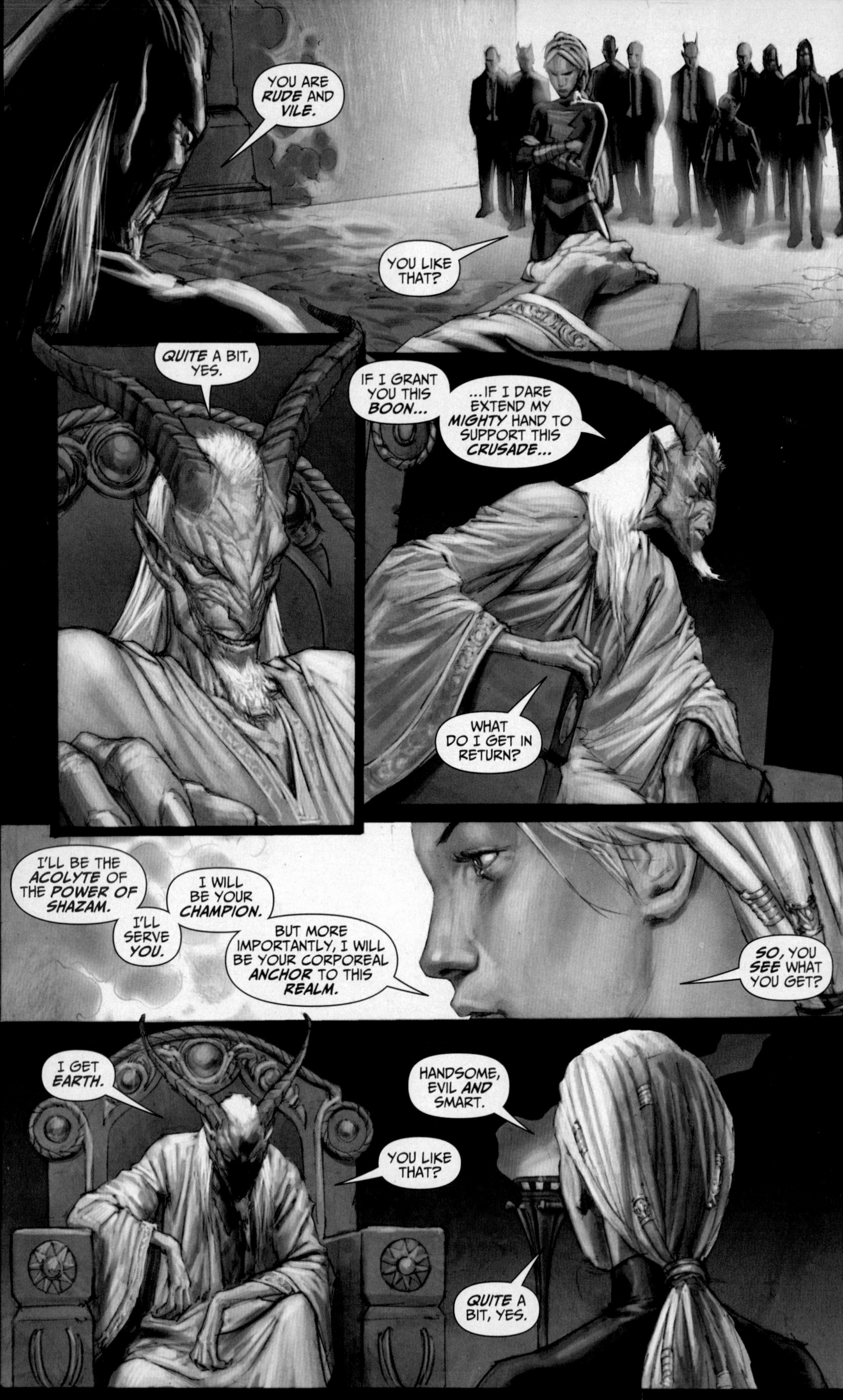
YOU ARE RUDE AND VILE.
YOU LIKE THAT?
QUITE A BIT, YES.
IF I GRANT YOU THIS BOON...
...IF I DARE EXTEND MY MIGHTY HAND TO SUPPORT THIS CRUSADE...
WHAT DO I GET IN RETURN?
I'LL BE THE ACOLYTE OF THE POWER OF SHAZAM.
I'LL SERVE YOU.
I WILL BE YOUR CHAMPION.
BUT MORE IMPORTANTLY, I WILL BE YOUR CORPOREAL ANCHOR TO THIS REALM.
SO, YOU SEE WHAT YOU GET?
I GET EARTH.
HANDSOME, EVIL AND SMART.
YOU LIKE THAT?
QUITE A BIT, YES.

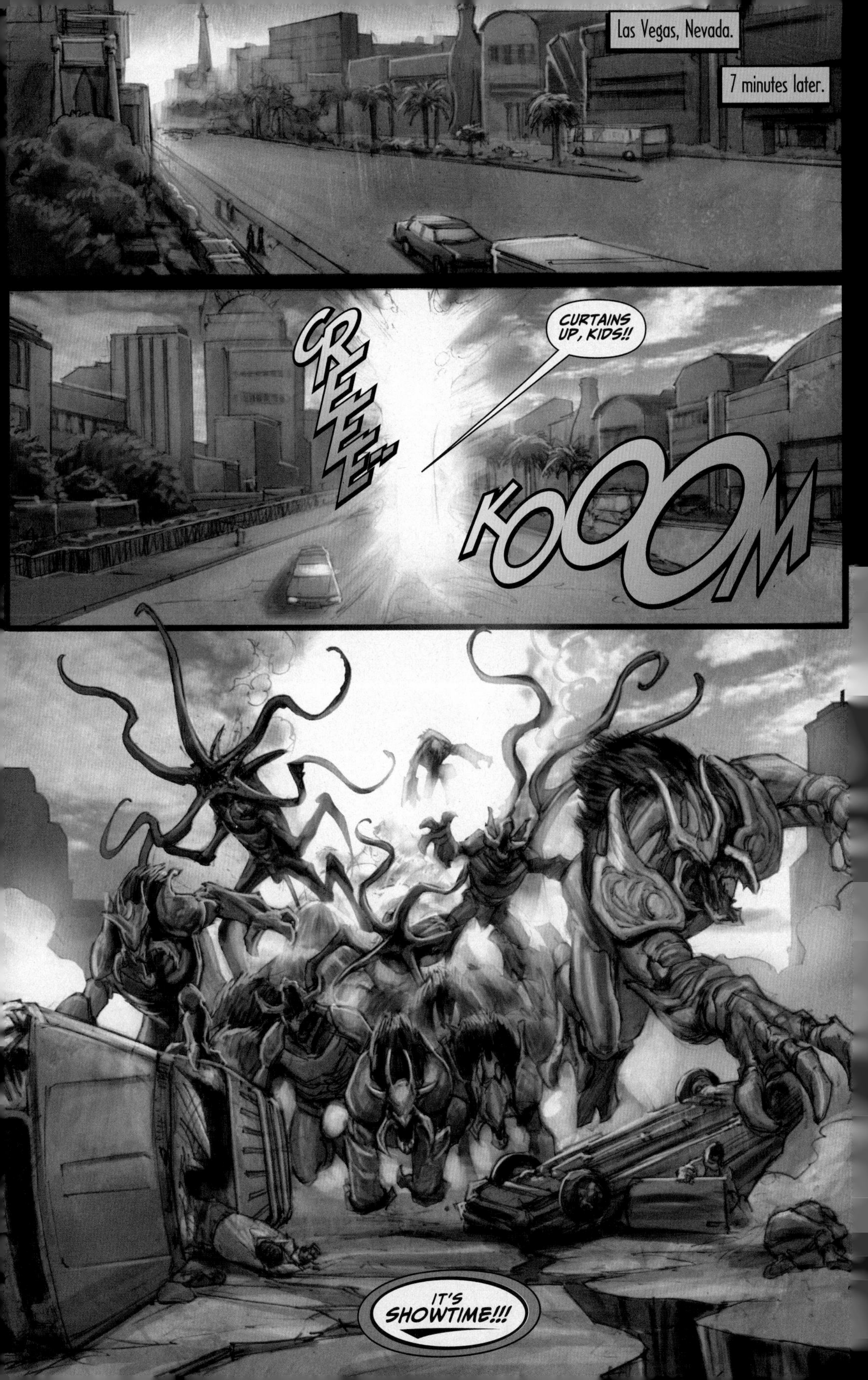
Las Vegas, Nevada.
7 minutes later.
CREEE...
CURTAINS UP, KIDS!!
KOOOM
IT'S SHOWTIME!!!

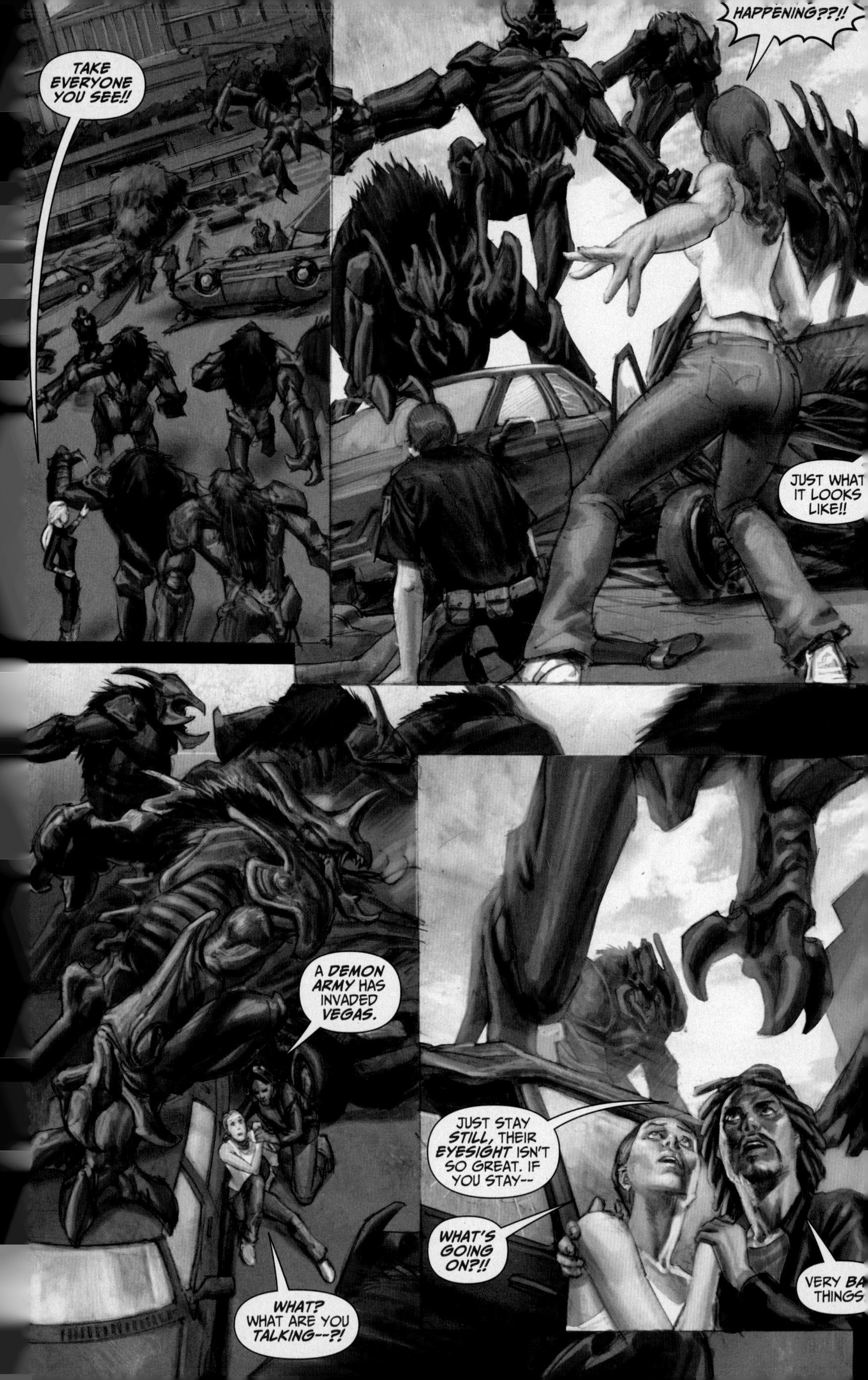
HAPPENING??!!
TAKE EVERYONE YOU SEE!!
JUST WHAT IT LOOKS LIKE!!
A DEMON ARMY HAS INVADED VEGAS.
WHAT? WHAT ARE YOU TALKING--?!
JUST STAY STILL, THEIR EYESIGHT ISN'T SO GREAT. IF YOU STAY--
WHAT'S GOING ON?!!
VERY BA THINGS

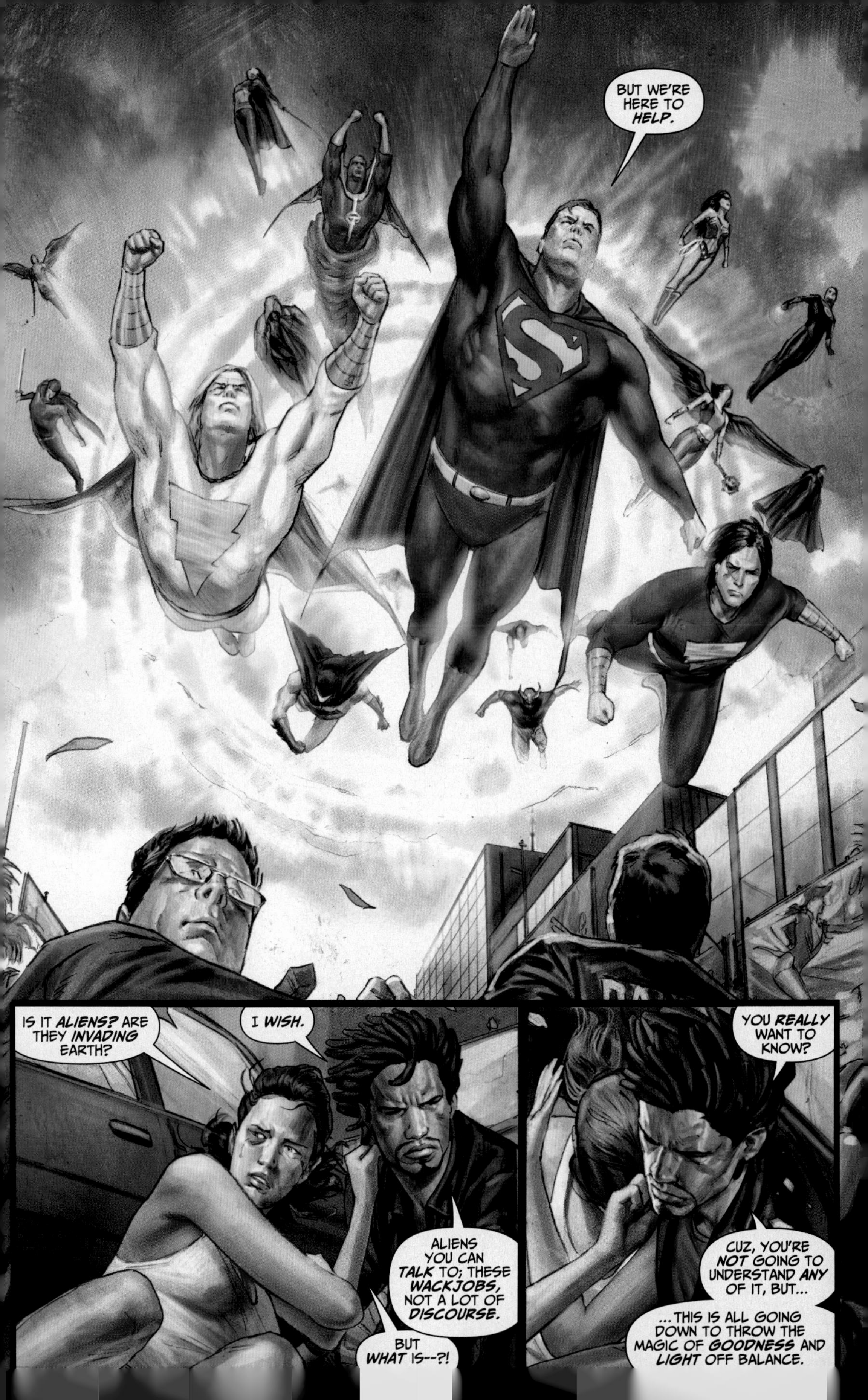
BUT WE'RE HERE TO *HELP.*
IS IT *ALIENS?* ARE THEY *INVADING* EARTH?
I *WISH.*
ALIENS YOU CAN *TALK* TO; THESE *WACKJOBS,* NOT A LOT OF *DISCOURSE.*
BUT *WHAT* IS--?!
YOU *REALLY* WANT TO KNOW?
CUZ, YOU'RE *NOT* GOING TO UNDERSTAND *ANY* OF IT, BUT...
...THIS IS ALL GOING DOWN TO THROW THE MAGIC OF *GOODNESS* AND *LIGHT* OFF BALANCE.

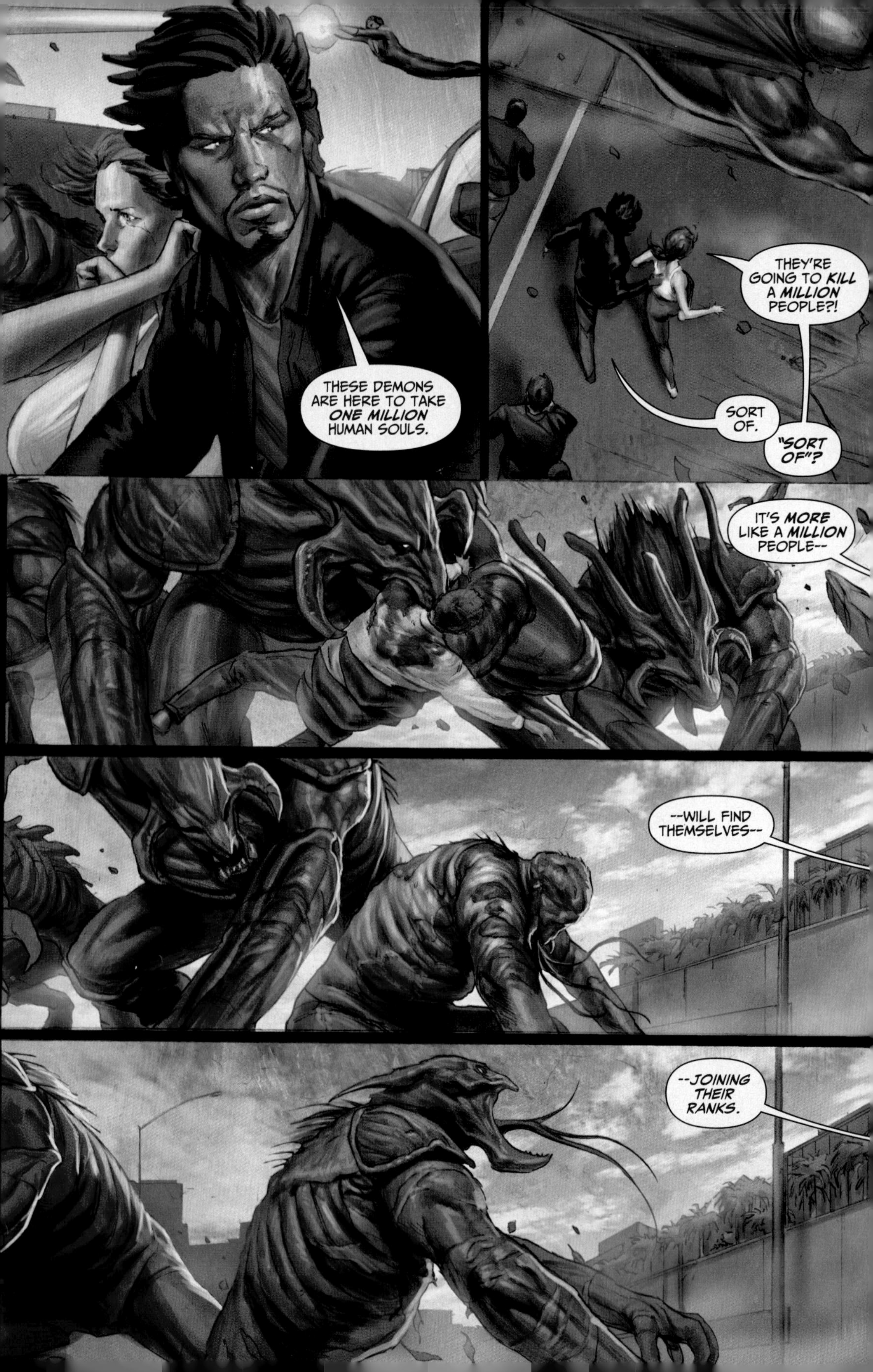
THESE DEMONS ARE HERE TO TAKE ONE MILLION HUMAN SOULS.
THEY'RE GOING TO KILL A MILLION PEOPLE?!
SORT OF.
"SORT OF"?
IT'S MORE LIKE A MILLION PEOPLE--
--WILL FIND THEMSELVES--
--JOINING THEIR RANKS.

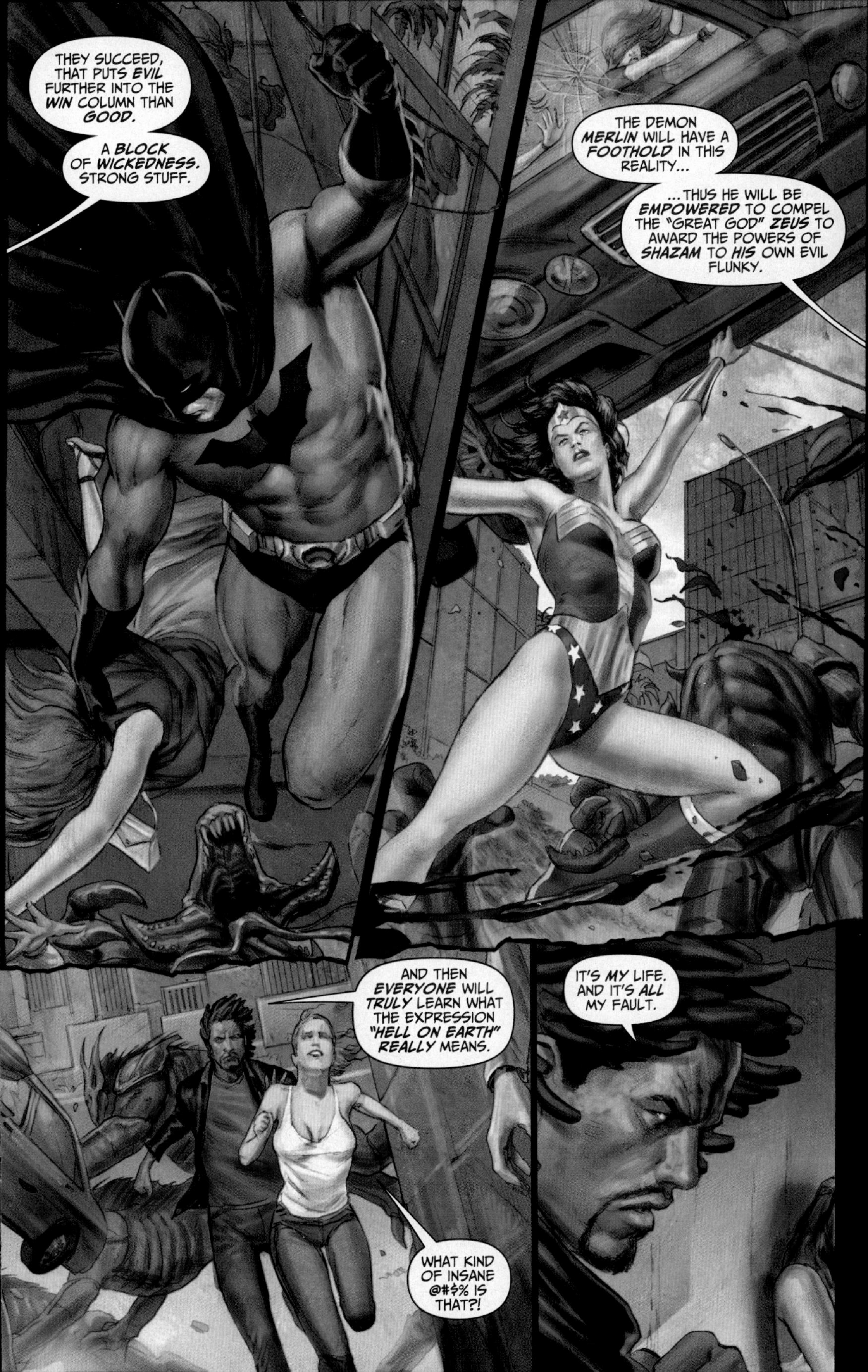
THEY SUCCEED, THAT PUTS EVIL FURTHER INTO THE WIN COLUMN THAN GOOD.
A BLOCK OF WICKEDNESS. STRONG STUFF.
THE DEMON MERLIN WILL HAVE A FOOTHOLD IN THIS REALITY...
...THUS HE WILL BE EMPOWERED TO COMPEL THE "GREAT GOD" ZEUS TO AWARD THE POWERS OF SHAZAM TO HIS OWN EVIL FLUNKY.
AND THEN EVERYONE WILL TRULY LEARN WHAT THE EXPRESSION "HELL ON EARTH" REALLY MEANS.
WHAT KIND OF INSANE @#$% IS THAT?!
IT'S MY LIFE. AND IT'S ALL MY FAULT.

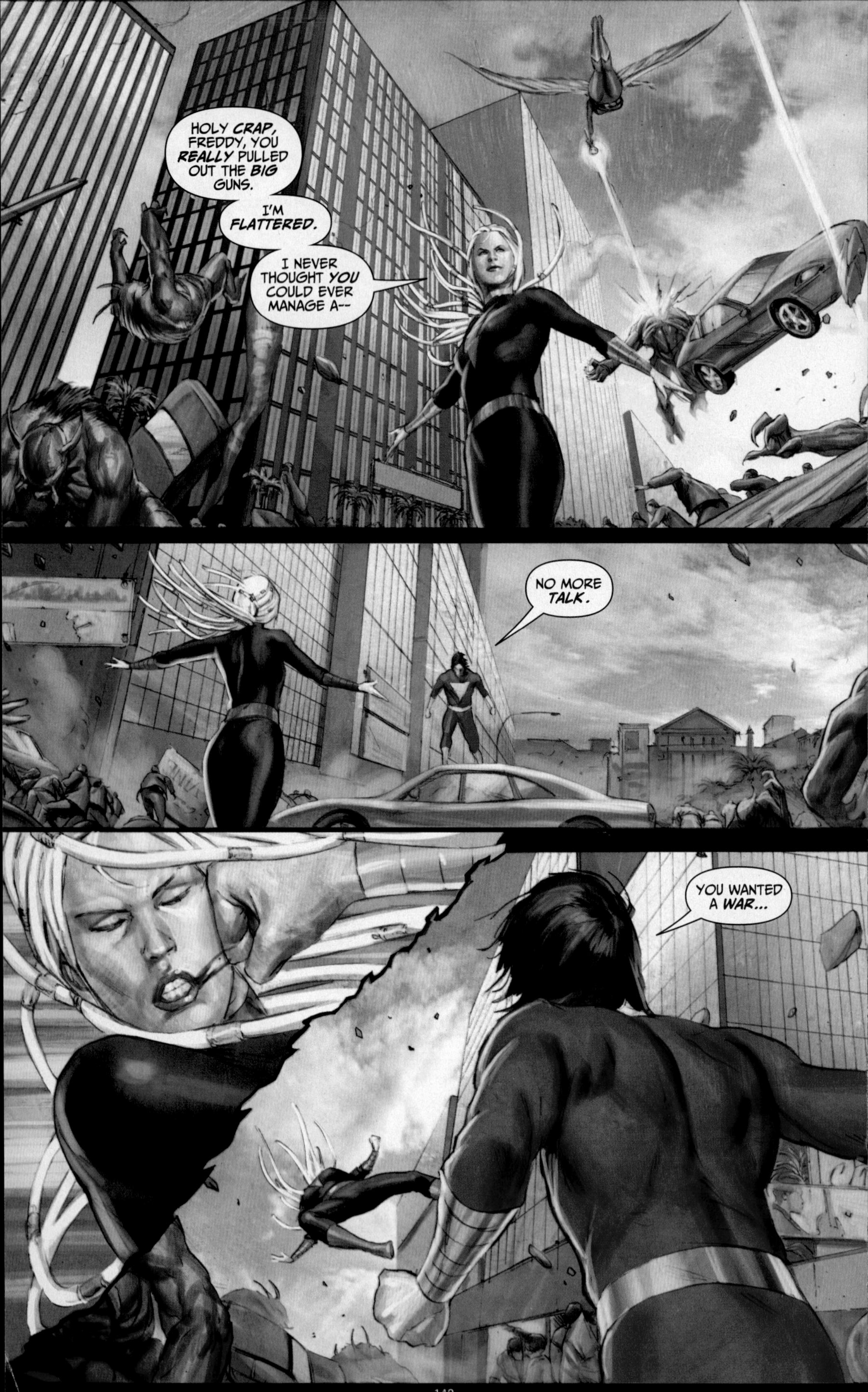
HOLY CRAP, FREDDY, YOU REALLY PULLED OUT THE BIG GUNS.
I'M FLATTERED.
I NEVER THOUGHT YOU COULD EVER MANAGE A--
NO MORE TALK.
YOU WANTED A WAR...

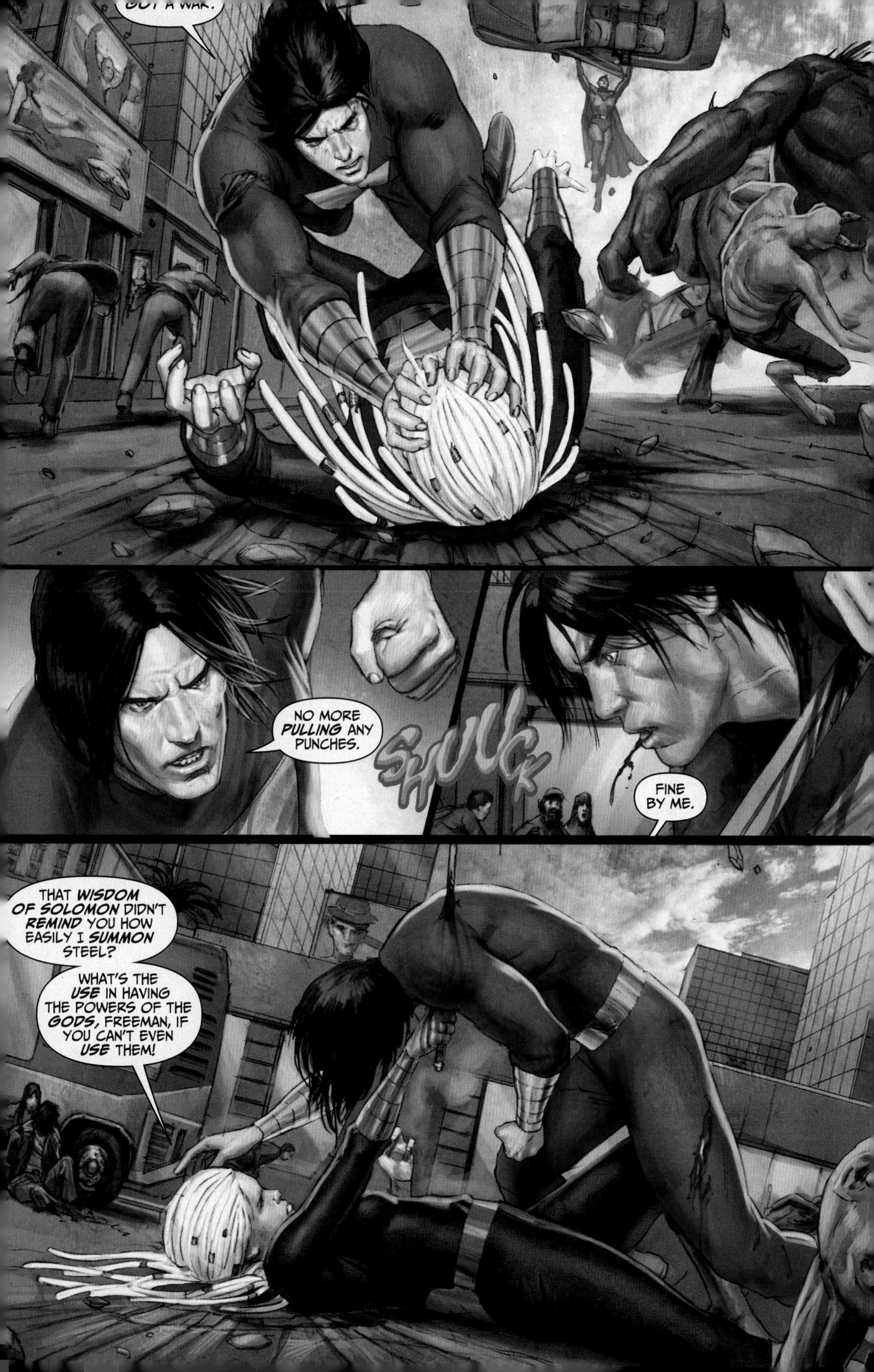
GOT A WAR.
NO MORE PULLING ANY PUNCHES.
SHUNCK
FINE BY ME.
THAT WISDOM OF SOLOMON DIDN'T REMIND YOU HOW EASILY I SUMMON STEEL?
WHAT'S THE USE IN HAVING THE POWERS OF THE GODS, FREEMAN, IF YOU CAN'T EVEN USE THEM!

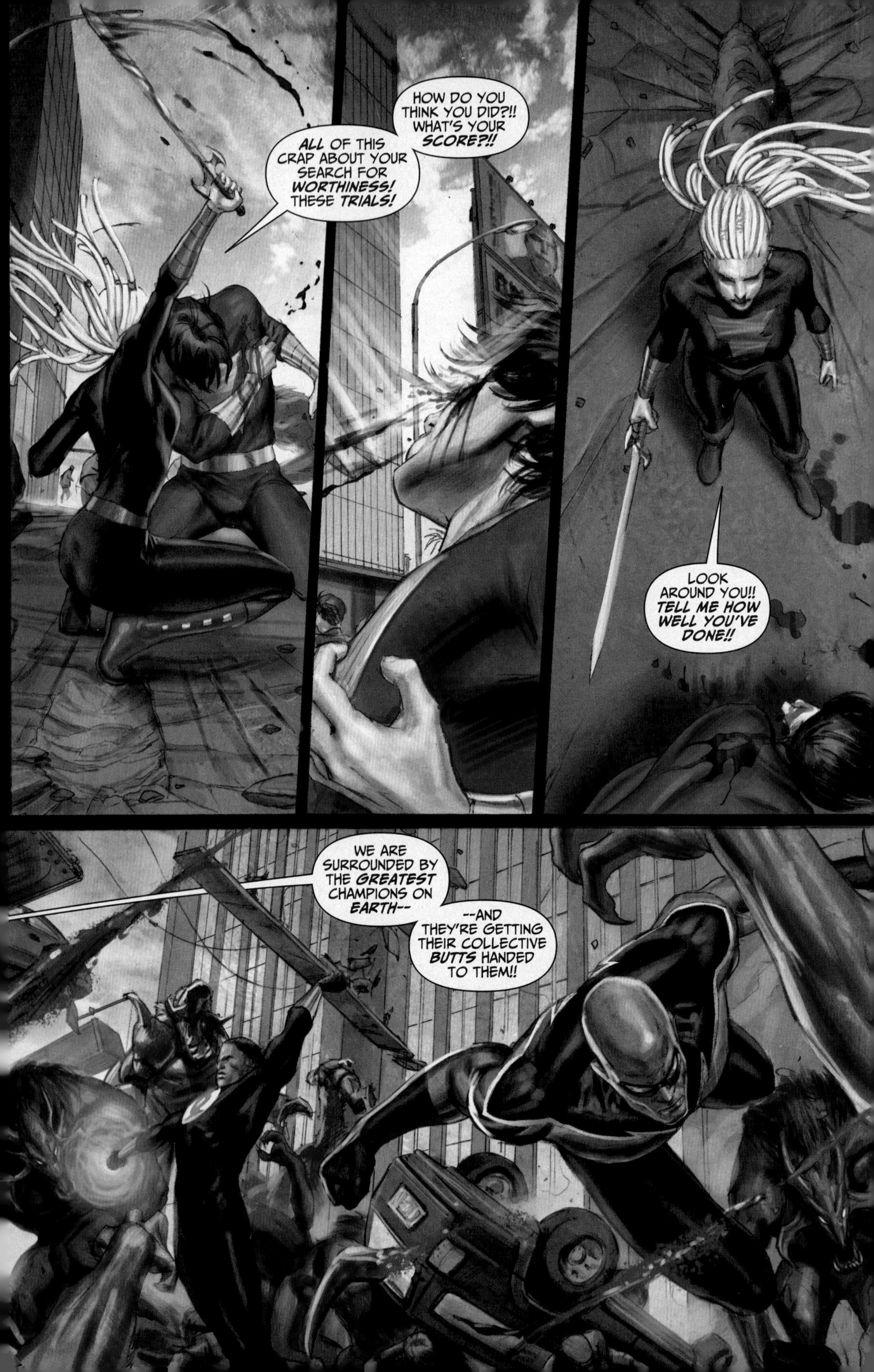
ALL OF THIS CRAP ABOUT YOUR SEARCH FOR WORTHINESS! THESE TRIALS!
HOW DO YOU THINK YOU DID?!! WHAT'S YOUR SCORE?!!
LOOK AROUND YOU!! TELL ME HOW WELL YOU'VE DONE!!
WE ARE SURROUNDED BY THE GREATEST CHAMPIONS ON EARTH--
--AND THEY'RE GETTING THEIR COLLECTIVE BUTTS HANDED TO THEM!!

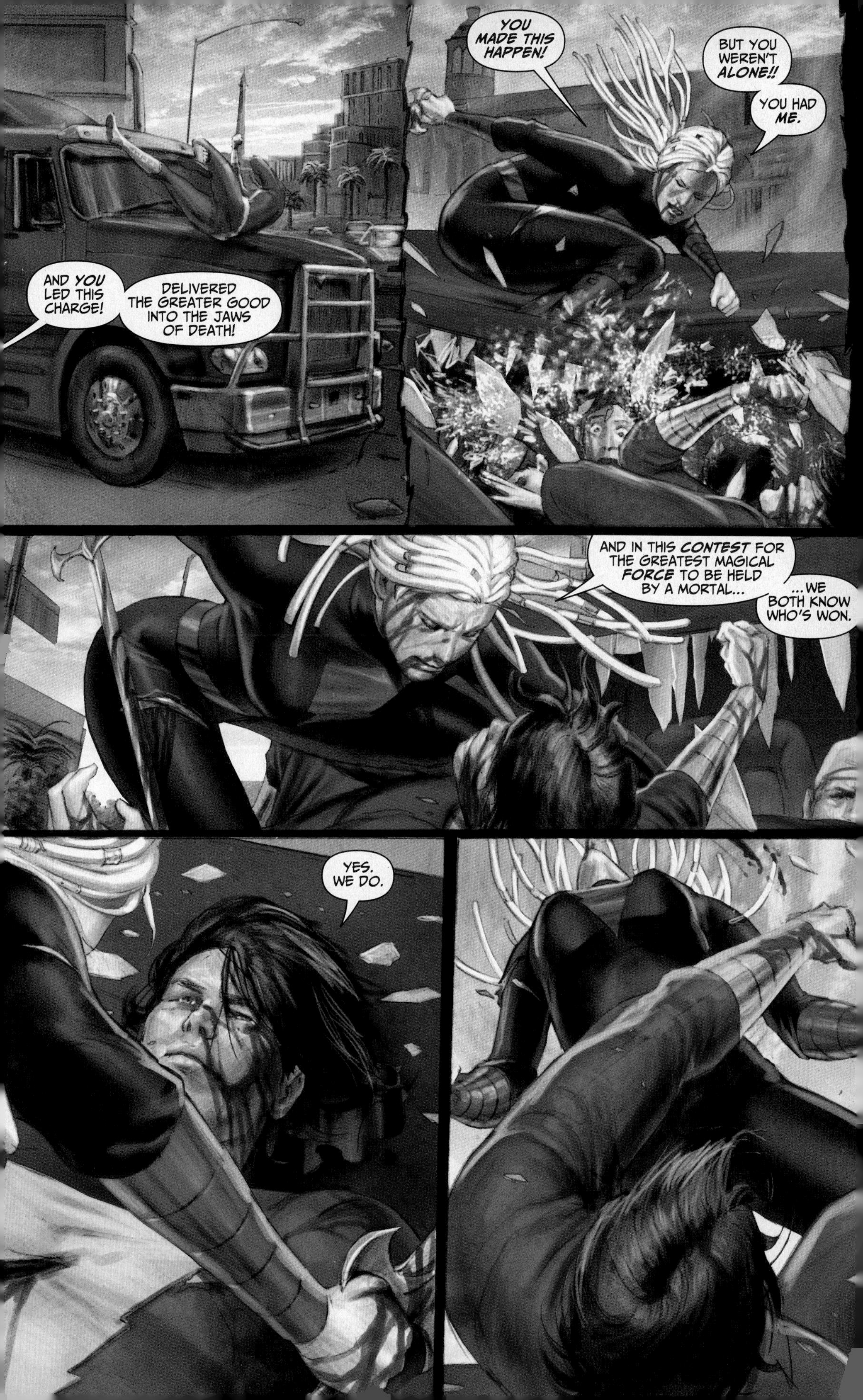
AND YOU LED THIS CHARGE!
DELIVERED THE GREATER GOOD INTO THE JAWS OF DEATH!
YOU MADE THIS HAPPEN!
BUT YOU WEREN'T ALONE!!
YOU HAD ME.
AND IN THIS CONTEST FOR THE GREATEST MAGICAL FORCE TO BE HELD BY A MORTAL...
...WE BOTH KNOW WHO'S WON.
YES. WE DO.

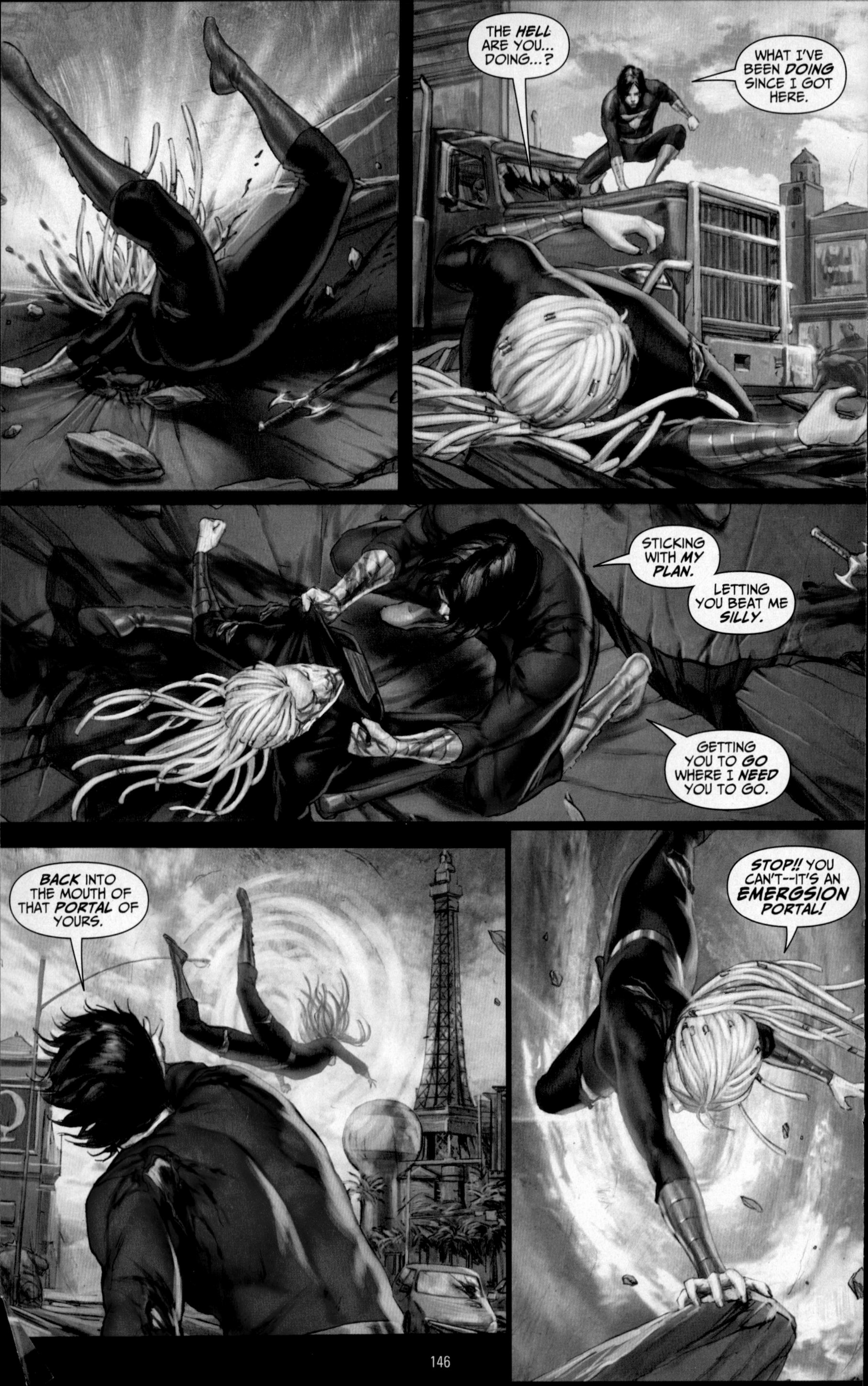
THE HELL ARE YOU... DOING...?
WHAT I'VE BEEN DOING SINCE I GOT HERE.
STICKING WITH MY PLAN.
LETTING YOU BEAT ME SILLY.
GETTING YOU TO GO WHERE I NEED YOU TO GO.
BACK INTO THE MOUTH OF THAT PORTAL OF YOURS.
STOP!! YOU CAN'T--IT'S AN EMERGSION PORTAL!

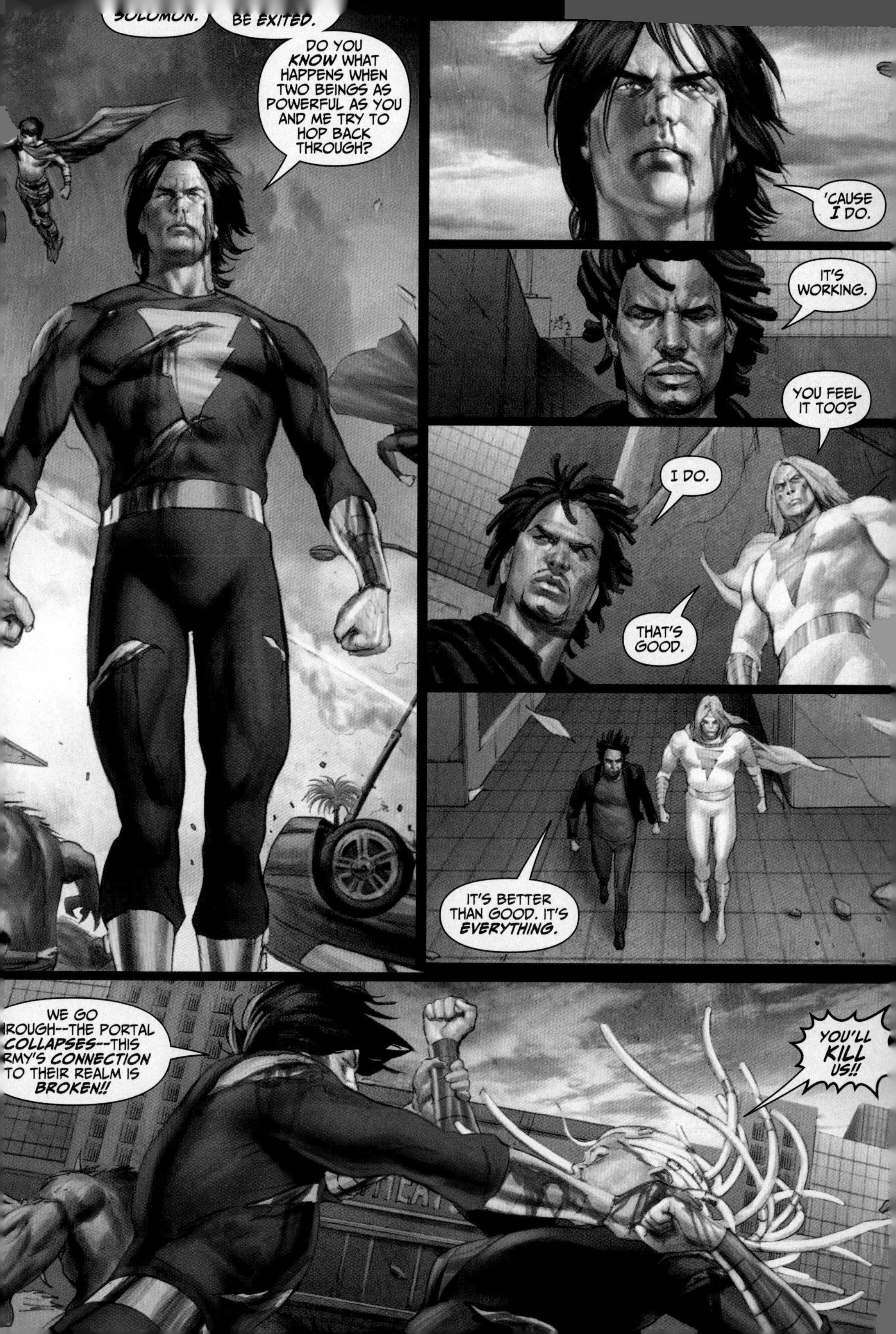

SOLOMON.
BE EXITED.
DO YOU KNOW WHAT HAPPENS WHEN TWO BEINGS AS POWERFUL AS YOU AND ME TRY TO HOP BACK THROUGH?
'CAUSE I DO.
IT'S WORKING.
YOU FEEL IT TOO?
I DO.
THAT'S GOOD.
IT'S BETTER THAN GOOD. IT'S EVERYTHING.
WE GO
ROUGH--THE PORTAL COLLAPSES--THIS
RMY'S CONNECTION TO THEIR REALM IS BROKEN!!
YOU'LL KILL US!!

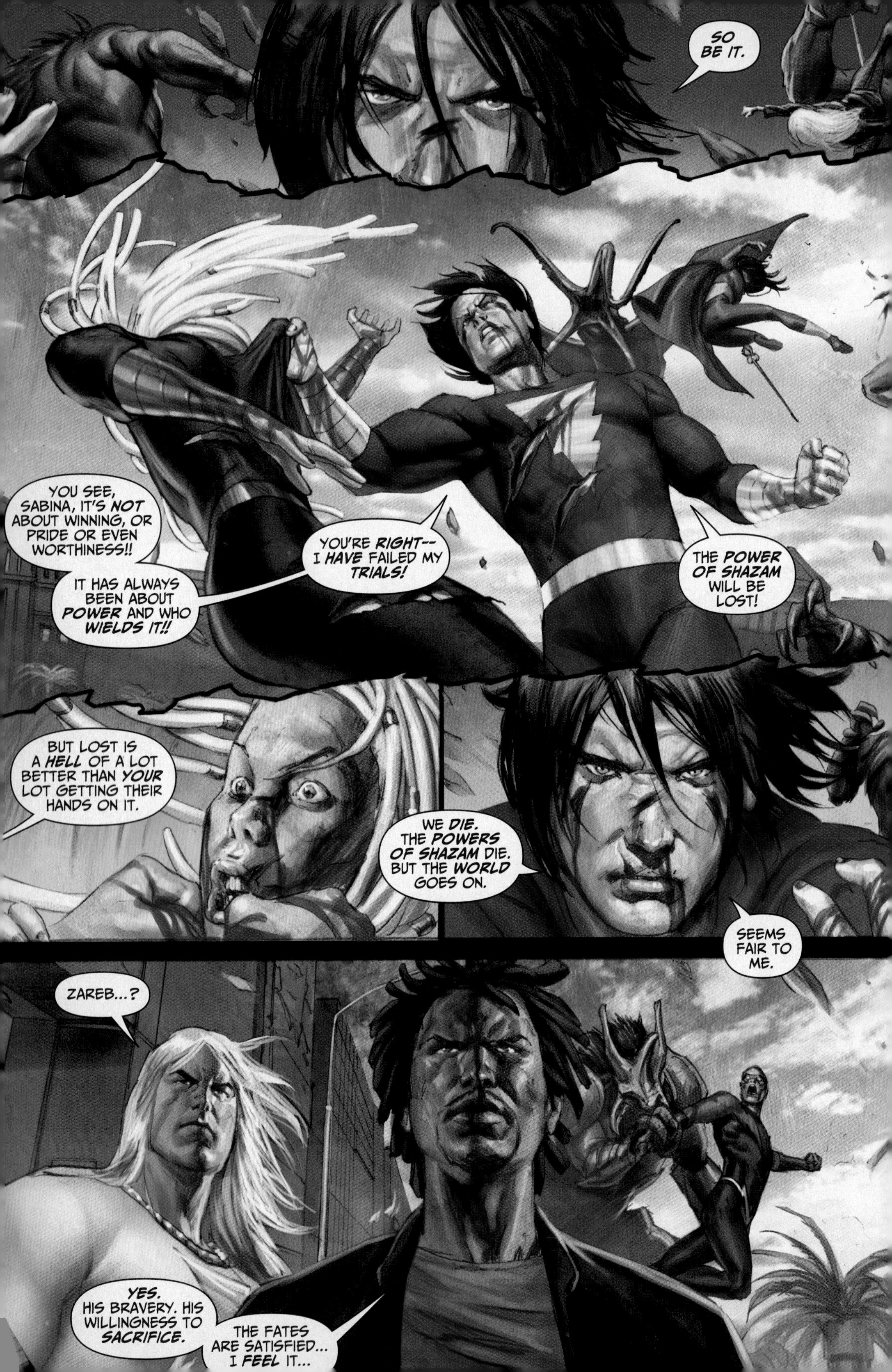
SO BE IT.
YOU SEE, SABINA, IT'S NOT ABOUT WINNING, OR PRIDE OR EVEN WORTHINESS!!
IT HAS ALWAYS BEEN ABOUT POWER AND WHO WIELDS IT!!
YOU'RE RIGHT-- I HAVE FAILED MY TRIALS!
THE POWER OF SHAZAM WILL BE LOST!
BUT LOST IS A HELL OF A LOT BETTER THAN YOUR LOT GETTING THEIR HANDS ON IT.
WE DIE. THE POWERS OF SHAZAM DIE. BUT THE WORLD GOES ON.
SEEMS FAIR TO ME.
ZAREB...?
YES. HIS BRAVERY. HIS WILLINGNESS TO SACRIFICE.
THE FATES ARE SATISFIED... I FEEL IT...

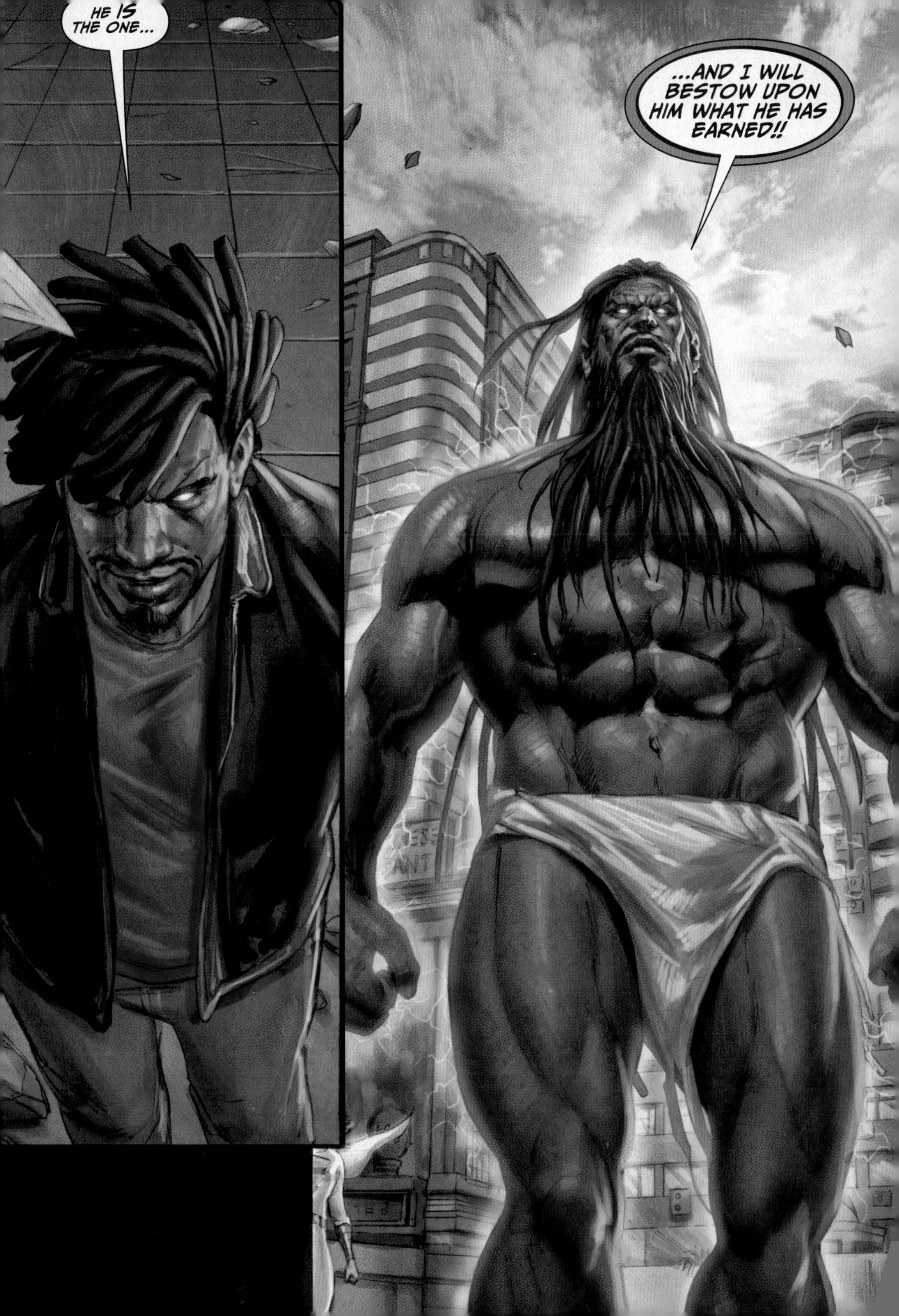
HE IS THE ONE...
...AND I WILL BESTOW UPON HIM WHAT HE HAS EARNED!!

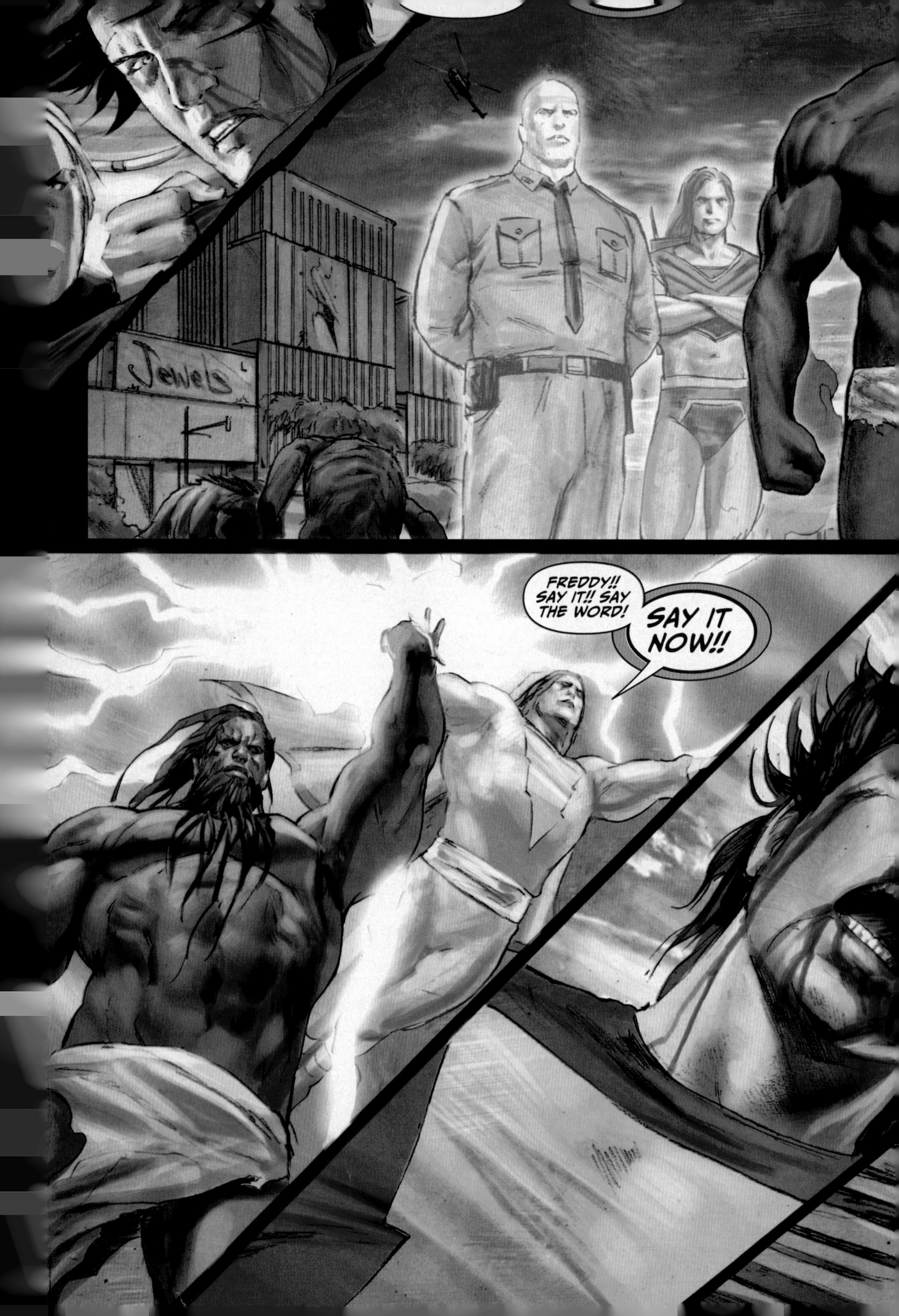
Jewels
FREDDY!! SAY IT!! SAY THE WORD!
SAY IT NOW!!

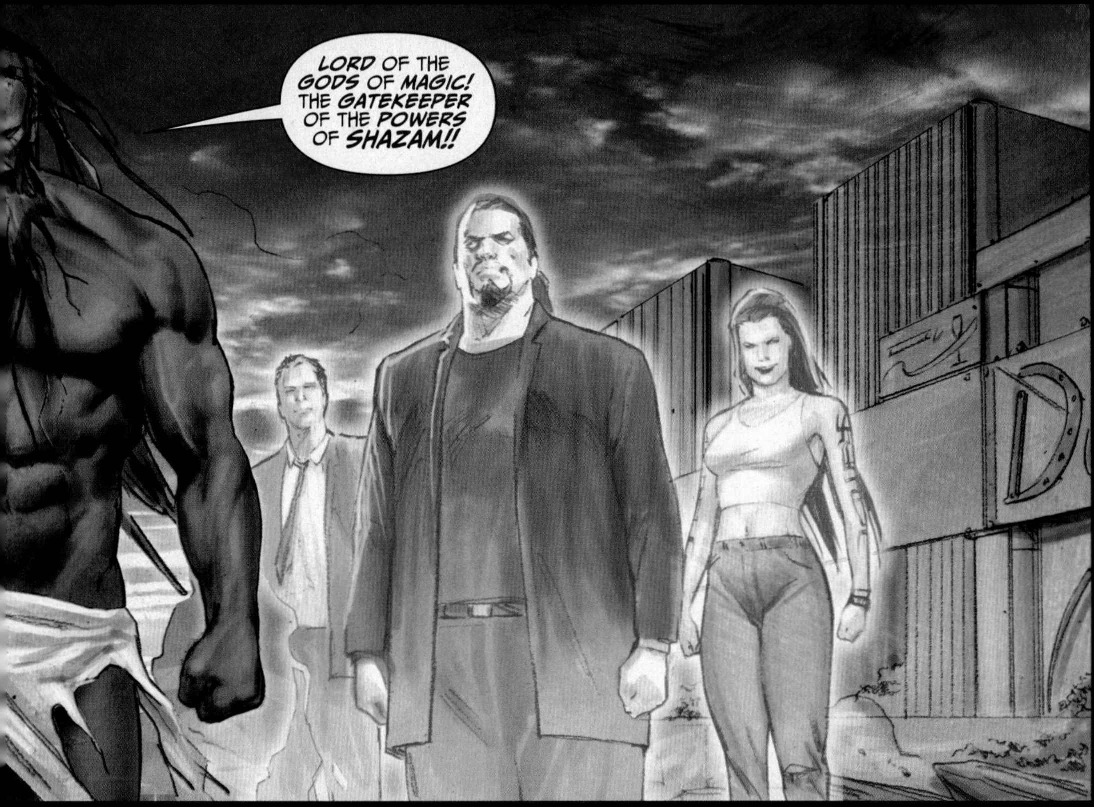
LORD OF THE GODS OF MAGIC! THE GATEKEEPER OF THE POWERS OF SHAZAM!!

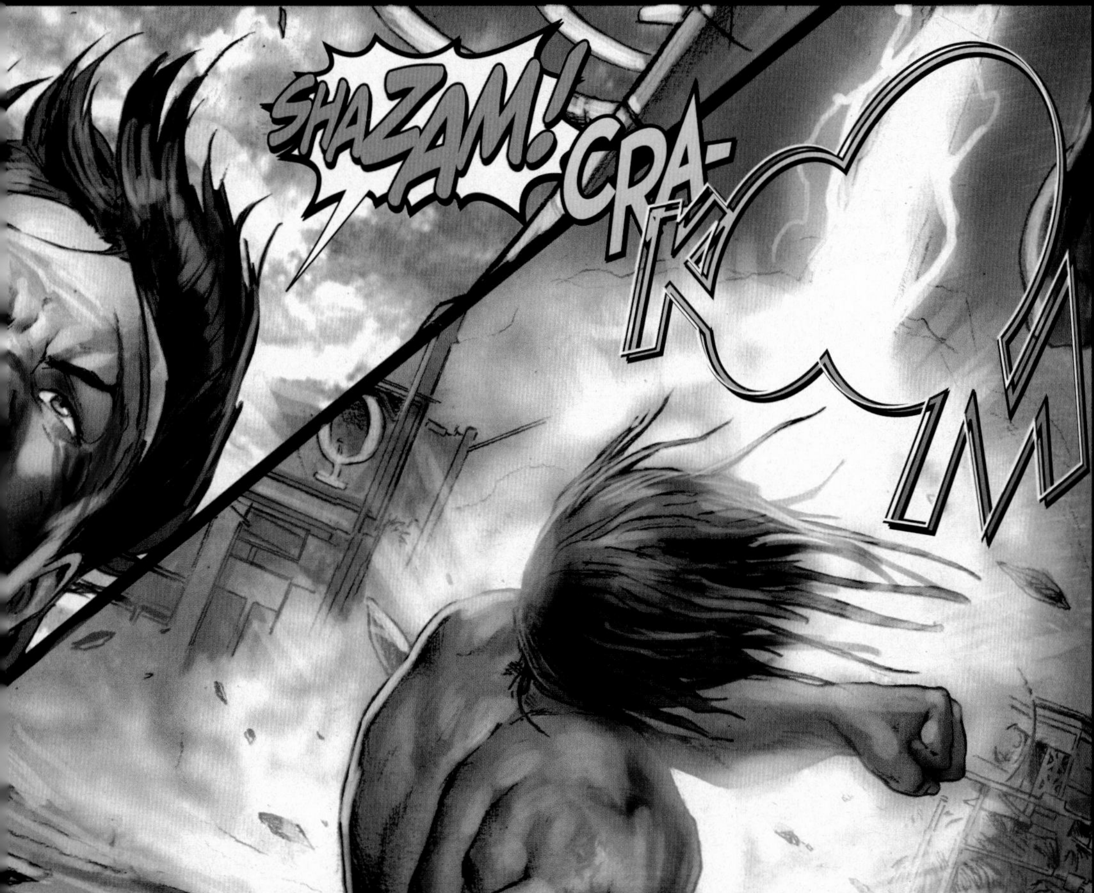
SHAZAM!
CRA-KOOM

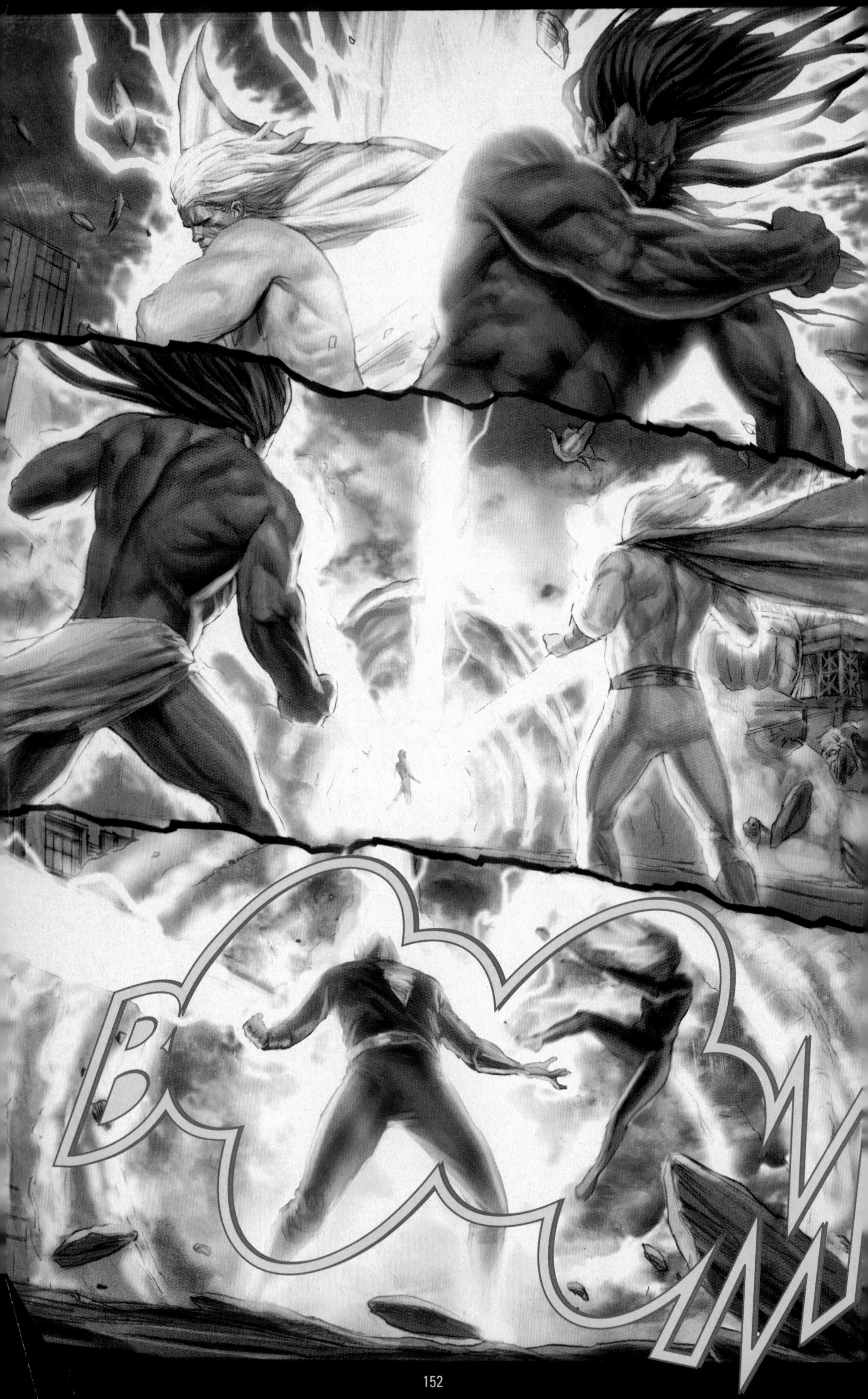
BOOM

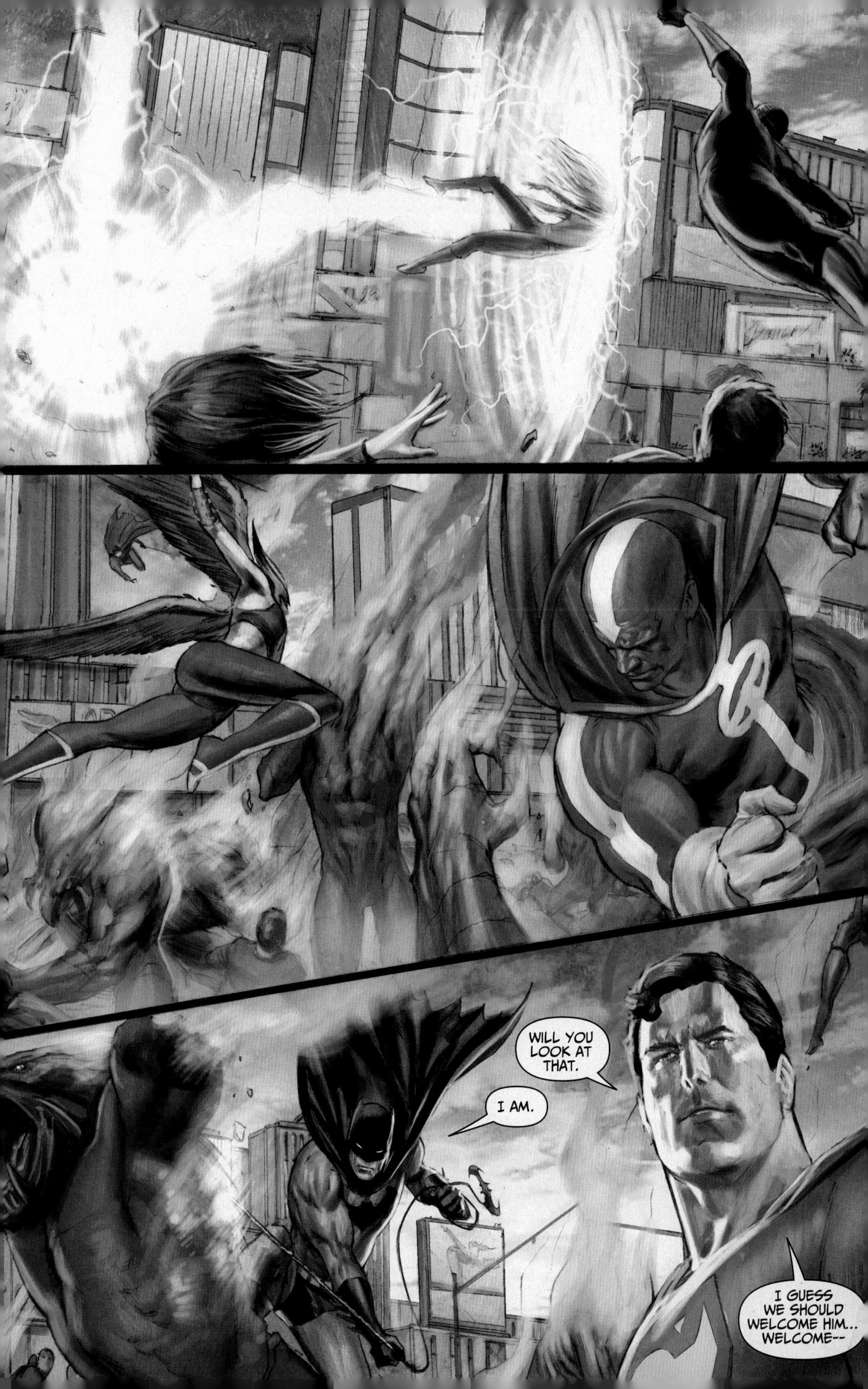
WILL YOU LOOK AT THAT.
I AM.
I GUESS WE SHOULD WELCOME HIM... WELCOME--

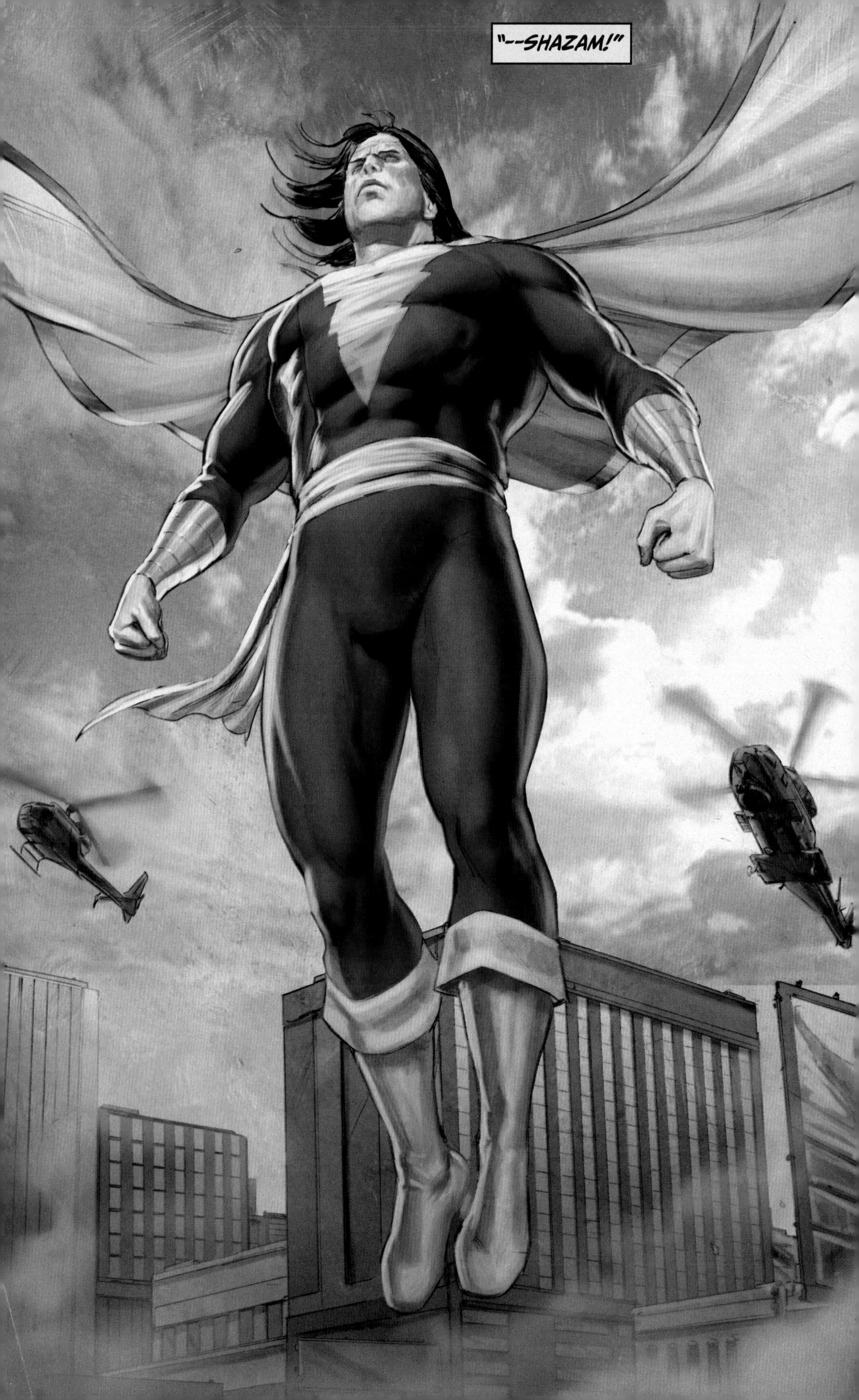
"--SHAZAM!"

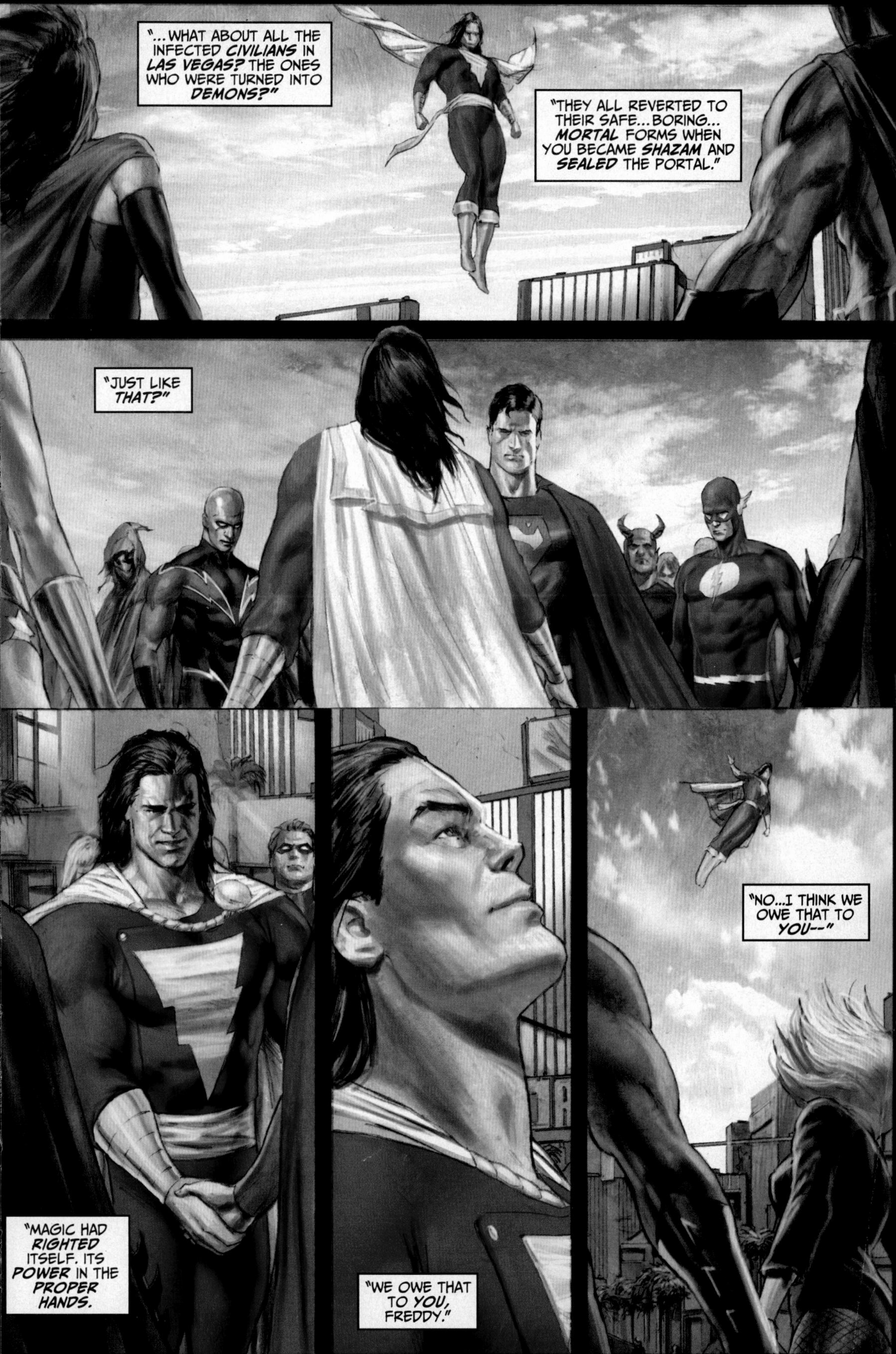
"...WHAT ABOUT ALL THE INFECTED CIVILIANS IN LAS VEGAS? THE ONES WHO WERE TURNED INTO DEMONS?"
"THEY ALL REVERTED TO THEIR SAFE...BORING... MORTAL FORMS WHEN YOU BECAME SHAZAM AND SEALED THE PORTAL."
"JUST LIKE THAT?"
"MAGIC HAD RIGHTED ITSELF. ITS POWER IN THE PROPER HANDS.
"WE OWE THAT TO YOU, FREDDY."
"NO...I THINK WE OWE THAT TO YOU--"

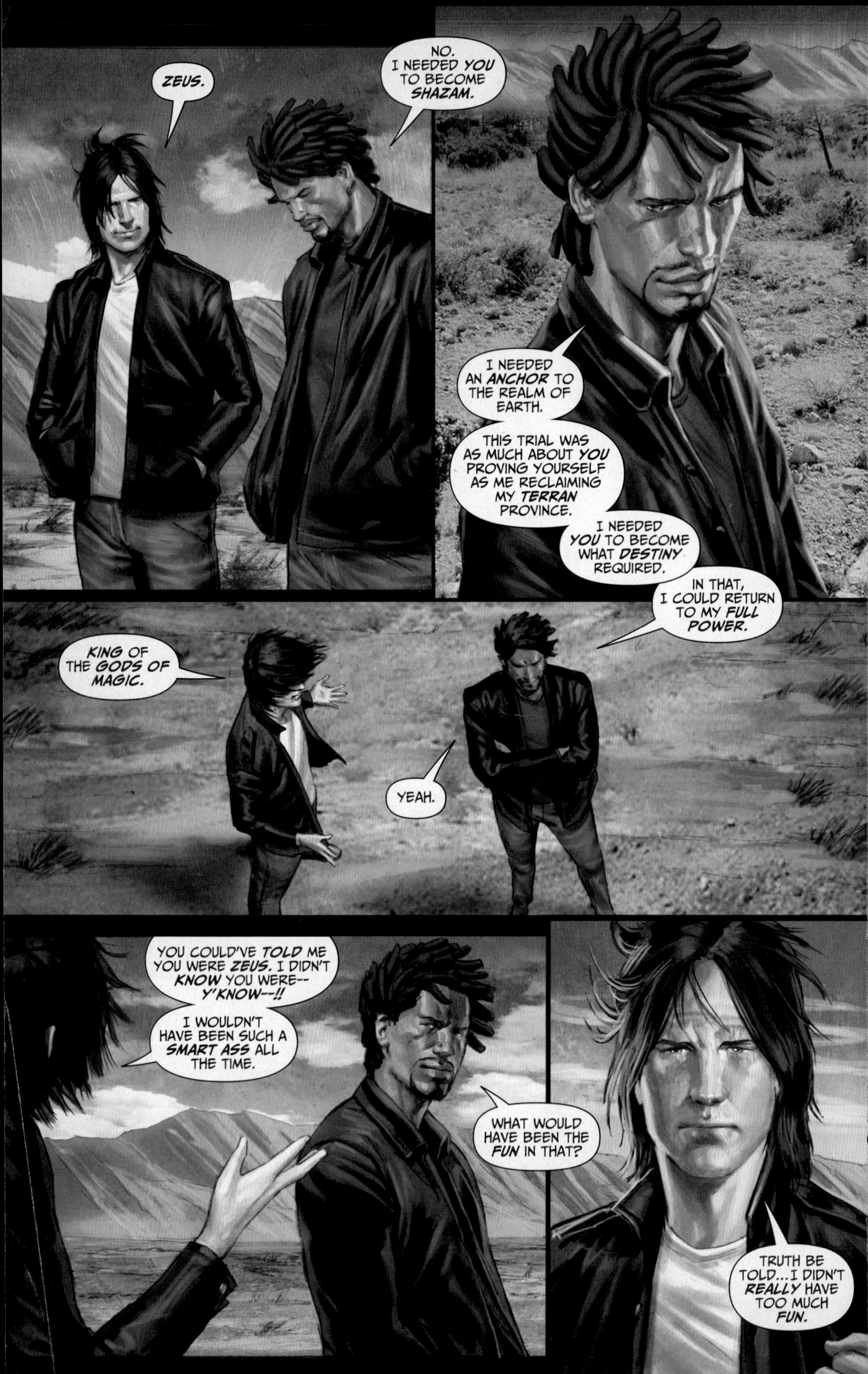
ZEUS.
NO. I NEEDED YOU TO BECOME SHAZAM.
I NEEDED AN ANCHOR TO THE REALM OF EARTH.
THIS TRIAL WAS AS MUCH ABOUT YOU PROVING YOURSELF AS ME RECLAIMING MY TERRAN PROVINCE.
I NEEDED YOU TO BECOME WHAT DESTINY REQUIRED.
IN THAT, I COULD RETURN TO MY FULL POWER.
KING OF THE GODS OF MAGIC.
YEAH.
YOU COULD'VE TOLD ME YOU WERE ZEUS. I DIDN'T KNOW YOU WERE-- Y'KNOW--!!
I WOULDN'T HAVE BEEN SUCH A SMART ASS ALL THE TIME.
WHAT WOULD HAVE BEEN THE FUN IN THAT?
TRUTH BE TOLD...I DIDN'T REALLY HAVE TOO MUCH FUN.

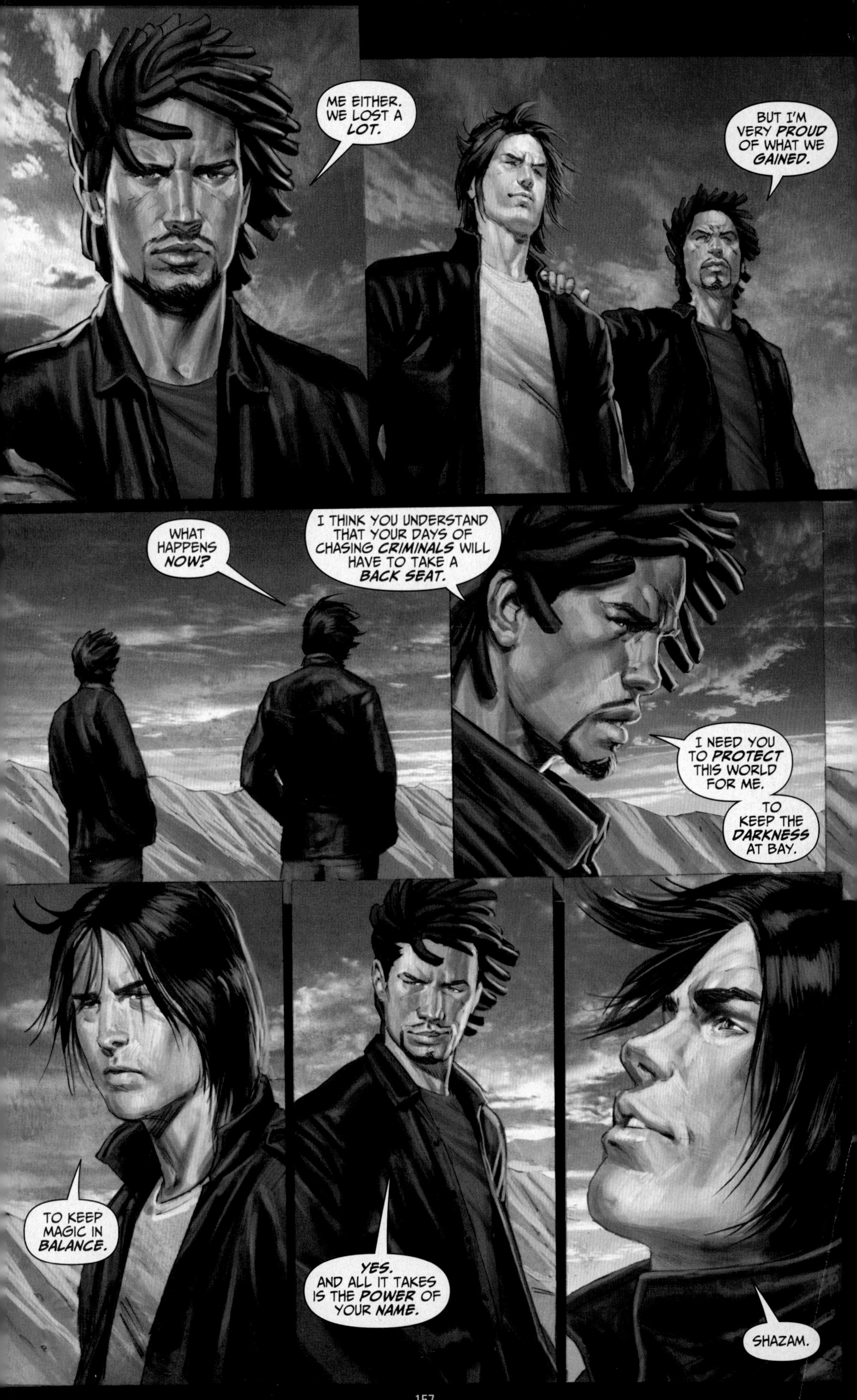

ME EITHER. WE LOST A LOT.
BUT I'M VERY PROUD OF WHAT WE GAINED.
WHAT HAPPENS NOW?
I THINK YOU UNDERSTAND THAT YOUR DAYS OF CHASING CRIMINALS WILL HAVE TO TAKE A BACK SEAT.
I NEED YOU TO PROTECT THIS WORLD FOR ME.
TO KEEP THE DARKNESS AT BAY.
TO KEEP MAGIC IN BALANCE.
YES. AND ALL IT TAKES IS THE POWER OF YOUR NAME.
SHAZAM.

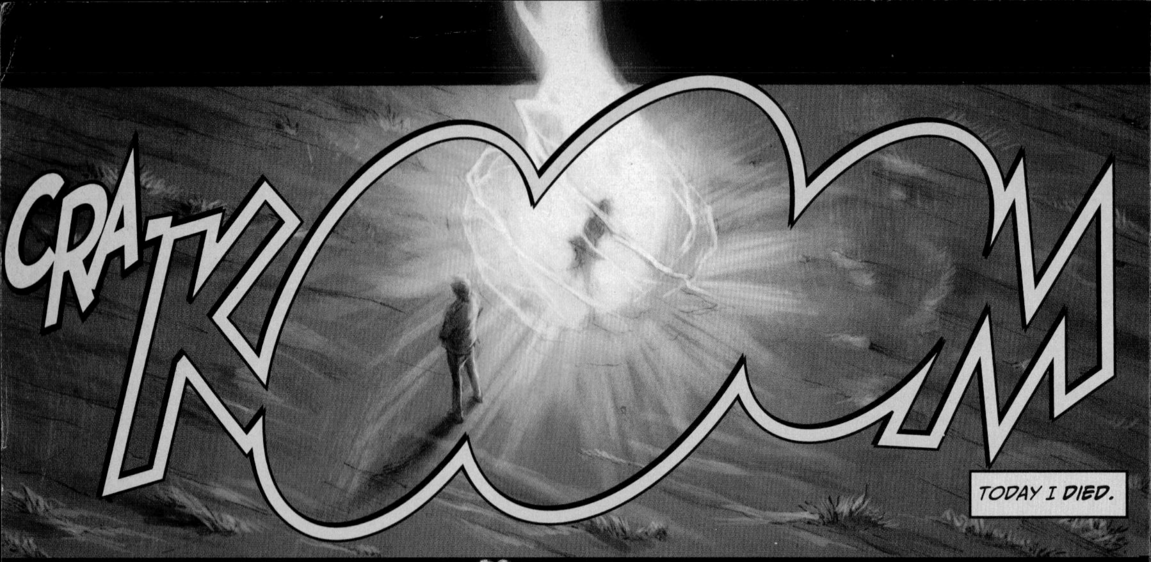
CRAKOOOM
TODAY I DIED.

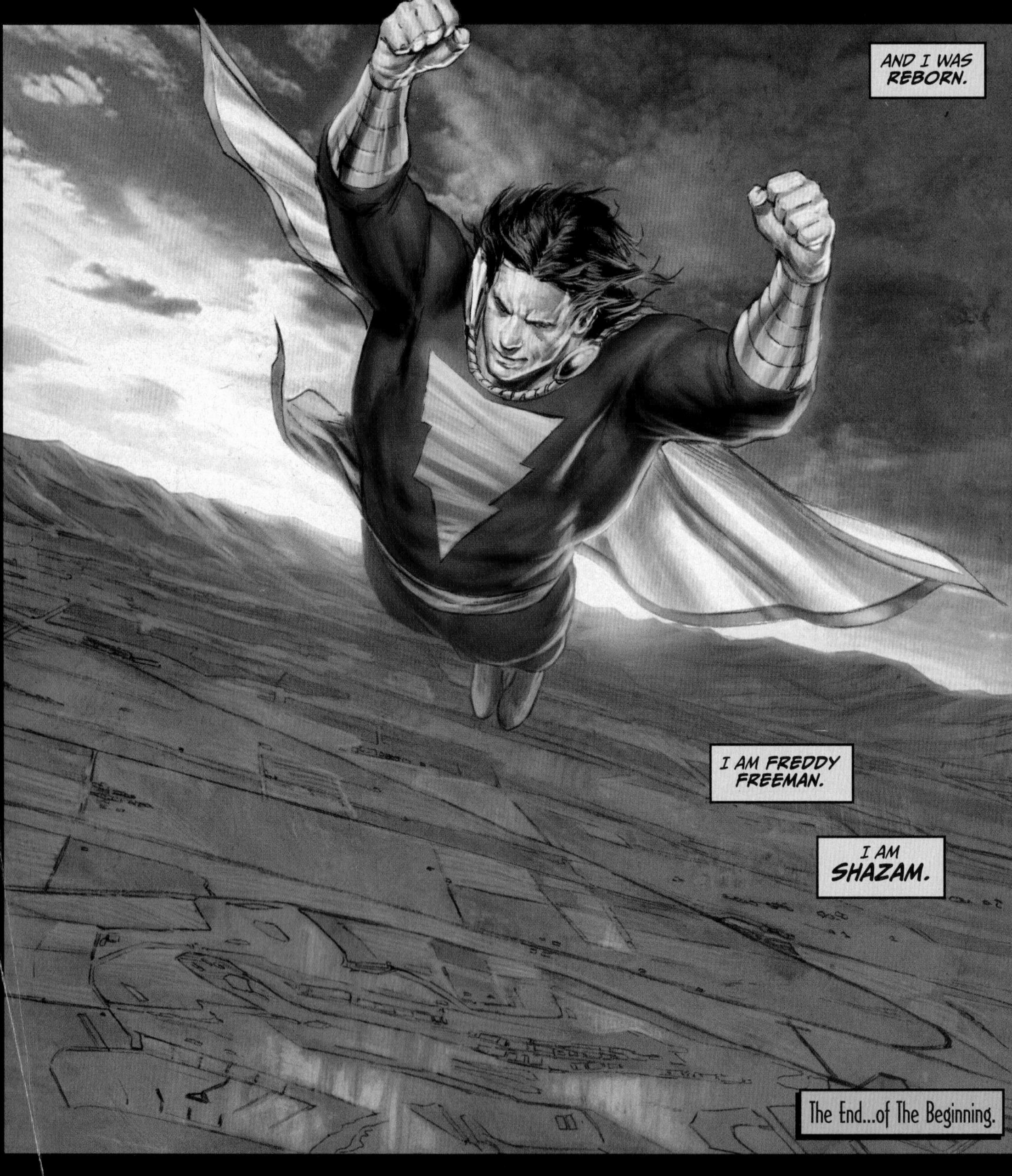
AND I WAS REBORN.
I AM FREDDY FREEMAN.
I AM SHAZAM.
The End...of The Beginning.

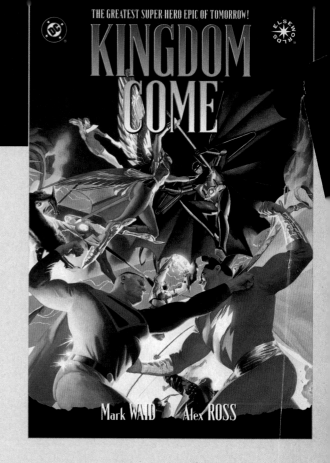
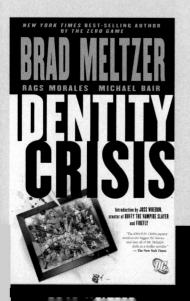